The Campaign for
Prohibition in
Victorian England

The Campaign For Prohibition in Victorian England

The United Kingdom Alliance
1872 – 1895

A.E. Dingle

CROOM HELM LONDON

© 1980 A.E. Dingle
Croom Helm Ltd, 2-10 St John's Road, London SW11

British Library Cataloguing in Publication Data

Dingle, A E
  The campaign for Prohibition in Victorian
  England.
  1. Prohibition — England — History — 19th century
  I. Title
  322.4'40942   HV5091.G7

ISBN 0-7099-0224-7

Printed and bound in Great Britain by
Redwood Burn Limited
Trowbridge & Esher

CONTENTS

INTRODUCTION

This book studies the attempt by a group of Victorian reformers to create what they perceived to be a better world, not only for themselves, but for society as a whole. The United Kingdom Alliance was formed in 1853 to campaign for the 'Total and Immediate Legislation Suppression of the Traffic in all Intoxicating Liquors' which would lead to an alcohol-free utopia. Prohibition has been called a 'particularly American aberration'[1] but this is not strictly true. While the United States was the first modern nation state to develop prohibitionist ideas, and most thoroughly implemented them, Finland, Norway, Iceland and Turkey also experimented with prohibition. In its modified form of local option or local permissive prohibition, a degree of prohibition was achieved in Sweden, Denmark, Canada, New Zealand, Australia and Scotland in the late nineteenth and early twentieth centuries. Victorian England also experienced a long and vigorous but ultimately unsuccessful campaign for prohibition which was organised and run by the Alliance.

Until recently most historians of nineteenth-century Britain ignored the Alliance and the temperance movement of which it was a part. Reasons for this neglect are not hard to find. Because the movement failed to realise its objectives it has left no obvious imprint on contemporary society and hence can find no place in a Whig interpretation of the process of historical change. From this viewpoint temperance was a Victorian 'dead end'. Fortunately recent research has rescued the temperance reformer from his unwarranted obscurity by demonstrating the impact and ramifications of his activities within the mainstream of Victorian social history.[2] No account of Victorian England which pretends to be comprehensive can afford any longer to ignore him. Nevertheless the historian is still faced with the difficulty of coming to terms with his beliefs and ideals. This problem is particularly acute with the prohibitionist because he appears to be such an alien and unsympathetic figure to later generations. The problem is compounded because the American experience with prohibition has

7

demonstrated to modern eyes the futility of this approach to social reform and clothed it in a faint aura of ridicule. Any sympathetic understanding of the prohibitionist must be founded on his undoubted honesty and enthusiasm and his demonstrable capacity to 'inspire hope and sincerity in intelligent men' of his era.[3] The Alliance was at once the embodiment of this hope and also the weapon forged to achieve prohibition in England.

Victorians were obsessed with alcohol. Among the literate and the articulate, the proper place of drink in society was debated with an intensity and an exhaustiveness which is now difficult for us to comprehend. Traditional drinking habits increasingly conflicted with the requirements of industrial work and urban living, and with changing concepts of what constituted acceptable standards of behaviour. While drinking continued unabated, it appeared to a growing number of people that the social costs involved were becoming intolerable. The result was an increasingly organised attack, first on excessive drinking, but increasingly on the consumption of all alcohol. From the 1820s onwards a variety of remedies was proposed. Each held the centre of the stage for a time before being challenged by an alternative. The seriousness with which the 'drink problem' was viewed and the urgency with which the search for a solution was conducted can be gauged from the fact that successive remedies became progressively more radical both in the degree of social reorganisation considered necessary and in the willingness of reformers to move beyond prevailing ideas on the scope of political action and the role of the state. Temperance reformers became pacesetters for social change.

The first of these remedies was free trade in drink. In its application to the drink trade in the 1820s it represented an early but neglected phase in the evolution of the practice of *laissez-faire*. In the following decade the temperance movement had its birth with the foundation of anti-spirits and teetotal societies. These worked for the moral regeneration of the individual through self-help and pioneered the individualist, Smilesian ethic, long before its better-known advocates had taken the field. The demand for prohibition grew out of what some regarded as the failure of this 'moral suasionist' phase of the temperance reformation. At a time when the doctrines of the 'Manchester School' were still dominant, prohibitionists began to develop a more positive interventionist concept of the role of the state which was expanded and formalised some thirty years later by T.H. Green and others. Prohibition in its turn had to compete with more radical alternatives which demanded even greater government intervention. In the 1870s Joseph Chamberlain advocated municipal ownership of the drink trade as an ingredient in his philosophy of municipal socialism, and by the end of the century socialists were demanding nationalisation.

A study of the Alliance throws light on a second feature of Victorian England, the concern with political power. Victorians disagreed about who should exercise control over whom and what form this control should take. One outcome of this disagreement was a proliferation of reformist pressure groups. In a socially differentiated society where political parties were unable or unwilling to articulate minority views, these became accepted vehicles for the exercise of political influence. Associations of people outside the formal institutions of government, and often also of party, used them as a way of influencing what went on in Whitehall and Westminster. Because prohibition required legislation and because prohibitionists were political outsiders, they were forced to adopt this approach. As a result of their efforts the Alliance eventually developed into one of the handful of powerful reformist pressure groups which played such a prominent part in political life during the nineteeth century. Indeed it was in this context rather than as a branch of the temperance movement that it first attracted serious attention from historians.[4]

Throughout this study the Alliance is viewed as a political pressure group and the work as a whole constitutes a case study of a pressure group striving to achieve its objectives within a particular socio-political environment. It examines how prohibitionists mounted their campaign and assesses their effectiveness and their impact on politicians, on political parties and political processes. Attention is focused mainly on the years between 1871 and 1895 because it was during this period that the Alliance was at its most active and influential and came closest to success. While it is to be hoped that these aims have not been interpreted too narrowly, this study has no pretensions to being a complete history of the temperance movement in late nineteenth-century England. Little is said of other important temperance organisations such as the Church of England Temperance Society and the curious but neglected Independent Order of Good Templars, except where they impinge on the activities of the Alliance. The same is true of trade interests, brewers, distillers and publicans, who felt their very livelihood threatened by the demand for prohibition and formed their own great defensive pressure groups.

The history of the Alliance during the nineteenth century falls neatly into two distinct phases. Initially it hoped to succeed by utilising approaches and tactics pioneered by earlier pressure groups in their campaigns against slavery and protection. It attempted to generate popular support for its cause and expected that the weight of public opinion would be sufficient to persuade a government to legislate. By 1871 mounting temperance pressure, generated in part by the Alliance, was sufficient to persuade Gladstone's Liberal government to bring in a Licensing Bill. While this Bill failed, a more moderate Licensing Act was passed the following year but it fell far short of what prohibitionists wanted. At this point Alliance leaders were reluctantly forced to recognise the inadequacy of their efforts to exert pressure on Westminster during the previous two decades. They had concentrated upon whipping up manifestations of popular support for prohibition, while remaining independent of both political parties, and all they had to show for it was a small reduction in pub opening hours. This early phase of activity lies firmly in the Anti-Corn Law tradition of pressure-group politics, but thereafter the Alliance changed its tactics. In 1872 prohibitionists decided that they should try to infiltrate the Liberal party, convert it to their viewpoint and then use it as a vehicle through which to achieve their legislative ambitions. Thereafter the Liberal party rather than parliament as a whole became the focus of the campaign. This change coincided with a period during which the Liberal party was slowly growing more responsive to the views of its provincial supporters and developing mechanisms through which their views could be adequately represented. The Alliance, along with other organisations such as the Liberation Society and the National Education League, played a part in this process of democratisation and forged new relationships between themselves and the Liberal party during the last quarter of the century.

The approach adopted in this study has been influenced by two books. The first, *Drink and the Victorians* by Brian Harrison, is a wide ranging study of the many facets of the temperance movement between 1815 and 1872 and includes an extended treatment of the history of the Alliance to 1872. Convinced that no good purpose is to be served by ploughing the same furrow twice, I have dealt only briefly with these early years. The second book, *Liberal Politics in the Age of Gladstone and Rosebery: A Study in Leadership and Policy* (1972), by D.A. Hamer, examines the difficulties faced by Liberal leaders attempting to formulate national policies in the face of pressure from various 'sections' within the party who were each trying to ensure primacy for their own pet reform. In order to maintain unity, leaders alternated between a policy of concentration on one single issue which transcended sectional demands, and the attempt to organise the demands of individual sections into a generally acceptable programme. This provides a useful framework within which to view prohibitionist efforts to manipulate the party. While Hamer looks at sectional interests through the eyes of Liberal leaders, the party and its leaders are here viewed through the eyes of one section which was attempting to push its own panacea. It was the intention of the Alliance to frustrate Liberal leaders in their efforts to subdue and discipline sectional interests.

I am indebted to the many people and institutions who have assisted me with my researches. This study would not have been possible without help of various kinds received from Lucy Brown, A.G.L. Shaw, Franca Goodwin and Bev Goodall. Brian Harrison, guide and mentor to many temperance historians, was generous with his friendship, help and guidance, and made valuable criticisms. I wish also to express my gratitude to Mr T. Garth Waite, secretary of the Alliance, for giving me access to the Minute Books of the Alliance, and to Viscount Harcourt for allowing me to work on the Harcourt Papers at Stanton Harcourt.

Monash University
Melbourne

Notes

1. W.W. Rostow, *The Stages of Economic Growth* (paperback edn, Cambridge University Press, 1965), p. 88.
2. The major contribution has been made by Brian Harrison in his *Drink and the Victorians. The Temperance Question in England 1814-1872* (1971) and other publications.
3. Andrew Sinclair, *Prohibition: The Era of Excess* (1962), p. 4.
4. H.J. Hanham in his influential *Elections and Party Management. Politics in the Time of Disraeli and Gladstone* (1959) was the first to outline the political impact of the Alliance in the 1870s and his interpretation was reinforced by G.Kitson Clark in *The Making of Victorian England* (1962).

Chapter 1

EARLY YEARS

The campaign for prohibition in England began in 1853. Two years earlier the state of Maine had introduced statewide prohibition and information about this experiment had been disseminated in England by visiting American prohibitionists. Nathaniel Card, a Quaker cotton manufacturer and member of the Manchester and Salford Temperance Society, was impressed by what he heard and early in 1852 he tried to interest other members of his society in starting a campaign for a 'Maine Law' in England. During a meeting at Card's house in June 1852 it was decided to form a 'National League for the Total and Legal Suppression of Intemperance'. After further private meetings and intensive lobbying for support among 'men of influence', the 'United Kingdom Alliance for the Suppression of the Traffic in all Intoxicating Liquors' was established. It held its first public meeting and made its first appeal for popular support in October 1853.[1]

The appearance of the Alliance was a new departure for a temperance movement which had been fighting against the evils of drink for almost a quarter of a century. Whilst the ultimate objective of an alcohol-free utopia remained unchanged, new methods were now to be employed in an attempt to realise it. Teetotallers had always sought to eliminate the demand for drink by persuading people to take a pledge of abstinence; this approach did not directly threaten either the drink trade or the licensing system. Prohibitionists in contrast wished to stop people drinking by eliminating the supply of drink. This represented a rejection of the belief, strongly held by early total abstainers, that man could control his own destiny by voluntarily renouncing the use of alcohol. Because the temperance reformation had not occurred prohibitionists concluded that in an environment filled with drinkshops the individual was powerless to improve his lot by his own unaided efforts. Licensing in any form was rejected as unsound and unworkable, and the drink trade became the target for a frontal assault aimed at its elimination. Thus after more than twenty years' concentration on the individual as the focus for all reforming efforts, a branch of the temperance movement now looked to legislation to effect a remedy. Parliament was to be the new battleground and the emphasis shifted from social regeneration within local communities to political campaigning on a national scale.

At the outset of the campaign for prohibition none of the leaders of the Alliance had a clear idea of how they could achieve their purpose. Echoing Benjamin Disraeli they assumed that 'all public questions pass through various stages. They are first popular, then parliamentary, and lastly governmental'.[2] While it was anticipated that the campaign would follow this pattern, no one had yet thought out how progress from one stage to another could be achieved. Nevertheless the first stage, that of popularising the principle of prohibition, presented few problems. The Alliance had at its disposal a heritage of techniques developed by the anti-slavery and anti-corn law campaigns which could be used to attract and demonstrate the existence of mass support. The public meeting, the petition and the deputation were all familiar to prohibitionists and they immediately began to employ them with skill and ingenuity.

The Alliance rapidly attracted support. Temperance pioneers such as Joseph Livesey, John Dunlop and Father Mathew were attracted to prohibition because it appeared to offer a political short cut to universal abstinence, and a means of rejuvenating the ailing teetotal movement.[3] Total abstainers followed their lead and began joining in large numbers. Within a year the Alliance had enrolled over 4,500 members, this rose to 21,000 in 1855 and 30,000 a year later. Membership was open to anyone willing to donate a shilling, regardless of whether they personally were total abstainers. This was condemned by some as hypocritical but the Alliance defended itself by arguing that it was engaged in a national crusade and 'to accomplish a general object, it must obviously be inappropriate to employ mere sectional effort'.[4] Its pool of potential support was thereby widened to include those who supported prohibition but still personally drank. Open membership allowed the Alliance to benefit from the services and support of people like Lord Brougham, Professor F.W. Newman and the future Cardinal Manning at a time when the last two had not yet renounced the use of alcohol.

The social backgrounds of those who gave money to the Alliance during its first twenty years have been examined by Brian Harrison.[5] Most came from the industrial counties of the north, particularly Lancashire. Manufacturers, particularly those in the textile industry, were the largest occupational group and provided the major single source of finance. Subscribers were almost exclusively Nonconformist in religion and Liberal in politics. There were a few Anglicans, large landowners, professional people and others from diverse backgrounds, but they tended to be untypical of their class. To the end of the century the prohibitionist campaign continued to draw the bulk of its support from Nonconformity and Liberalism.

Alliance subscription lists greatly underestimate support for prohibition. Many more people were content to turn up to the numerous Alliance meetings, of which 500 were held in 1855 alone, in order to demonstrate their approval. The evidence of these meetings and the results of canvasses in the provincial cities convinced Alliance leaders that their cause enjoyed wide popular support. They believed they had the backing of the aristocracy of labour as well as the lower middle class of shop keepers and clerks. Some even asserted that those of the unregenerated, drunken 'residium' would also, in their more sober moments, give prohibition their blessing. Sir Wilfrid Lawson insisted that the demand for prohibition came 'absolutely from the people themselves. It has sprung from them'.[6] Such claims were perhaps somewhat extravagant, but by the 1860s the campaign had harnessed some of the money-power of northern manufacturers and was attracting support from two groups whose political influence was in the ascendancy. Nonconformists were at last putting their political quietism, born out of long years of social and political exclusion, behind them. The stage was set for the emergence of 'militant dissent' and the Alliance was to be one of its vehicles. Likewise the articulate working man was flexing his political muscles through trade unionism and the Reform League, before being enfranchised in large numbers in 1867.

As donations poured into Alliance coffers, £4,427 in 1855 rising to £15,290 by 1869, the foundations for the campaign were gradually established. An Executive Committee (hereafter referred to as the Executive) in Manchester was entrusted with control of the movement. A number of energetic individuals filled key roles; Samuel Pope, a Nonconformist businessman turned lawyer, became the first secretary. When he later became honorary secretary his place as secretary was filled by the vegetarian accountant and former commission agent T.C. Barker. The Baptist minister and temperance historian Dawson Burns, a founder member of the Alliance, became metropolitan superintendent of the campaign. The Radical activist James Hayes Raper was appointed parliamentary agent in 1860 and Henry S.

Sutton, a vegetarian poet and disciple of Swedenborg became editor of the prohibitionist newspaper *Alliance News* in 1854. As funds allowed, a network of district agents was established and by 1870 there were nineteen of them covering the whole country. In addition to this, autonomous Alliance auxiliaries sprang up in towns wherever there were enough enthusiastic prohibitionists to establish one.[7]

As support increased and an effective organisation was established, the next stage of the campaign was to convince parliament of the benefits of prohibition. Prohibitionists identified parliament, still in the fifties and sixties predominantly aristocratic in composition and indifferent to the evils of drink, as the main obstacle to progress and it was here that the first major problems were encountered. The resources at the disposal of the Alliance, impressive though they appeared, were not immediately equal to the task. The Nonconformist background of most Alliance leaders was a handicap because their history of political disabilities left them without knowledge or experience of government processes. The Executive reluctantly conceded that 'temperance men are mostly inexperienced in the wiles of political struggle'.[8] Consequently they were forced to approach their task blindly and, by a process of trial and error, endeavour to locate the seat of political power. It soon became clear that no further progress could be made until the Alliance acquired a parliamentary leader willing to push its cause, and a specific legislative proposal which incorporated the principle of prohibition and could be introduced into the House of Commons.

Sir Walter Trevelyan the eccentric Anglican naturalist and landowner had become the first president in 1853. He was asked if he would become an MP and lead the cause in the Commons but he was not interested in undertaking so onerous a task. Samuel Pope wished to do so but he was defeated in his attempts to get elected for Stoke-on-Trent in 1857 and 1859. The problem was eventually solved when Wilfrid Lawson, the young MP for Carlisle since 1859, agreed to take on the job. A large landowner, keen amateur sportsman and 'a cobdenite of the Cobdenites', his reasons for doing so are obscure. 'I did not take up the question' he declared, 'the question took me up', but then somewhat equivocally added, 'I certainly would not have taken the part which I did if anyone else would have undertaken it.'[9] Although at first regarded as a stopgap, he remained to lead the Alliance in the Commons for over forty years.

The second difficulty, that of embodying the aims of the Alliance into a specific legislative demand, was overcome with the emergence of the Permissive Bill. This gave ratepayers in any locality the power to ban the trade in drink in their district if a two-thirds majority of them desired it. A vote for prohibition would then automatically result in the suppression of all licensed premises. The idea of permissive legislation had first been proposed in an anonymous article in 1855 (the brewer Charles Buxton later admitted authorship). At the Alliance annual meeting in 1857 many suggestions for a 'Voluntary Maine Law' had been made, some of them extremely complex, but the Bill as it finally emerged was largely the work of Lawson, though he was given some assistance in drafting it by J. H. Raper. It was brief and simple containing one permissive prohibitory clause and nine others suggesting machinery for its operation.[10]

The Permissive Bill was in some ways quite different from the 'Maine Law' which had been the rallying cry in earlier years. The advocacy of a national and imperative change had now been replaced by a proposal that was both local and permissive. The immediacy of the demand for prohibition was thereby inevitably reduced. Total abstainers of the 'moral suasionist' school, who had enthusiastically pinned their hopes on prohibition as a once and for all short cut to national sobriety, were alienated by the change. Their most prominent spokesman, Joseph Livesey, complained that 'the Permissive Bill is about the strongest symptom of Alliance weakness of anything that has transpired with it'. He saw it as an admission that national prohibition was impossible and believed that to campaign for it would simply 'prolong a hopeless agitation'.[11] Alliance leaders did not see matters in the same light. While national prohibition remained their ultimate objective, they reluctantly realised that without much preparatory legislation it was not a practicable reform in the 1860s. All was not well with prohibition in Maine where the law had been repealed in 1856 only to be re-enacted again in 1858. J.B. Gough the prominent American temperance orator had toured England in 1857 under the auspices of the 'moral suasionist' National Temperance League and greatly embarrassed the Alliance by declaring the 'Maine Law' to be a 'dead letter'.[12] The Permissive Bill was designed to avoid the pitfalls to which prohibition in Maine had proved susceptible. Because it was local it could only be adopted 'wherever the condition of a favourable local sentiment existed'.[13] There was then less chance of it subsequently being repealed. An additional reason for initially preferring a local to a national measure was highlighted in correspondence between Lord Stanley and Samuel Pope which was published in *The Times* in 1856. Stanley argued that immediate national prohibition would bring a large part of the country's commercial and fiscal system to a halt because the drink trade was so extensive and drink taxes were the largest single source of government revenue. The Alliance was reluctantly forced to agree with him, but the Permissive Bill overcame this difficulty as even the most enthusiastic prohibitionists accepted that it would not be adopted immediately in every part of the country. Consequently the extent of the dislocation would be minimised.

The Permissive Bill emerged as a temporary compromise with political realities intended to pave the way for total prohibition. While it alienated some temperance men it also greatly broadened the appeal of the Alliance among many who had previously been disinterested.[14] The Bill contained two elements, the demand for prohibition, and the insistence on local self-government as the machinery by which this would be carried out. These demands attracted considerable support, not only because they were seen as desirable in themselves, but also because they offered a way of achieving a wide variety of wishes for changes in society. Nonconformist businessmen expected that prohibition would benefit them economically. Sober workmen would be more disciplined and productive and, once drink expenditure had been eliminated from their budget, could purchase more consumer goods. Such a stimulus to domestic purchasing power would benefit both employers and workers by increasing business profits, employment opportunities and working-class living standards. Working-class leaders such as Thomas Burt supported the Alliance for different reasons. They believed that drink stupefied workers, making them the pawns of unscrupulous employers. A sober working class would be better able to organise in order to protect its interests. Many artisans and those of the lower middle class also believed they could benefit from prohibition. Dr Kitson Clark has drawn attention to an important division in Victorian society between those who aspired to respectability and those who did not.[15] Personal abstinence was an ideal to which the respectable aspired as a means of differentiating themselves from the rest of society. This was not easily achieved amid the temptations of a drink-sodden environment, but by eliminating the public house, the Permissive Bill promised to improve the local environment and make personal abstinence easier. Prohibitionists always minimised the barriers to social advancement. They argued that the worker and the capitalist began life similarly equipped with skills and intelligence, but the latter developed 'superior self-control, and prudence, and economy'.[16] Permissive prohibition promised to make such virtues easier to achieve and consequently more widespread.

Prohibitionists identified drink as the root cause of most social ills. They believed that its elimination would create a society in which it was possible to lead a civilised and respectable life and enjoy to the full the fruits of industrialisation. The Permissive Bill was their weapon, but it was a weapon which demanded state intervention in an age when *laissez-faire* was the ruling philosophy. Prohibitionists believed that free trade, while expanding national income, was deficient in that it 'regarded the development of wealth as if it were the chief, if not the sole end of a nation's existence'. Because the 'moral progress of the nation' had been neglected, increases in wealth were 'appropriated to luxury, self-indulgence, and intemperance' and became 'the instrument of the people's demoralization and impoverishment'. By advocating state intervention to eliminate social abuses, prohibitionists anticipated the views of T.H. Green (who later joined the Alliance) in regarding the state as an organic body; 'it is the representative and protector of society, acting on behalf of its constituency, and in this capacity carrying out the people's will, and so ensuring to its people their collective as well as their individual rights'.[17] The mechanistic concept of individuals and the state as separate entities whose interests might clash, was rejected. The individual was a part of the state, therefore he could not complain that legislation designed to promote the general good was an infringement of his personal liberty. If the actions of the individual clashed with the good of society, this was not a question of liberty but of wrongdoing. The cry of freedom was 'the cry of revolution . . . The reign of terror was heralded in France by shouts of freedom'.[18]

The fear of revolution pervaded Victorian society and obsessed many reformers. Because the nation was becoming morally corrupt, a 'modern Babylon', a dose of abstinence was needed to rejuvenate it. The experiment in political democracy could not work while people were in a drunken and degraded state. Self-interested drink manufacturers and religious apathy were sowing the seeds of social catastrophe. 'The "have-nots" and the "lack-lands" are the hands and feet of the revolution' wrote Cardinal Manning, 'but the sharers in the welfare of a people are men of order and peace'.[19] If left untouched the 'drink curse' would lead to class conflict by creating 'a heaving, seething mass of discontented, disaffected, moody passionate socialists; regarding the rich with hate, brooding over the "tyranny" of capital, and ready to bury the social edifice in ruins'. Capitalist indifference to the lure of the gin palace and public house was 'a process by which Communists are being manufactured where good citizens and good Christians would otherwise flourish'.[20] The breach between capitalist and worker was thus seen to result as much from the neglect of the former as the drunkenness of the latter, and was not in the best interests of either. The second feature of the Permissive Bill was its emphasis on local self-determination. This attracted support because it was regarded as a means by which local initiative could be strengthened and extended and also as a way of attacking the privileged governing classes. While the Bill required state intervention, it was only necessary for central government to establish the principle of prohibition which would then be administered by the locality which was in the best position to know its own requirements as regards drink. It was the area of *local* responsibility that would be enlarged thus making it 'worth the while of able educated men to devote their lives to the prosperity of great local communities — larger than ancient Athens or Sparta'.[21] As a result of their history of exclusion, many Nonconformists viewed Westminster with suspicion. They had made their mark instead in the provincial cities, as captains of industry, philanthropists, or councillors within the existing machinery of local government, and they simply wished to extend the scope for such work. The Permissive Bill was also democratic because it gave local ratepayers the power to control their own fate as regards the supply of drink; by exercising this power they would learn to be good and responsible citizens. Cardinal Manning went further. Believing that drink and social revolution were intimately linked, he was convinced that the decentralisation fostered by the Permissive Bill would stave off revolution in Britain. While drunken London might fall to the mob, sober responsible self-governing provincial centres would be counter-revolutionary.[22]

In the 1860s the assumption behind popular Radicalism was that a natural community of interest existed among all those who were not members of the old privileged classes. Wealthy Nonconformists still believed they had much to gain from a political alliance with the 'labour aristocracy', particularly in an attack on privilege. Lawson, the parliamentary leader of the Alliance, typified this belief. He shaped his political career so as 'to go against all political privileges'.[23] The Alliance acted as a vehicle for this assault because the Permissive Bill campaign provided an opportunity to attack a variety of attractive targets including unrepresentative MPs, the licensing system, magistrates, monopolistic brewers and landed aristocrats.

While provincial liberalism was strongly Nonconformist and Radical by the 1860s, the parliamentary Liberal party was still predominantly Whig and Anglican and thus did not adequately represent the views of many of its constituents. The Alliance sought to overcome this problem in two ways. First it bypassed local MPs and attempted to influence parliament directly, in the same way that the Anti-Corn Law League had done. Joseph Chamberlain supported it at this time simply because it appeared to be an organisation capable of forcing governments to legislate. Secondly, as will be seen later, prohibitionists in the 1870s organised themselves into constituency electoral associations and tried to force Whig MPs to support the Permissive Bill in return for their votes. In this way Whigs could be forced to bow to Radical demands.

The licensing system was seen as a gigantic conspiracy by wealthy landowners and brewers directed against the interests of the working class. It allowed brewers and landowners to avoid their share of the national tax burden and place it instead onto the shoulders of the wage earner. Furthermore, through the agency of the magistrate, large numbers of public houses were established in working-class areas, thus boosting demand for the landowner's barley and brewer's beer. The misery caused by drink augmented the burden of poor relief and police rates, but because ratepayers had no control over licensing they were unable to gain any relief from such tax burdens. Thomas Burt was suspicious of those 'who demand that the working man shall have his beer, when I find that those who are so anxious in this direction are unwilling to give the working man his political rights, the power to educate his children, and other things far better for him than his beer'.[24] The licensing system was a symbol of the power of the governing classes. The government itself was a 'sleeping partner' in the drink trade because it upheld the system and benefited from any increase in drinking through increased revenue. The Permissive Bill was thus seen both as a way of undermining the power of the privileged and also of rescuing the state from its immoral dependence upon the drink trade.

The fury of the prohibitionist attack on magistrates was second only to that directed against the brewers and publicans. Licensing magistrates determined how many licences should be issued in an area, yet they were not elected, they did not live near public houses or have to put up with the disturbance and reduction in property values that this entailed, nor did they personally use the facilities which they administered. For these reasons they could not accurately gauge the real needs of a community and were regarded as irresponsible political appointees representing no one but their political masters. G.O. Trevelyan pointed out that while they were keen to punish the poacher they were loath to convict the publican who flouted licensing regulations.[25] The wealthy never had to suffer the inconvenience of living near a public house. They surrounded themselves with parks, influenced licensing magistrates or drew up building leases which excluded public houses. Large landowners went even further. Many of them, including Palmerston, Shaftesbury and Prince Albert on the royal estates at Windsor, absolutely prohibited the sale of drink on their estates. They were exercising a power much more despotic than anything the Permissive Bill proposed. All that the Bill wished to do was to allow 'the rich and the poor to stand on the same footing' by giving the working man the same power to control his environment as 'the rich man enjoys and derives so much advantage from'.[26]

Such were the attractions of the Permissive Bill and the way in which the measure was pushed heightened its appeal. The Alliance believed it was leading a holy crusade against the slavery of drink. It was important to fight the good fight because 'in the face of great social evils, apathy is a crime, and despair is the one great sin that cannot be atoned for'. The conflict was seen as a life or death struggle: 'If we do not destroy [the drink trade], it will destroy us as a people and nation.'[27] Because the campaign was depicted as an essentially religious endeavour it attracted militant Dissenters and provided them with a means of airing their ideas in Westminster.

Wilfrid Lawson introduced the Permissive Bill into the House of Commons for the first time in 1864 and it was defeated by 292 votes to 35. This was the first serious setback to the campaign. Prohibitionists had expected hostility from publicans and brewers, but not from so many MPs, prominent intellectuals and the bulk of the national press. The debate on the merits of the Bill was far more than merely a clash of vested interests, prohibitionists on one side and trade interests on the other. What was at stake was the much wider issue of what constituted good and just government. Opposition to the Bill was comprehensive in scope and embraced objections to the principle of prohibition and local self determination, as well as to the machinery by which these principles were to be implemented. While the full range of objections was not aired during the first debate in 1864, this is a suitable point at which to summarise some of the major arguments raised during the next 25 years.[28] Such arguments were a serious obstacle to the Alliance simply because they were articulated by those to whom prohibitionists looked to implement the Permissive Bill. It was the inability of the Alliance to convert the House of Commons to its viewpoint by the persuasiveness of its arguments that led to the major changes in campaign strategy which will be discussed in the next chapter.

The attack on the principle of prohibition stemmed from a radically different concept of individual liberty to that embraced by prohibitionists. John Stuart Mill believed that personal liberty was increased with every lessening of government control. People could only progress morally if their freedom of choice remained unfettered, so drunkenness should only be punished when it was contrary to the public interest. Prohibition was an intolerable interference with personal liberty and dangerous because it was capable of indefinite extension. 'There is no violation of liberty which it would not justify', argued Mill, because 'the doctrine ascribes to all mankind a vested interest in each others' moral, intellectual, and even physical perfection, to be defined by each claimant according to his own standard'.[29] This objection was echoed by many others. Lord Neave complained that the Permissive Bill was 'a Bill to permit you to prevent me doing what you don't like and I do', while Lord Derby denounced it as 'sheer tyranny and intolerance of the worst sort'. In his view it differed little from religious persecution: 'It would be just as reasonable to lay it down that where two-thirds of the population of any district were Protestants, no Catholics should be allowed to open a place of worship'. Fears concerning the coercive powers of a majority within a local democracy were widespread in a society which was as yet undemocratic. Conservatives were most concerned about this, but the Whig Bishop of Peterborough, William Magee, also expressed a 'sneaking kindness for minorities' and a desire to see their rights defended.[30]

There was widespread concern at any attempt to make men sober by Act of Parliament. Frederic Harrison attacked the attempt 'to effect by force and law a moral and social reform which can only be healthily promoted by moral and spiritual agencies', because it resulted in 'that abandonment of moral effort for material penalties which is one of the most fatal tendencies of our age, a tendency which brutalises government whilst it discredits religion'. John Newman likewise believed that the withdrawal of such matters from the 'jurisdiction of religion' was tending to 'the destruction of religion altogether'.[31] William Magee made one of the most celebrated attacks on the Permissive Bill when he declared that 'it would be better that England should be free than that England should be compulsorily sober'. He preferred freedom to sobriety 'because with freedom we might in the end attain sobriety; but in the other alternative we should eventually lose both freedom and sobriety'. The principle of abolishing temptation was 'precisely the one which the Church of Rome used long ago for burning heretics'. Many politicians believed that lasting temperance reform could not rely upon legislation. Men as different as John Bright and Lord Salisbury agreed that temperance men should stay out of parliament and achieve their objectives 'by their own preaching and ministrations'.[32]

Those of a more pragmatic frame of mind concerned themselves with the practicality of the Permissive Bill rather than its morality. Joseph Chamberlain believed that 'in the present state of society, and having regard to the social habits of the people, it is impossible to enforce a prohibitory law'.[33] Many sincere temperance reformers, including those of the Church of England Temperance Society, agreed with him, as did the Lords *Select Committee on Intemperance* (1879). Even some who had joined the Alliance in the hope that its campaign might force a government to act, were sceptical of the value of the Bill. There were fears that if prohibition was passed without widespread popular support people would continue to drink secretly and wholesale evasion of the law would then bring the whole system of laws into disrepute and endanger the social fabric. The eventual revolt against prohibition would also damage the cause of moderate temperance reform. The Alliance replied that its Bill could operate only if it won a two-thirds majority, but this did not placate opponents. Because there was no precedent in English legislation for the Permissive Bill, its likely effects were unknown, and both opponents and supporters looked to the United States as an example of what could be expected. There followed a protracted debate over the effectiveness and benefits of prohibition in America, but by the 1870s it was clear that permissive prohibition had worked most effectively in the sparsely populated rural states. Opponents therefore concluded that the Permissive Bill would only be adopted in rural areas where it was least needed. In the cities, where the problem was most urgent, the drink-sodden slum dweller could not be expected to deprive himself of one of his few solaces in life.

The Permissive Bill offered ratepayers only a limited degree of local control. They had the option of voting either for the *status quo* or for the prohibition of all licences. Politicians and moderate temperance men pointed out that 'the great number of respectable and intelligent persons who favour restriction, but are disinclined to prohibition, would have no opportunity whatever of expressing their real opinion'.[34] The only people actually consulted would be the respective partisans. In order to avoid this, moderates wanted the inclusion of an option to reduce licences. Prohibitionists replied that if this were done the Permissive Bill would degenerate into a mere licensing measure and this would be a denial of all that the Alliance stood for. Its very existence was a protest against three centuries of unsuccessful attempts to regulate the sale of drink.

It did not escape the notice of critics that the Permissive Bill proposed to prohibit the retailing of drink, but not its consumption, manufacture, or import. This was regarded by some as a serious inconsistency. Even the Bristol Radical, Handel Cossham, a vice-president of the Alliance, pointed out that 'if the right to drink intoxicating drinks is conceded, the right to sell these drinks follows as a matter of course'.[35] Conversely Hartington, Ritchie and others pointed out that if prohibitionists sincerely believed drink to be injurious, they should demand the prohibition of its manufacture, importation and consumption. The Alliance claimed that the distinction it drew between the trade in and consumption of a commodity was one observed in all laws affecting the circulation of injurious articles, but there were also tactical reasons for drafting the Bill in this way. Prohibitionists could thereby avoid being accused of promoting a sumptuary law, and also side-step objections concerning the liberty of the individual raised by Mill, Magee and others. The distinction might appear to be a nice one, but it appealed to the argumentative mentality of prohibitionists. However this approach laid the Alliance open to the charge that it was promoting class legislation. By attacking the drink trade it was trying to abolish the public house, the main drinking place of the poor, but the rich man's cellar or club, stocked largely by imported wines and spirits, would be unaffected. The difference between a West End dining room and an East End pub was, as a brewers' representative pointed out, one 'of manners, not of purpose'.[36] George Potter, while sympathetic to the Alliance, believed it went too far in attempting to deprive the poor man of his glass of beer. With the growth in class consciousness towards the end of the century the class bias of the Permissive Bill and similar legislation was vigorously criticised by Socialists.[37]

By the 1870s support for the principle of local control was growing in both political parties. Liberals and Radicals, given their social background, were naturally sympathetic and the Tory government after 1874 made wide use of permissive legislation which Disraeli considered 'the characteristic of a free people'. Temperance men of all opinions agreed on the desirability of local control, even though they differed on most other matters. However there was much disagreement as to how local control could best be implemented. The Alliance proposed a periodic referendum. This horrified those steeped in the English tradition of representative government. Joseph Chamberlain believed this to be 'entirely contrary to, and subversive of, the principles of representative government. Our whole system is based on the assumption that representatives freely elected are the proper persons to deal with the questions submitted to them.' Consequently a referendum would be 'injurious to the character and efficiency of the representation'.[38] Given the strength and persistence with which interested parties on both sides were likely to push their respective viewpoints, MPs were concerned that impartiality would be difficult to maintain. Drink would become the major issue in local politics and successive referenda would simply result in repeated clashes between publicans and temperance reformers and 'repeated instances of turmoil . . . detrimental to the peace and quietude of every neighbourhood in England'.[39] For this reason most MPs of both parties preferred that any measure of local control should be exercised by existing local government agencies, rather than by periodic votes of ratepayers.

It was objections such as these which prompted MPs to vote overwhelmingly against the Permissive Bill on its first introduction into the Commons in 1864. The vote in favour was 'not quite equal to Sir Wilfrid's expectations', and the Executive was also bitterly disappointed. Alliance leaders were forced to face the possibility that Lawson might never succeed in passing the Bill, but they took comfort from the fact that neither Villiers nor Cobden had ever persuaded the Commons to pass a resolution in favour of repealing the corn laws, yet a government had been forced to act. Nevertheless parliamentary hostility had exposed the naivete of the Alliance approach. The Executive had regarded parliament as a corporate body and had too easily assumed that if it was bombarded with sufficient evidence of popular support for prohibition, legislation would result. Lawson had confidently assumed that a petition bearing several thousand signatures would be a sufficiently powerful weapon to persuade a home secretary to act.[40]

The Executive concluded that 'the first necessity of the agitation in Parliament is to secure a full representation of its [i.e. the Permissive Bill's] principles, by sending there men who . . . fully understand and identify themselves with the interests of the movement'.[41] This was an attempt to shift the emphasis of the campaign away from parliament viewed as an organic whole and towards its constituent parts, that is, the individual MP. Potentially one of the most valuable resources at the disposal of the Alliance was the voting power of its members. This had early been recognised. In 1859 Dawson Burns laid down a carefully thought out blueprint for future political action. Convinced that 'our strongest public efforts will prove inadequate until, along with them we treat each Member of Parliament as a distinct element in the settlement of this question', he urged temperance men to mobilise and organise their electoral strength. Burns envisaged the setting up of constituency organisations which would deliver a bloc vote to favourable candidates; 'organisation is power' he emphasised, 'and in vain shall we boast of our electoral influence unless it is embodied'. Only in this way could the electoral influence of the publican be counterbalanced, and candidates persuaded that the support of temperance men was worth having. In 1862 Thomas Begg went further and suggested that prohibition candidates be introduced into likely constituencies.[42]

Prohibitionists had made sporadic attempts to exert electoral pressure almost from the beginning of their campaign. During the general election of 1857 some candidates had been asked to pledge their support for the Permissive Bill, but as the measure had not yet reached the Commons, any pledge given was hardly binding. Encouraged by the strategy outlined by Dawson Burns, the Executive urged prohibitionists to form electoral Permissive Bill associations in the constituencies. It was intended that these would consist of voters pledged to vote only for candidates who supported permissive prohibition. Agents and local enthusiasts in various parts of the country carried out canvasses to identify Alliance supporters and scrutinised electoral registers to make sure that eligible temperance men were properly enrolled. Such associations emerged wherever enough enthusiasts could be found but most of them were ephemeral. The basic difficulty — one that was to bedevil Alliance electoral work for the rest of the century — was to persuade prohibitionists to ignore party loyalties and cast their vote on the temperance question alone. The dilemma surfaced whenever a Liberal candidate favoured temperance reform but was unwilling to go so far as to pledge his support for the Permissive Bill. If Alliance men, overwhelmingly Liberal in inclination, withheld their votes, they simply helped a Tory who was likely to be hostile to all reform.

The strategy adopted by Alliance men varied from place to place. Sometimes they abstained, at other times they united behind whichever candidate came nearest to their position. Local circumstances and local enthusiasm determined the outcome. The Executive was incapable of giving a lead as it also wavered between these two alternatives at different times.[43] Most of the impetus for electoral organisation came from local prohibitionists rather than the Executive and so efforts were not effectively co-ordinated. Even the pledges extracted from association members varied from place to place. The Executive was unable to mount an effective national electoral campaign because as yet many Alliance leaders were not convinced of the necessity for such a step. Dawson Burns frankly recognised that until 'a large body of the General Council are ready to make a surrender of all their other political preferences, it would be out of place for them to urge this surrender upon the Temperance-loving electors of the nation'.[44] In the meantime the campaign concentrated on generating popular support.

The 1865 election cruelly exposed the electoral weakness of the Alliance. Lawson lost his seat at Carlisle and Samuel Pope failed to get elected at Bolton where he had stood as a Liberal. Prohibitionists had not been enfranchised in sufficient numbers to make their support valuable to a candidate, nor were they distributed in a way that would enable them to make their presence felt in selected constituencies. The Executive had long been convinced that effective electoral pressure could only be exerted after electoral reform. As early as 1859 it claimed that any extension of the franchise which included 'the cream of the working classes' would allow them to 'sweep all before us in the House of Commons'. Not only would the number of temperance voters be increased, the electoral influence of publicans would be diluted. However even after the extension of the franchise the Executive was forced to admit that in the general election of 1868 the 'full strength of the Alliance could not be put forth'. Most of the new electors, temperance men among them, had followed Gladstone's lead and cast their votes on the Irish Church issue, relegating temperance reform to a position of secondary importance.[45]

Nevertheless the 1868 general election was a turning point. Lawson was returned to the Commons and Benjamin Whitworth, a member of the Executive, was elected as Liberal MP for Drogheda. The new House was more sympathetic to the demands of temperance reformers. Debates on the Permissive Bill when it was introduced in 1869 and 1870 reflected a change in the climate of opinion; serious criticism replaced the ridicule and contempt of earlier years. The majority against the Bill was 106 in 1869 and only 31 in the following year. After the failure of the Liverpool experiment, where local magistrates had tried to free the trade in drink, the free trade solution was finally discredited in the eyes of most MPs. Jacob Bright noted that 'a strong feeling appears to have sprung up in favour of a strong bill'. Most MPs put this down to the persistent agitation of the Alliance.[46] Political leaders had for some time recognised the need for licensing reform. H.A. Bruce mentioned that a draft Bill, approved by successive Home Secretaries, had lain in the Home Office for some years. It had not been introduced because 'successive Governments have not felt sufficient confidence in their ability to carry it through the House, for as is well known, the influence of the publicans both in the boroughs and counties has always been very strong'. However the extension of the franchise had diluted this and Bruce believed that if he could mobilise growing temperance sentiment behind a measure of reform, his chances of success would be high.[47]

Thus by 1870 the Liberal government had been brought to the point of action, and the Alliance could justly claim that its activities had materially contributed to this. At this juncture however the different assumptions of the Alliance and of most parliamentarians became crucial. While many MPs saw something of value in the Permissive Bill, the overwhelming majority of them, Liberal and Conservative, were opposed to its provisions. Philip Munz, MP for Birmingham, probably voiced the thoughts of many in believing that the Permissive Bill was 'merely a manifestation' of the need for action.[48] They were convinced that restriction and regulation was the best method of alleviating drunkenness and dealing with the just claims of the drink interest. Prohibitionists saw the situation in a different light and were in no mood to accept what they regarded as a compromise measure from a government which they believed had only been prodded into action by their efforts. Their attitude to Bruce's promised Bill was typified by F.W. Newman when he warned that:

> The Government was aiming at an object different from ours. We were for prohibition, and the Permissive Bill was only a means to that end. That end which we desired the Government feared; therefore we must be intensely jealous and suspicious of what was being done by the Government.[49]

For the Alliance, the Permissive Bill *was* a practical compromise. It was a minimum demand.

The temperance world was divided as to what legislation was most desirable and there was certainly no unanimity of support for the

Permissive Bill. Some important teetotallers, including Joseph Livesey, were sceptical of the value of any legislation. Others favouring a middle way between free trade and prohibition threatened the Alliance's position as the only national temperance body committed to legislative reform. The threat took on two dimensions, internal and external. Many friends of the Alliance tried to persuade it to moderate its position and support a measure which would gain wide public acceptance. Such overtures were gently but firmly rejected. The Executive argued that temperance men should not reduce their demands to conform to the existing state of public opinion, but rather raise public opinion to the 'required' level.[50]

An alternative approach was to form new organisations and several emerged in the 1860s. The Central Association for Stopping the Sale of Intoxicating Liquors on Sundays, the Licence Amendment League, and the National Association for Promoting Amendment in the Laws relating to the Liquor Traffic, all offered moderate alternatives to the Permissive Bill and thus attracted moderate men. Many temperance men were members of several organisations, including the Alliance, and concentrated their efforts on whichever proposal they felt had the best chance of success. Consequently the temperance movement was unable to speak with one voice and attempts to push a range of alternative legislative proposals were mutually destructive. The petition movement for the Permissive Bill in 1869 was seriously curtailed because most temperance men preferred to petition for Ryland's Sunday Closing Bill. The Executive was alarmed 'lest efforts which are now being made, and in which Alliance men are very extensively participating, should rob us of the fruit of our bygone labour and stultify the action we have been earnestly advocating now for many years'.[51] The Licence Amendment League was reproached for being too moderate, and the Scottish Temperance League accused of shirking all active support for the Permissive Bill. Attempts to amalgamate the Licence Amendment League with the National Union for the Suppression of Intemperance were enthusiastically promoted but came to nothing.[52] The Alliance could neither swallow up the smaller moderate societies nor silence them.

It was against this background that Bruce introduced his Intoxicating Liquors (Licensing) Bill in 1871. The measure was a comprehensive one. It proposed to give back to magistrates responsibility for licensing. Opening hours were to be reduced and, if a three-fifths ratepayer majority so wished, these could be cut still further, and complete Sunday closing imposed. Regulations governing the conduct of public houses were to be tightened up and a public-house inspectorate established to ensure that these were effectively kept. The most radical of Bruce's proposals was for a reduction in the number of licences. Justices were to decide if any new licences were required for their district, and if so how many. A three-fifths majority of local ratepayers could then, if they wished, insist on a reduction of this number down to a ratio of one licence to 1,000 inhabitants in towns and one licence to 600 inhabitants in rural areas. This opened the way for a drastic reduction as there was one on-licence for every 201 persons in England and Wales in 1871. In order to compensate existing licence holders for the loss of their monopoly, they were to be given a ten-year possession of their licences before any reductions could become effective. This was known as 'time compensation'.

The reaction of the drink trade was immediate and hostile. Convinced that the Alliance had captured the ear of Bruce in framing the measure they mobilised their resources for a massive campaign against it. The Country Brewers Society attracted many new members and built up a fighting campaign of £21,000 in its defence of the rights of property. The result was impressive; *The Times* doubted 'if any trade or interest in the country could have got up a stronger agitation than we now see ... Confiscation is the only term applied to its provisions, and the walls and hoardings of every town in the Kingdom are covered with vigorous and stirring appeals to all classes of the population in favour of universal resistance'.[53] Petitions opposing the Bill far outweighed those in its favour. The drink trade was able to overlook its internal differences sufficiently to demonstrate its strength as a pressure group in defence of its vested interests.

Temperance reform was regarded at this time as a non-party issue so Bruce could not expect to have the Liberal party united behind him. Consequently he needed strong and united temperance support if he was to stand any chance of success. This was not forthcoming. The initial reaction of the Alliance was one of disappointment and hostility. Regretting that Bruce had 'not dealt with this momentous question in a more sagacious and statesmanlike manner', it objected to the proposal for 'time compensation' which it believed would create a vested interest in a licence where none had existed previously. However the Executive was forced to come to grips with political realities and the consequences of its own previous actions. Prohibitionists realised that the local control clauses were included as a concession to them and that the Alliance had frequently promised 'to sustain any advance in the direction of legislative action'. A few eminent supporters such as Archbishop Manning were prepared to honour this promise and support the Bill. In order to prevent any split in the ranks the Executive decided to appear to be supporting Bruce while actually doing nothing. Supporters were urged not to oppose the second reading, but to try to insert complete local control and get rid of compensation at the committee stage. No agitation was mounted on behalf of the Bill, all energies were directed instead to whipping up support for the Permissive Bill which Lawson introduced once again in 1871.[54]

The moderate temperance bodies, which had been advocating just those kinds of reforms which Bruce introduced, tried to provide him with adequate backing, but without success. Attempts by the National Association to ensure united temperance action were spurned by the Alliance; Sir Robert Anstruther appealed to prohibitionists not to leave Bruce 'in the lurch', but to no avail. The most the Executive was prepared to do was provide £25 towards the cost of a meeting held by the National Association. The lack of wealth, influence and support for moderate organisations was clearly exposed. Bruce attracted support from many MPs, both Liberal and Conservative, and from sections of the press, but this was not enough. Without the backing of a powerful body capable of whipping up popular support and counteracting the drink trade campaign, the Bill had to be dropped without reaching a second reading.[55]

By 1871 the Alliance had marshalled its resources with sufficient effect to become a power to be reckoned with at Westminster. The Bruce Bill was a recognition of this, but it was a compromise which failed because of the attitudes taken to it by two powerful and opposing pressure groups. The Executive believed that the failure of the Bill was to its advantage for several reasons. First, temperance reform had become a major political issue; 'it has invaded the Home Office, and cannot be rejected until it has won a just and satisfactory solution'. *The Times*, while not supporting the Permissive Bill, agreed that 'the question will not sleep, nor, indeed be long suspended'. Secondly, the Alliance was convinced that trade interests in opposing the Bruce Bill 'never so completely alienated themselves from public sympathy and never won a more disastrous victory'. Once again, more impartial observers agreed; by demonstrating the enormous difficulty of reforming the licensing system the drink trade had 'given an argument to those who would reform it out of the land'. Trade hostility also made the enthusiasm and energy of prohibitionists more attractive and valuable to any government contemplating temperance reform.[56]

Thirdly, the failure of the Bruce Bill had, at least temporarily, discredited moderate reforms and those temperance organisations which had supported them. The Alliance strengthened its position both politically and within the world of competing temperance societies. Lawson was convinced that 'Mr. Bruce has no chance of carrying a bill that will do good to the country unless he enlists the prohibition party in his cause'.[57] In order to do that Bruce would have to draft something very like the Permissive Bill. By the end of 1871 Lawson's Bill was the only independent runner still in the field. The *Daily News* was afraid that because of this, prohibitionists had gained the initiative.

We cannot shut our eyes to the fact, that it is a definite, logical, and resolute policy; that its advocates are numerous, influential and earnest, and that they thoroughly believe in their scheme. These qualities make any movement dangerous to those whom it opposes, but they become ten times more so when everybody else is hesitating what to do. Any definite policy has recommendations to a nation waiting for a policy; and even the Permissive Bill may come to be accepted, if all other expedients should be discouraged and fail.[58]

Prohibitionists had 'made licensing reform their own especial property'.[59] Increased parliamentary support for the Permissive Bill in 1871 was interpreted as an indication of this. The campaign for prohibition appeared to be close to victory.

Notes

N.b. References to *Hansard* are all to 3rd series unless otherwise stated.
Minutes of the Executive Committee of the United Kingdom Alliance are hereafter referred to as *Minutes*.
Reports of the Executive Committee of the United Kingdom Alliance are hereafter referred to as *Annual Reports*.

1. *1st Meeting of the Members of the General Council of the United Kingdom Alliance 1853*, pp. 5-8.
2. *7th Annual Report 1859*, p. 2.
3. Brian Harrison, *Drink and the Victorians: The Temperance Question in England 1814-1872* (1971), p. 211.
4. *5th Annual Report 1857*, p. 4.
5. Brian Harrison, 'British Prohibitionists 1853-1872. A Biographical Analysis', *International Review of Social History*, vol. 15, no. 3 (1970), pp. 375-467.
6. *Hansard*, vol. 278, c.1283; ibid., vol. 251, cc.503-4; cf. Harrison, 'British Prohibitionists', p. 394.
7. Detailed biographies of all Alliance personnel can be found in A.E. Dingle, 'The Agitation for Prohibition in England' (Monash University PhD 1974), biographical appendix.

8. *7th Annual Report 1859*, p. 17.

9. Harrison, *Drink and the Victorians*, p. 252; G.W.E. Russell, *Sir Wilfrid Lawson. A Memoir* (1909), pp. 69, 74.

10. (Charles Buxton), 'How to Stop Drunkenness', *North British Review*, February 1855; J.D. Hilton, *A Brief Memoir of James Hayes Raper, Temperance Reformer* (1898), p. 51.

11. Quoted in H. Carter, *The English Temperance Movement. A Study in Objectives* (1933), p. 98.

12. For the resulting controversy between Gough and F.R. Lees of the Alliance see Harrison, *Drink and the Victorians*, pp. 212-14.

13. W.S. Caine, Dawson Burns and W. Hoyle, *Local Option* (1885), p. 16.

14. The attractions of the Permissive Bill are more fully discussed in Dingle, 'Agitation for Prohibition', ch. 2.

15. G. Kitson Clark, *The Making of Victorian England* (1962), pp. 126-8.

16. *Alliance News*, 24 June 1871, p. 405.

17. William Hoyle, *Our National Drink Bill* (1884), pp. 160-3, 165, 182-3.

18. H.E. Sutton in *Alliance News*, 6 January 1872, p. 13.

19. A.E. Dingle and B.H. Harrison, 'Cardinal Manning as Temperance Reformer', *Historical Journal*, vol. XII, no. 3 (1969), p. 505.

20. A.M. Sullivan in *Alliance News*, 28 October 1871, p. 702.

21. F.W. Newman in ibid., 25 March 1871, p. 674.

22. Dingle and Harrison, 'Cardinal Manning', pp. 505-6.

23. *Alliance News*, 4 February 1871, p. 67.

24. *Hansard*, vol. 251; c.464.

25. *Alliance News*, 16 December 1871, p. 839.

26. Lawson in *Hansard*, vol. 251, cc.447-8.

27. T.H. Barker in *Alliance News*, 8 April 1871, p. 210.

28. The arguments against permissive prohibition are more fully discussed in Dingle, 'Agitation for Prohibition', ch. 2.

29. J.S. Mill, *On Liberty* (1966 edn), pp. 108-10.

30. Lord Neave, quoted in Caine, Burns and Hoyle, *Local Option*, p. 57; Lord Derby in *Alliance News*, 13 January 1872, p. 32; William Magee in ibid., 11 May 1872, p. 357.

31. Frederic Harrison, *Realities and Ideals* (1908), pp. 196-7; John Newman quoted in T. Kenny, *The Political Thought of John Henry Newman* (1957), p. 172.

32. William Magee in *Alliance News*, 11 May 1872, pp. 354-5, 357; Lord Salisbury quoted in Paul Smith, *Disraelian Conservatism and Social Reform* (1967), p. 211.

33. Quoted in *25th Annual Report 1877*, p. 27.

34. Joseph Chamberlain, *Fortnightly Review*, vol. 25 (1876), pp. 638-9.

35. *Minutes*, 1 October 1873.

36. National Association for the Promotion of Social Science, *Conference on Temperance Legislation* (1886), p. 22.

37. See Harrison, *Drink and the Victorians*, ch. 17; Dingle, 'Agitation for Prohibition', pp. 445-59.

38. *Alliance News*, 11 July 1885, p. 434.

39. Wheelhouse in *Hansard*, vol. 251, c.475.

40. George H. Dyer, *Sir Wilfrid Lawson : His Life, His Humour and His Mission* (n.d.), p. 6; *12th Annual Report 1864*, pp. 11-12.

41. Ibid., pp. 3, 5.

42. *7th Annual Report 1859*, pp. 30-4; *10th Annual Report 1862*.

43. For early attempts at electoral action, see D.A. Hamer, *The Politics of Electoral Pressure. A Study in the History of Victorian Reform Agitations* (1977), ch. 9.

44. *7th Annual Report 1859*, p. 33.

45. Quoted in Harrison, *Drink and the Victorians*, p. 222.

46. *Hansard*, vol. 196, cc.656-71.

47. Ibid., cc.675-7.
48. Ibid., c.672.
49. *Alliance News*, 29 October 1870, p. 346.
50. *17th Annual Report 1869*, p. 10; *15th Annual Report 1867*, pp. 26-7.
51. *Alliance News*, 26 February 1870.
52. E.g. *Minutes*, 26 April 1871.
53. *Times*, 25 April 1871.
54. *Alliance News*, 15 April 1871, pp. 230-1; 6 May 1871, p. 287; *19th Annual Report 1871*, pp. 8, 13-14.
55. *Minutes*, 3, 11 and 24 May 1871; the 1871 licensing crisis is dealt with in greater depth by Harrison, *Drink and the Victorians*, ch. 12.
56. *19th Annual Report 1871*, pp. 2, 15-16; *Daily News*, 19 May 1871; *Pall Mall Gazette*, 21 September 1871.
57. *Alliance News*, 9 December 1871, p. 815.
58. *Daily News*, 19 May 1871.
59. *Manchester Courier*, 4 September 1871.

Chapter 2

NEW DIRECTIONS, 1872-1874

Although the Alliance attracted most of its support from Radicals and Liberals, at the foundation of the organisation it had been emphasised that it would be independent of any political party. Because prohibitionists were working in the national interest, 'the great interests of sobriety, involving all other political and social interests must be superior to the claims of a mere party policy'. After the failure of the Bruce Bill in 1871 the Executive believed that if a resolutely independent stance could be maintained, victory would result. Lawson declared, 'we throw off all party ties now; we are done with party'. This was a warning to Bruce that any future initiative of his would gain prohibitionist support, only if it was framed according to their wishes.[1]

However attempts were made at this time to forge closer links between the Liberal party and the Alliance. The young Radical G.O. Trevelyan, a 'recent recruit' to the temperance movement, toured the country at the end of 1871 speaking from Alliance platforms. His message was that 'the Liberal party, in spite of its antecedents and fancied interests, must ere long become a temperance party' because 'liberalism cannot permanently live if divided from temperance'. He claimed that the Bruce Bill had begun a polarisation of attitudes to temperance reform along party lines. Drink interests were now voting *en bloc* for Conservatives at elections, and the Conservative party was welcoming such support. To counteract this, temperance men had to capture the Liberal party. George Melly came to the same conclusion. Trevelyan warned that Nonconformists had been 'too considerate, too loyal' to the government and the inadequate Bruce Bill was their 'reward'. They must therefore 'take care that no Liberal candidate, whose Liberalism did not go far enough . . . should ever become a Liberal representative on any condition whatsoever'.[2]

Trevelyan did not simply desire temperance reform, his aims were much more ambitious. He saw in this issue a means of radicalising the Liberal party and making it more thoroughly representative of Nonconformist and working-class interests. The Liberal party, he believed, had done little for the average working man, nor would it, until working men united behind some great scheme of reform and worked towards its success, without relying, as they had in the past, on 'Peers and wire-pullers'. The demand for the Permissive Bill was just such an issue. He believed that it enjoyed working-class support and also embodied what he saw as 'the great ruling doctrine of Liberalism ... the paramount and unlimited authority of popular control'. With the aid of the secret ballot the Liberal party could be forced to swallow not only the Permissive Bill but also the wider Radical viewpoint of its Nonconformist and working-class adherents. The party was likely to suffer temporary damage during its conversion, but would emerge greatly strengthened.[3]

Trevelyan spoke to Alliance audiences 'not in the character of a Temperance man, but of one who was a Radical from the core outwards'. The Tory prohibitionist Bishop Ellicot objected and pointed out that Trevelyan was forcing the Alliance to become even more of a party-political organisation that it had been hitherto. Alliance leaders were embarrassed and immediately denied that there was anything more than the 'slightest tinge' of party politics about their organisation. Despite the strength of his Liberalism, Lawson was prepared to assert that 'the Alliance is as free from any admixture of party politics as any association ... we will', he added, 'accept the aid of anybody'. T.H. Barker, the secretary, repudiated the views expressed by Trevelyan and drew a distinction between what was said in the *official* publications of the Alliance and what was said by individuals on Alliance platforms. The former was a true guide to policy, but he could exercise no control over, nor claim responsibility for the latter.[4] The Executive, convinced that it was in a strong position, had no wish to take new initiatives which might alienate people for no useful purpose. After this rebuff Trevelyan took no further part in the Alliance campaign. His stand had already caused him a great deal of trouble in his constituency where many electors objected to the importance he attached to the Permissive Bill.[5]

Meanwhile early in 1872, Sir Henry Selwin-Ibbetson introduced a Bill to codify and simplify the licensing laws. The government, anxious to forestall this move, hastily drafted its own Bill which was introduced into the House of Lords by Kimberley. This was a much more moderate measure than its 1871 predecessor. It proposed to have magistrates as the sole licensing authority, to reduce opening-hours and tighten up policing provisions, but it did not repeat the attempt to reduce the number of licences and allow an element of local control.

Kimberley was convinced that in 1871 Bruce had 'altogether over-esti-mated the forces of the Temperance agitators, and underrated the power of the traders in liquor', and framed the Bill accordingly.[6] As an attempt to meet the 'just wishes of the Trade',[7] it failed because most brewers and publicans remained hostile, but it did not give rise to the ferocious opposition encountered in 1871. The Alliance on the other hand was dismayed at the Bill's timidity and made no attempt to support it. Nevertheless without outside backing Kimberley and Bruce managed to pilot the Bill successfully through both Houses. They received considerable help from Conservatives such as Selwin-Ibbetson and attracted the hostility of some Liberals, particularly W.V. Harcourt.[8]

This was a shattering blow for prohibitionists. True the govern-ment had been forced to legislate, as was expected, but Liberal leaders demonstrated that they were by no means bankrupt of independent ideas on temperance reform and were quite capable of acting effec-tively without the aid of prohibitionists. Alliance leaders were forced to face the fact that their existing strategy and tactics had failed. Bringing pressure to bear on parliament as a whole, and MPs *within* parliament, mainly by means of public meetings, petitions and printed propaganda, had led only to the two unsatisfactory measures of 1871 and 1872. If the Permissive Bill or a similar measure were ever to be passed, the Alliance must adopt a new strategy and new tactics. This much was realised, but deciding on what these should be proved a long and difficult process. During the next eighteen months new methods of attack were slowly developed in the face of hostility from politicians and major differences of opinion among prohibitionists themselves.

During the debate on the 1872 Bill, Kimberley, speaking on behalf of the government, frankly informed an Alliance deputation; 'we must think what we can carry . . . at the moment we think you are the weaker party'. This angered Alliance leaders who interpreted it as a direct challenge to organise 'the voting power which the friends of temperance and the Permissive Bill possess'. Lawson told prohibi-tionists that they could continue to hold meetings and draw up peti-tions if they so desired, 'but if they are in earnest and determined, they will vote, and vote alone, for the man who will go against the liquor traffic'. He was saying in effect that the Permissive Bill was now to be the paramount electoral issue, and only those parliamentary candi-dates who pledged their support for it could hope to win the votes of prohibitionists.[9]

At first sight this demand appears to be simply a reaffirmation of suggestions which had appeared sporadically in Alliance literature from the late 1850s onwards. Organised, non-party electoral activity had always, theoretically, been a weapon used by prohibitionists. However 1872 did in fact mark a new departure in several ways. To begin with the Executive for the first time mounted a concerted effort to ensure that this policy was implemented effectively and on a national scale. This involved diverting an increasing proportion of Alliance resources of men and finance into electoral work. The *Alliance News* contained exhortations to act and practical advice as to how this might be done. In areas where Alliance auxiliaries did not exist committees were to be formed, their task being to set up organisations of electors in their respective constituencies. Agents equipped themselves with Parliamentary Registers and became electoral organisers. By these means it was hoped 'to give confidence to temperance electors', and also 'make an impression upon politicians'. William Hoyle, a member of the Executive, visited various parts of the country urging the necessity of vigorous action. His message gained in urgency because the Executive believed there was a possibility of an early dissolution. Thus the tactics outlined by Dawson Burns thirteen years earlier were being put to the test on a national scale for the first time.[10]

The year marked the beginning of a new departure in a second way. Alliance leaders had come to recognise what they had refused to accept from the mouth of Trevelyan the previous year, that polarisation along party lines was taking place on the temperance issue. The Executive concluded that

> It cannot be concealed that the publicans are determined, if possible, to humiliate the Government which has dared to interfere with them, while some politicians on the other side are eager to avail themselves of the opportunity so afforded. If the publican interest succeeds in identifying itself with the politics of a party, *it must be so fought*.[11]

The rapidity and the extent of the permanent move of trade interests into the Conservative camp has been the subject of debate among historians. It now appears that it took place slowly and was never entirely completed.[12] Nevertheless between 1871 and 1874 Conservatives had benefited greatly from trade support in a series of by-elections. There was an obvious opportunity here for Conservatives to exploit the difficulties experienced by the government over temperance reform.

Kimberley complained that, 'Dizzy knows well what a prodigious advantage the rage of the publicans gives the Tory party'. While the Conservative party as a whole did not back trade interests whole-heartedly, many individuals within the party did offer their aid and sympathy.[13]

The Alliance interpreted this as evidence of a *permanent* alignment of interests between the Conservative party and the trade. In order to counteract this it was therefore imperative that prohibitionists should align themselves with the Liberal party, the only difficulty being that the Liberals had so far shown no desire to welcome them. T.H. Barker explained just what was involved in the attempt to persuade the Liberal party to change its mind.

> The Permissive Bill men, though organised, will find themselves opposed by the Tories, and not taken up heartily and as a whole by the Liberals. They can only exclaim with Luther, 'In the name of God here we stand'. They may not be a majority in any constituency, but they are a minority powerful enough, by standing aside, to teach very salutory lessons. This policy may lead to many a reverse having to be sustained, and perhaps so by the party that many hoped most from. But until that party sees its way to manfully adopt the principle we demand, it cannot be otherwise. We have then to prepare for a crisis, and for, it may be, just that class of defeat that has ever been necessary to prepare the way for future victory.
>
> We would now inquire: Will the Liberal party in such a case allow itself permanently to dissolve rather than take up our principle? And to the inquiry may we not fearlessly answer, never? So soon as we make those who lead in such matters feel that we are in earnest, on the same principle of self-preservation that has led parties and governments to adopt measure after measure in the past, will they not adopt ours? How soon this will be so remains with ourselves.

Here in a nutshell was the aim and justification for this new departure. It was designed to capture the Liberal party for temperance. Barker believed that if prohibitionists would be content to 'let principle come first and be our watch word . . . the question of party will right itself'.[14]

An unexpectedly early opportunity to try out the new policy occurred close to the seat of Alliance power, at a by-election at Preston in September 1872. Initially neither candidate was favourable to the

Permissive Bill. The Conservative, Holker, opposed it and publicly attacked it, while the Liberal, Major German, would not give it his public support. The Alliance sent a deputation including William Hoyle, Charles Thompson and J.H. Raper to organise electoral action among the estimated 1,000 to 1,500 temperance electors in the constituency. Special placards showing Lancashire 'Drink Facts' and 10,000 leaflets were also supplied. This was a considerable show of strength. Lawson strongly urged that the Alliance should field its own candidate, or failing this, persuade temperance voters to abstain from voting altogether. Peter Spence, a strong Alliance supporter, was approached by local temperance men with a view to his standing as an independent Liberal. In order to avert this possibility, German agreed to support the Bill with stringent qualifications. As a result most local temperance electors agreed to vote for him, although a few seem to have abstained. Despite this, German lost the election.[15]

Lawson was disappointed but concluded that because two straight party men were standing, neither of whom really liked his Bill, the Alliance would not have gained materially even if the Liberal had won. He contrasted this with what had happened in the Aberdeen by-election a few months earlier. Here neither party candidate had favoured the Permissive Bill and John Farley Leith was persuaded to stand as an independent Liberal. With the help of 1,000 temperance votes he topped the poll.[16] As a result of the promptings of Lawson, a special meeting of the Executive framed the following resolution:

> That whenever a vacancy occurs in the representation of any constituency, the electors are recommended to put in nomination a candidate favourable to the Permissive Bill, and the Council of the United Kingdom Alliance pledges itself to give such candidate every possible support, by deputation, lectures and the distribution of publications. In the event of any constituency being unable to procure a suitable candidate, the Council pledges itself to find candidates, so as to afford every elector an opportunity of recording his vote in favour of the Permissive Bill, until the question be decided.[17]

It is not clear what Alliance leaders expected would follow from this resolution. From the views of Barker, which have already been quoted, it would appear that some regarded it mainly as a means of forcing the Liberal party into line, but others may have been more optimistic about the possibility of forming a viable and independent prohibition party. The long-term implications of this new policy were not carefully thought out at the time. Both Lawson and the Executive had taken up a more uncompromising stand than anything they had previously contemplated, seemingly more in anger and disappointment over the Licensing Act of 1872 rather than as a result of realistic discussions about its practicality.

Once the support of W.C. Trevelyan, the Alliance president, had been obtained, the resolution was placed before the annual meeting in October 1872. This provided the first real opportunity for rank-and-file Alliance men to voice their opinion of the new strategy. It soon became clear that a vocal group, led by Thomas Whittaker, Handel Cossham and Charles Pease, were opposed to it. As staunch Liberals they felt unable to set aside their Liberal convictions and cast their vote on the Permissive Bill alone. Handel Cossham pointed out that

> we are not only temperance reformers, we are citizens of a free country, and bound by every obligation of duty and self-interest to express our opinions through our representatives in Parliament on all questions that affect the well-being of society; but how can this be done if we only vote for Permissive Bill men? Surely, because I feel it right to abstain from intoxicating drinks I do not cease to hold opinions on other questions.[18]

They realised that as most prohibitionists were Liberals, it would be the Liberal party that would be most severely damaged if the policy of abstaining or running independent candidates was carried out on a large scale. Even Samuel Pope was dubious about this method of seeking to win over the Liberal party because it 'would involve us in a contest with all our accustomed political associations', and work to the benefit of Conservative candidates. He reluctantly supported the new initiative but realised that it must be made to work, or the Alliance would become a joke.[19]

Alliance leaders chose to ignore these differences of opinion and with enthusiastic backing from the more uncompromising supporters who put prohibition before party, the resolution was passed. The work of forming associations of temperance electors throughout the country began at once. J.W. Owen was hired as an electoral and organisational agent in order to co-ordinate activities, Lawson toured the country endeavouring to whip up support for the electoral policy, and canvasses were begun in some constituencies in search of voters willing to join electoral associations. Joseph Malins was approached in order to get the help of Good Templar Lodges. A conference between Alliance and Good Templar representatives decided not to enter into any formal arrangement, but work informally through their respective agents at the constituency level.[20]

During the following year the new policy came under fire from politicians and the Press. Alliance involvement in the Preston by-election had already been attacked by both Liberals and Conservatives. The former complained that because the Liberal candidate had been forced by prohibitionists to pledge half-hearted support for the Permissive Bill, he earned the hostility of all local publicans who then helped to defeat him at the polls. Conservatives on the other hand were convinced that the Liberal did not really support the Permissive Bill, indeed he personally owned some public houses, consequently they argued that Alliance support was being given purely on party grounds. The Alliance in other words was no more than a party political organisation.[21] The more usual Liberal complaint, heard at by-elections during 1873, was that prohibitionists helped Conservatives to victory by abstaining when a Liberal candidate did not support the Permissive Bill. The 'miserable defection' of prohibitionists was held responsible for Liberal defeats at East Staffordshire and Hull.[22] Some suggested that the 'political ingratitude' of the Alliance towards the party that had done most for it was in large part responsible for the Tory comeback in by-elections during 1873. Liberal candidates were caught both ways. If they repudiated prohibitionists, they forfeited their votes, but if they supported the Permissive Bill they earned the united hostility of local publicans who threw all their weight behind the Tory candidate.[23]

The Press quickly realised that drink trade and prohibitionist pressure in the constituencies was polarising positions on temperance reform along party lines. The *Manchester Examiner* concluded that because of Alliance pressure 'the most eligible of candidates is a brewer'. While brewers were being forced to look to the Tory party, Liberals were being driven 'into the arms of the Temperance party'. The danger was that elections could turn upon a 'small' issue rather than major national ones, as should be the case. The temperance-oriented *Western Morning News* observed that 'the publican henceforth will determine to know nothing about Imperial or local politics', but the Alliance could, with more justice, be accused of 'deliberately ignoring patriotism and public policy' because it had initiated the battle by insisting on the political primacy of the Permissive Bill.[24]

MPs expressed their feelings on Alliance activity by subjecting the

Permissive Bill to a crushing defeat in 1873 when only 81 voted for it and 321 against. This was the lowest level of support it had attracted since 1864. The Executive concluded that 'the politicians themselves have thrown down the gauntlet. No one can doubt that the division ... was expected to crush the political action of the Alliance'. In view of the possibility of an early general election, the 'triple force' of Bruce, Disraeli and the brewers had combined in opposition. Ever ready to sense a political conspiracy the Executive believed that 'the word has passed along both sides of the House, in such a way as to be equivalent to a bid to secure the liquor party in future emergencies'.[25]

Attempts to implement the new electoral policy at times ran into difficulties. There were three by-elections at Bath during 1873. In the first, won by the Tories, neither party fielded a candidate favourable to the Permissive Bill. Consequently 150 voters formed the Bath Permissive Bill Electoral Association to organise united action by temperance voters. In the second election the same situation prevailed. Temperance men then threatened to run William Hoyle as an independent candidate and were only dissuaded from doing so by a promise from the Liberal committee that in the next election the official candidate would support the Permissive Bill. Temperance electors were then left in a quandary as to what to do. A majority voted in favour of abstaining, but many did not abide by this decision and voted for the Liberal purely on party grounds. However the Tory was again successful.[26]

In the final election of the year the official Liberal, Haytor, again opposed the Permissive Bill, despite previous promises to the contrary. This so infuriated a group of local temperance men that they persuaded Charles Thompson, a member of the Executive, to run as an independent. This created a split within the local temperance community as many preferred 'their party to their principles' and felt that Thompson's candidature would seriously damage the official Liberal's chances. J.H. Raper, who was on the spot, reported to the Executive that the result was likely to be a fiasco because local temperance men were so divided, consequently the Executive made no real effort to aid Thompson's candidature and took care not to become too closely identified with it. Thompson was prevented from holding any public meetings because of the disruptive and intimidatory tactics of Haytor's supporters and eventually polled only 57 votes, only one-third the number of those who had enrolled in the Bath Electoral Association earlier in the year. The rest voted for Haytor who won, thus demonstrating that it was possible for a Liberal to succeed without pledging support for the Permissive Bill.[27]

Events at Bath indicated that the new electoral policy would be difficult to implement wherever party loyalties were fiercely held. The resulting conflict of interest meant that united action by temperance men could not be guaranteed. In such a situation a prohibition candidate stood no chance of success. A by-election at Liverpool earlier in 1873 provided a marked contrast and indicated the gains which could result from working closely with the Liberal party, providing the official candidate supported the Permissive Bill. Here W.S. Caine, a strong Alliance supporter, had originally attempted to get Hugh Mason, a vice-president of the Alliance, to stand as Liberal candidate with Alliance encouragement. When this failed he reluctantly stood himself with the active backing of the Alliance. Caine felt that his youth (he was thirty), and his advocacy of the Permissive Bill would not make him a good candidate. He was advised to soft-pedal on the Permissive Bill but refused to do so and consequently gained the votes of nearly 6,000 temperance supporters, 2,000 of whom were reputed to be Conservatives. While failing to win the seat he was more successful than anyone had expected, increasing the Liberal vote by 1,400.[28] The Executive immediately recognised this as a precedent which might be profitably emulated and both parties were requested to provide a list of prospective candidates so that their views on the Permissive Bill might be vetted.

After these varied experiences Alliance men gathered together for the annual meeting in October 1873 to discuss once again the electoral policy. Lawson, its original promoter, was unrepentant. He argued that the main charge laid against it, that it would break up the Liberal party, was unjust. Other groups had adopted the same tactics, but they had not been criticised in this way. He concluded from this that the Alliance had attracted such criticism only because it was so powerful; it bothered the 'wire-pullers', a group of politicians he particularly despised. Nevertheless some important lessons had been learned from the events of the previous year and the policy was significantly modified. There was a partial retreat from the original resolution which the Executive claimed had never been intended, 'to induce electors to throw over all other convictions ... and bring forward candidates distasteful to the general body of politicians, simply as Permissive Bill candidates'. It was explained that prohibitionist candidates were unlikely to appear in any numbers. This meant that the Alliance abandoned any hopes that may have been entertained in 1872 about the possibility of founding a separate prohibition party to contest elections. The strong political affiliations of so many temperance men clearly made this impracticable. The Executive realised that if disastrous splits among prohibitionists were to be avoided the electoral policy could not be enforced indiscriminately and without due regard for local circumstances. It could only be used if a majority of Alliance men in any constituency wished to implement it. This concession did not silence moderates who were concerned at the damage which might be inflicted on the Liberal party but it was sufficient to prevent them breaking away from the Alliance altogether.[29] The *Saturday Review* drily noted that 'the report of a breach in the Alliance was unfounded'.[30]

In a further attempt to maintain unity the Executive insisted that its resolution in 1872 'did intend to recommend that the electors should secure the nomination ... of a candidate who, to his party qualifications, added the support of the Permissive Bill'.[31] While the original resolution had not been interpreted in this way, the Executive in 1873 did urge prohibitionists to infiltrate their local party association and endeavour to influence the selection of candidates. This meant in effect that a new dimension had been added to the electoral policy. Not only would organised groups of prohibitionists seek to persuade a candidate to support the Permissive Bill by threatening to withhold their votes if he did not, they would also attempt to influence the initial selection of the candidate. If successful, this latter approach would eliminate any possibility of a clash between prohibitionist principles and party loyalties because only supporters of the Permissive Bill would become candidates.

After the poor vote on the Permissive Bill in 1873, the Executive realised that its best chance of success lay in getting the Bill accepted as a plank in the platform of either major party. It could then be officially promoted by the party. This placed the intended aims of electoral organisation into much clearer perspective. The aim was to demonstrate to both parties the voting power which the Alliance could command, as a means of persuading them to adopt the Permissive Bill. The Executive pointed out that

at present, when party leaders want to select candidates, every working politician knows how carefully the balance is weighed between the opposition and support which the advocacy of any opinion not yet recognised as a party requirement will arouse. Too often the question is not, 'Are those views right?' but, 'Can we win without them?'. The two points on which politicians must be satis-

fied are — 1. Is the Alliance resolution real? 2. Are the adherents
of the resolution strong enough to make their support worth
having?[32]

Given the political affiliations of most prohibitionists this could
only mean that the Liberal party was the main target. Both Pope and
Leatham frankly recognised this at the annual meeting and urged
prohibitionists to press on with the task of making the Liberal party a
temperance party, however uncongenial the work might be for loyal
party men.[33] There were other reasons why the Alliance had little
choice but to look to the Liberals. The Conservative party was not a
realistic target because, although its record on temperance reform up
to the early seventies was in no way inferior to that of the Liberals, it
had proceeded along different lines. Intemperance had been attacked
as a threat to public order, but landowners, reliant on brewers'
demand for their barley, disliked the temperance movement. Conservatives did not share the Liberal enthusiasm for self-help, local self-
government, or attacks on local magistrates which the prohibitionist
approach to reform involved. The few Conservatives in the ranks of
the Alliance were convinced that a Tory government was more likely
to pass a Permissive Bill than a Liberal one. They remembered that
Conservatives had been eager to 'dish the Whigs' in 1846 and 1867,
and hoped the same would happen with the Permissive Bill. However
the bulk of prohibitionists, overwhelmingly Liberal in inclination,
refused to take such predictions seriously.[34]

A further reason for looking to the Liberal party stemmed from the
fact that most support for the Permissive Bill in the Commons already
came from this source. If the divisions on the Bill in 1869 and 1873 are
taken as examples, in 1869 it was supported by 92 MPs, of whom 76
were Liberals, while in 1873 it was supported by 88, of whom 75 were
Liberals. Thus the new policy was as much as anything a recognition
of political realities. The licensing crisis of 1871-2 had very little
impact on either the over-all level of support, or its party complexion.
Both in 1869 and 1873 Liberal support for the measure consisted of
about 20 per cent of total Liberal voting strength in the Commons. In
the 1873 division almost half of all Liberal support was drawn from the
'Celtic fringe'. Of the English Liberals, all but three of the 39 voting in
favour (including the teller Lawson) sat for borough seats. Most were
large provincial towns, the average number of voters in each being
over twice as numerous as the average for all English borough seats.
Only 14 of the constituencies voting in favour had fewer than the

national average of borough votes. The small volume of Tory support, 16 out of a party strength of 279 in 1869, came mainly from Ireland. Between 1869 and 1873 the number of English Conservative supporters fell from six to one, this last being Hugh Birley, MP for Manchester, home of the Alliance.[35]

By the end of 1873 the Alliance had settled upon an electoral policy which was designed to apply both external and internal pressure on the Liberal party, with the intention of making it the party of permissive prohibition. Existing parliamentary support for the Permissive Bill was limited to a small group of Radical and Nonconformist MPs who reflected the sources of support upon which the Alliance was able to draw in the constituencies. Whigs and moderates had still not been won over, but rather than spend more time on their conversion, the Alliance had now decided to try to eliminate them by working towards a Liberal party dominated by Radicals and Nonconformists. In order to ensure that only the right kind of MPs reached the Commons, there was a marked shift in the focus of activity, away from parliament itself to the constituencies.

Thus the electoral strategy worked out between 1872 and 1873 was extremely ambitious. It sought to do nothing less than change the whole complexion of the parliamentary Liberal party, but because the Alliance was without influential support within the party, it had to mount its attack as an outsider. Its campaign fell into three clearly definable stages. First, the Liberal sympathies of most Alliance supporters had to be turned into an effective electoral asset. This meant either the establishment of electoral associations to pressure parliamentary candidates into supporting the Permissive Bill, or infiltration of local Liberal associations as a means of influencing the initial choice of candidates. Secondly, and as a result of constituency activity, the small knot of Radical and Nonconformist support in the Commons had to be enlarged until it comprised virtually the whole of the party, or at least a majority of it. Lastly, it was necessary to win the active support of Liberal leaders. This was vital if legislation was to be passed, but in the absence of personal links between prohibitionists and the leadership, this could only be achieved after the first and second stages had been completed. Leaders were unwilling to listen to the demands of the Alliance, but they could not lightly dismiss the views of their party.

The Alliance put its new policy to the test on a wide scale for the first time in the 1874 general election, but before looking at this it is necessary to assess how effectively it had been implemented prior to

the election. While prohibitionists already held positions of importance in some local Liberal associations there was no time to effect
more extensive infiltration because barely three months elapsed
between the annual meeting at which this policy had been decided
upon in October 1873 and the election. Progress in this direction was
not discernible until the mid-seventies. Attempts at electoral organisation had been underway for somewhat longer. The *Alliance News*
recorded the establishment of one new electoral association between
January and June 1871, two more were set up between July and
December 1871 and a further two between January and June 1872.
The greatest advance came after the formal acceptance of the new
policy when 23 new associations were formed between January and
December 1873. Clearly the Executive was successful in urging
prohibitionists in the constituencies to unite. While it is not possible to
discover exactly how many electoral associations existed by the end of
1873, there were probably more than fifty. Some had been formed in
the late 1860s as a result of local initiatives and still operated, while in
other places Alliance Auxiliaries reorganised themselves for electoral
action without changing their name.

However the mere spread of electoral associations does not demonstrate their effectiveness. Most were not put to the test before the
general election, but in the few places where they were, the unanimity
of viewpoint implied by the existence of an association sometimes
proved illusory. The example of what happened at Bath has already
been examined. A similar clash between prohibitionist principles and
party loyalties erupted in Exeter when the local auxiliary decided to
adopt the new electoral policy because both sitting MPs were opposed
to the Permissive Bill. Some staunch Liberals believed this to be a 'sui-
cidal course' and one local prohibitionist urged everyone to 'stick to
our good old Liberal cause and try to stamp out the Tories'. In a by-
election for East Staffordshire neither candidate supported the Bill, so
the Alliance and Good Templars decided to abstain. Many Good
Templars attacked this decision and Joseph Malins had to intervene in
order to persuade them to toe the line. This they did, thus helping to
defeat the Liberal by a large majority. The Executive saw this as cause
for congratulation. At the Hull by-election local temperance men
decided to abstain only after a lengthy discussion, and by a fairly small
majority, but once the decision had been taken almost everyone seems
to have abided by it. Once again the Liberal was defeated and all the
local publicans voted for the Conservatives. The new policy was being
made to work, but not without considerable difficulty. It certainly

could not be assumed that any electoral association would act as intended when the time came.[36]

Immediately after the 1873 annual meeting, the Alliance began to make detailed preparations in anticipation of a general election. William Hoyle and some of the leading financial contributors decided to start a fund 'to aid the expenses of suitable candidates who agree to contest eligible constituencies in the interests of the Permissive Bill'. A committee consisting of Benjamin Whitworth, William Saunders and Hoyle was formed to allocate the fund of nearly £4,000. Hoyle also drew up a list of constituencies 'with a view of some definite action at the General Election'. These included Whitehaven, Middlesborough, Northallerton, Scarborough, Whitby, York, Leeds, Hull, North Riding of Yorkshire and Hartlepool. Contact was made with supporters in each area to see what could be done.[37]

However the general election was called before the organisation of these constituencies had been completed and it proved impossible to concentrate all the energies and resources of the Alliance in these areas. Alliance *Minute Books* indicate that during the election the Executive acted as a clearing house for electoral intelligence, provided speakers and pamphlets, and suggested possible candidates for various constituencies, while the *Alliance News* kept local men informed of developments elsewhere and served to keep them up to the mark on the tactics to adopt. Such was the rush however that speakers most heavily in demand, particularly Raper and Hoyle, could do no more than fulfil a fraction of the requests for their services. The Executive was largely in the hands of local supporters and auxiliaries and much depended on local energy and enthusiasm. Some auxiliaries and agents were wildly over-optimistic in assessing their likely influence over events but the Executive had to rely on their reports, as neither time nor people were available to make a more impartial assessment of the situation. Consequently resources were frequently absorbed by areas which had no chance of influencing the outcome of the election.

However the policy advocated was clear; whichever candidate pledged his support for the Permissive Bill was to receive the help and votes of Alliance supporters. If the officially endorsed Liberal candidate did so, there was usually no problem and the contest could proceed along normal party lines. If the Tory supported the Bill and the Liberal did not, as happened at Grimsby, prohibitionists were urged to vote for the Conservative. Most of them seem to have done so in Grimsby as a Liberal majority in 1868 was converted into a narrow Tory victory in 1874. If no candidate was pledged, then supporters were to abstain. In some cases the mere threat of this was sufficient to win some concessions as at Oxford and Bath.[38] But once again there were clashes between party loyalties and temperance sympathies; if local temperance men were staunch Liberals as at Hove, little could be done to influence the election. In a few constituencies Alliance men realised their limitations and were prepared to work quietly for candidates who had privately shown themselves to be favourable or neutral as was the case in Ayrshire and Woodstock; the active hostility of publicans therefore was not aroused.

In instances where no candidates were prepared to support the Permissive Bill, the Executive was often requested by local supporters to find someone who would. Before making any move in this direction it took care to ensure that there was sufficient support to make it worthwhile. If there was not, local men were urged to abstain. Any attempt to run a Permissive Bill candidate was discouraged. All those suggested as possible candidates combined support for the Permissive Bill with a wider appeal to voters, indeed most requests from local men specified that they needed a Nonconformist, disestablishment candidate, as well as one who was sound on the Permissive Bill. The following names were suggested as possible candidates for one or more constituencies during the 1874 election:

Hugh Mason	Sir George B. Pechell
J.S. Wright	W.R. Callender
Arthur Pease	W. Hoyle
* W.S. Caine	Alderman Tatham
William Saunders	Fielden Thorpe
Angus Holden	Charles Thompson
** Alex M. Arthur	* Handel Cossham
W.C. Trevelyan	Alfred Illingworth
* F.R. Lees	James Clark
T. Milner-Gibson	Alex Balfour
* Prof. Thorold Rogers	* Joseph Chamberlain
J.A. Partridge	* Edward Vivian
* contested the election	** were elected

Usually local men asked the Executive to suggest several possible names but occasionally they requested it to use its influence on a particular candidate, whom local supporters had already approached, in order to persuade him to stand. This was the case with Chamberlain while he was thinking of standing at Leicester and

Angus Holden at Paisley. W.R. Callender, an Alliance supporter and son-in-law of Samuel Pope the Honorary Secretary, was the only Conservative proposed; the rest were Liberals or Radicals who would appeal to one or more of the advanced sections of the Liberal Party. Their links with the Alliance varied; eight were Vice-Presidents in 1874, but the connections of others were more distant. The proposal that W.C. Trevelyan should become a candidate was half-hearted and came to nothing as he was not interested. With the exception of Benjamin Whitworth, none of those intimately connected with the day-to-day running of the Alliance finally stood. Both Hoyle and Raper believed that they were of more value in ensuring the smooth running of the Alliance during the election. An attempt was made to persuade Samuel Pope to contest a London borough, but he refused. Only seven of those suggested eventually became candidates, some of them not in constituencies for which they had originally been proposed. Only two, Alex M. Arthur and W.R. Callender, were selected. Only three of those put forward became endorsed Liberal candidates, while Callender was an official Conservative candidate in Manchester. The rest went forward in competition with the endorsed Liberal. The Alliance was one of several groups putting up unofficial candidates but it was careful to involve itself in situations of this kind only when the endorsed Liberal was unsympathetic. When three Liberal candidates looked like coming forward at Stoke-on-Trent, all pledged to support the Permissive Bill, the Executive was alarmed. Local supporters were urged to get rid of one candidate in order to 'avert a disaster'.[39] Unofficial candidates put forward by other groups were also given help by Alliance men provided they supported the Permissive Bill and official candidates were opposed. Several of those put forward by the Labour Representatation League, including Henry Broadhurst at High Wycombe, John Kane at Middlesborough and Benjamin Lucraft in Finsbury, were given enthusiastic support; so also was Mottershead at Preston although he was involved in a straight fight with two Tories.

As a result of the general election a Conservative government was returned with an overall majority of 50 seats. Immediately after his defeat Gladstone laid most of the blame on the trade, claiming he had been 'borne down in a torrent of gin and beer'. However John Bright believed that the Alliance was responsible for the movement of publicans and brewers into the Tory camp and therefore for the Liberal defeat. *The Times* agreed and concluded that 'the declamations of the Alliance are impotent as compared with the resolute opposition of a trade in arms'. Prohibitionist 'fanaticism' had been no match for trade 'self-interest'.[40] The Alliance accepted that 'beer and bible' had contributed to the result but attempted to play down the importance of the trade campaign. Lawson believed that trade strength had been augmented because 'they had formed an alliance with all sorts of discontented people throughout the country'.[41] Certainly the Liberal government had alienated other sectional interests as well as the brewers; trade unionists, and Nonconformists disgruntled with the Education Act defected in some numbers. Furthermore there was some disenchantment with the 'tameness' of foreign policy and Gladstone's financial stringency. In his study of the election Professor Hanham has endorsed the verdict of the Alliance and played down the importance of the brewers to the extent that the trade was actively hostile to Liberal candidates only in those constituencies where they supported the Permissive Bill.[42]

Because it was prepared to support the claims of independent Radicals against party candidates, the Alliance undoubtedly contributed to the downfall of some Liberals. Twenty-two constituencies in England and Wales were affected by Liberals standing against each other and in twelve of these Liberals would have won if all Liberal votes had been cast for the one candidate.[43] The Alliance was involved in most of these cases and therefore helped split the Liberal vote. This was exactly what its electoral policy was *designed* to achieve whenever the official candidate was not favourable to the Permissive Bill but two facts are worthy of note in this context. First, prohibitionists were not completely united behind the electoral policy during the election and, as was later admitted, some gave party loyalty precedence over temperance considerations.[44] Secondly, when the efforts of *all* pressure groups supporting independent candidates are weighed in the balance, they are still not enough by themselves to explain the Liberal defeat. If they can be held responsible for the loss of all twelve seats, the failure of the Liberals to hold these was not decisive as they suffered a net loss of 64 seats.

However the independence displayed by Radicals certainly did not help the Liberal cause in 1874. The constituency workers on whom the Liberal party relied were of two types,

> Those who have faith or hope in the party as such; and the men of 'isms', who expect the party will support the special measures which they believe would be beneficial to the community ... It is this belief which imparts activity ... and maintains political vitality.[45]

This latter group, 'the men of "isms" ' attached to groups such as the Alliance, were often the most energetic of constituency workers and their defection cost the Liberal party dearly. This did not happen only in constituencies where independents were standing, there was a general feeling that 'leaders without a policy and statesmen without principles find their natural results in followers without loyalty'.[46] Because Liberal leaders had failed to come up with an issue behind which the party could unite, reformist groups felt justified in pushing their own panaceas. The contrast with the 1868 general election was marked, for then the Irish Church issue had been powerful enough to override sectional demands and unify the party.

The Alliance was by no means the only pressure group which looked to the Liberal party to implement its demands; in addition to the Liberation Society and the National Education League there were many others of varying size and degrees of formal organisation. All were seeking to persuade the Liberal party and its leaders that their own particular concern was of greater urgency and importance than any other. The methods they adopted differed somewhat. Professor Hamer has suggested that in general two choices were open to them. They could either force themselves upon the Liberal party and its leaders by aggressive and threatening electoral action, as did the Alliance and the Liberation Society, or they could behave loyally and responsibly and thereby hope to earn the gratitude of the leadership, as did Welsh MPs in the eighties under the careful leadership of Stuart Rendel.[47]

However it would be a mistake to assume that the Alliance in the seventies had any such choice of tactics open to it. The resources at its disposal dictated that a concentration on electoral activity was the only course of action available, once the methods used up to 1871 had been discredited and discarded. No leading prohibitionist possessed the patience, spirit of compromise, and willingness to see sectional activity in a wider context, that Rendel displayed. Although an equally fervent Liberal, Lawson was not a 'party' man in the same sense. Confessing to being 'only an agitator' rather than a legislator, he considered it his political duty to act as the conscience of his party. By holding up before it everything that was right and good he hoped to ensure that it always remained a party of principle. To do this effectively he had to maintain a certain detachment from mundane political considerations in order, if necessary, to point out to the Liberal party the error of its ways. Lawson would 'far rather be the nuisance of a party than its solicitor general'. The art of political compromise was foreign to him and he was ever ready to brand it as 'wire-pulling' and intrigue. He was a political outsider who never really understood the political motivations of others, or the art of influencing Liberal leaders.[48]

Even if Lawson had wished to adopt tactics similar to those employed by Rendel he would have found it impossible to do so. The Alliance drew the bulk of its support from among provincial Nonconformists. Like Lawson, such people regarded politics as an activity dominated by questions of principle and morality. From this stemmed their great energy, enthusiasm and drive, but also their dogmatism, inability to entertain compromises and unwillingness to discuss detail. With political horizons necessarily limited to the provincial environment in which they lived and worked, their support could only be retained if the Alliance continued to uphold a principle, turn down all compromises, and also provide an outlet for the energy and enthusiasm they possessed. This could be most effectively and easily achieved by concentrating agitation at the constituency level where they were at home, rather than at Westminster which was unfamiliar to most of them. Any attempt to persuade such people to hold themselves in check and await developments in the Commons was always likely to lead to discontent and a falling off in support for the Alliance such as was to take place in the 1880s.

Lawson's freedom of action was constrained in a second way. Welsh MPs were conscious of belonging to a distinctive group within the Liberal party because they, and they alone, represented Welsh interests, but the Liberal MPs who between 1869 and 1878 cast their vote for the Permissive Bill did not regard themselves in the same way. The Alliance always assumed that the annual division on the Permissive Bill was a true measure of the support it enjoyed in the Commons, but this cannot be accepted uncritically. MPs could, and did, vote for the Bill without genuinely believing in its efficacy. For some it was a way of bringing pressure to bear on the government to bring in a more moderate measure of its own. This is borne out by the increase in support enjoyed by the Permissive Bill in 1871, which was partly a protest vote at the government's failure to persevere with the Bruce Bill introduced earlier in the year. Aware that it could not succeed, others voted for the Bill simply to placate prohibitionist voters.[49] H.A. Bruce estimated that not more than a quarter of those who voted for it, genuinely favoured it. Samuelson thought that all its supporters apart from Lawson believed it to be impractical and John Bright observed that 'almost all who vote for it condemn it in private conversation'.

Bruce concluded that the true opinion of the House of Commons had never been ascertained. Weary of the rush of MPs leaving the chamber before a division could be taken after a Permissive Bill debate, he urged them to stay and express their true opinion, but to no avail.[50]

The Bill was not a party measure, nor was it an exclusive indication of an MP's commitment to temperance reform. It was possible to be a sincere temperance reformer and still refuse to vote for the Permissive Bill. The situation in the Commons was a reflection of that in the country as a whole where there were many temperance societies with competing legislative proposals from which to choose. Because those who supported the Permissive Bill did so for a wide variety of reasons, the Bill could not act as a unifying force or provide the basis for a discernable section within the parliamentary Liberal party. The primary political allegiances of those MPs who voted for Lawson usually lay elsewhere. This was not what the Alliance had hoped and expected. The fact that some MPs were cheerfully prepared to vote for the Bill, clearly without understanding the principles on which it was based, worried some prohibitionists.[51] They urged that the Alliance should work towards building up a group of really committed MPs, even though they might be few in number, but Lawson rejected this as unrealistic. He felt that if they waited until the House of Commons became teetotal, they would 'wait until doomsday'.[52] The evil was too great to allow such a delay. But this did mean that Lawson was not the acknowledged leader of a distinct section of temperance MPs, in the way that Rendel was. Consequently it was futile for him to adopt Rendel's policy, because he had no parliamentary following whose loyalty he could pledge. Whatever weight he carried in the Commons derived solely from the fact of his being an individual MP and the leader of the Alliance, an extra-parliamentary pressure group. Lawson's inability to gather around him a group of really committed temperance Liberals was a serious weakness which subsequently greatly hindered the progress of the Alliance. Prohibitionist loyalists in the constituencies had adopted electoral strategies which created in the Commons a group of MPs who were too often reluctant supporters of the Permissive Bill. There was no possibility that these MPs would be willing to do in the Commons what prohibitionists were doing in the constituencies, and put temperance reform above all other considerations.

Notes

1. *12th Annual Report 1864*, p. 20; *Alliance News*, 9 Dec. 1871, p. 815.
2. *Alliance News*, 9 Dec. 1871, p. 814; 21 Oct. 1871, p. 676; 16 Dec. 1871, pp. 837, 839; 25 Nov. 1871, p. 768.
3. Ibid., 2 Dec. 1871, p. 795; 21 Oct. 1871, p. 676.
4. Ibid., 25 Nov. 1871, p. 768; 20 Jan. 1872, p. 47; 27 Jan. 1872, pp. 67, 70.
5. Many of them believed this was contrary to earlier promises he had made. Opposition was organised by a local licensed grocer. The Executive offered to intervene on his behalf but Trevelyan declined the offer, presumably because he did not wish to invite further trouble.
6. John Wodehouse, First Earl of Kimberley, 'A Journal of Events during the Gladstone Ministry 1868-1874', ed. Ethel Drus, *Camden Miscellany*, vol. XXI (1958), pp. 29-30.
7. Bruce quoted in *20th Annual Report 1872*, p. 18.
8. The passing of the Bill is discussed in Brian Harrison, *Drink and the Victorians. The Temperance Question in England 1814-1872* (1971), pp. 271-6 and Paul Smith, *Disraelian Conservatism and Social Reform* (1967), pp. 166-70.
9. *20th Annual Report 1872*, pp. 38, 46; *Alliance News*, 22 June 1872, p. 466.
10. Ibid., pp. 460-1; *Minutes*, 15 May 1872.
11. *20th Annual Report 1872*, p. 38 (original emphasis).
12. See R.C.K. Ensor, *England 1870-1914* (1936), pp. 20-2; H.J. Hanham, *Elections and Party Management. Politics in the Time of Disraeli and Gladstone* (1959), pp. 222-5; Harrison, *Drink and the Victorians*, pp. 279-85.
13. Kimberley, 'Journal', p. 22; Smith, *Disraelian Conservatism*, pp. 166-71.
14. *Alliance News*, 13 July 1872, p. 508.
15. *Minutes*, 28 Aug. 1872; for a report of the election campaign see *Alliance News*, 31 Aug. — 14 Sept. 1872.
16. Ibid., 19 Oct. 1872, p. 735; 6 July 1872, p. 493.
17. *Minutes*, 30 Sept. 1872. This was almost verbatim a copy of the resolution moved by the Anti-Corn Law League in 1843.
18. *Alliance News*, 4 Oct. 1873, p. 635.
19. Ibid.
20. *Minutes*, 28 May 1873. This was simply a recognition of the cooperation between the two bodies which was already taking place at the local level, e.g. *Minutes*, 29 Jan. 1873. Good Templars probably did not wish to create tighter links with the Alliance for fear of losing their independence of action. There were also occasional frictions between members of the two bodies which may have hindered closer ties, e.g. *Minutes*, 19 March 1873; 11 June 1873.
21. *Saturday Review*, 21 Sept. 1872, p. 346; *Alliance News*, 21 Sept. 1872, pp. 675-6.
22. Ibid., 21 Sept. 1873, p. 535; *Manchester Guardian*, quoted in ibid., 1 Nov. 1873, pp. 704-5; *Leeds Mercury*, 24 Oct. 1873.
23. *Alliance News*, 6 Sept. 1873, p. 561; 17 Jan. 1874, p. 42.
24. Quoted in ibid., 30 Aug. 1873, p. 552 and *21st Annual Report 1873*, pp. 1, 33.
25. Ibid., pp. 4, 14-15.
26. Alliance activity in by-elections at this time is discussed in D.A. Hamer, *The Politics of Electoral Pressure. A Study in the History of Victorian Reform Agitations* (1977), ch. 9 and the Bath elections are examined in some detail in pp. 184-8.
27. *Alliance News*, 4 Oct. 1873, p. 625; 17 May 1873, p. 316; 11 Oct. 1873, p. 654; *Minutes*, 8 Oct. 1873.
28. John Newton, *W.S. Caine M.P. A Biography* (1907), pp. 47-59.
29. *Alliance News*, 18 Oct. 1873, pp. 658-60; *21st Annual Report 1873*, p. 2.
30. *Saturday Review*, 18 Oct. 1873, p. 502.

31. *21st Annual Report 1873*, p. 2.

32. Ibid., p. 4.

33. *Alliance News*, 18 Oct. 1873, p. 658.

34. E.g. see Thomas Hutton in ibid.

35. Calculations based on figures derived from McCalmont, *Parliamentary Poll Book*.

36. *Alliance News*, 14 June 1873, p. 380; 9 Aug. 1873, pp. 502-3; 23 Aug. 1873, p. 535; 11 Oct. 1873, p. 640; 18 Oct. 1873, p. 661; 1 Nov. 1873, pp. 704-5.

37. *Minutes,* 22 Oct. 1873; 24 Oct. 1873. An independent fund was necessary because the Alliance constitution pledged that its general fund could not be used to pay anyone's electoral expenses. It is difficult to discover how much of the special fund was spent or who benefited. The total fund was probably not utilised, but Professor Thorold Rogers at Scarborough, A.M. Sullivan in Louth County and Thomas Mottershead at Preston appear to have been given financial assistance.

38. During the election the Executive sat continuously (from 26 Jan. to 4 Feb.) consequently the large volume of electoral information entered in the *Minutes* cannot be referred to with precision. However the observations in the next four paragraphs are culled from this source.

39. *Minutes*, 28 Jan. 1874.

40. Gladstone quoted in Philip Magnus, *Gladstone: A Biography* (1963 edn), p. 228; Bright quoted in *22nd Annual Report 1874*, p. 8; *Times*, 14 Feb. 1874.

41. *22nd Annual Report 1874*, p. 4; *Alliance News*, 17 Oct. 1874, p. 658.

42. Hanham, *Election and Party Management*, pp. 222-7.

43. Trevor Lloyd, *The General Election of 1880* (1968), p. 146.

44. *Alliance News*, 28 Oct. 1876, p. 694.

45. W. Saunders, *The New Parliament* (1880), pp. 180-1.

46. Joseph Chamberlain in *Fortnightly Review*, vol. 20 (Sept. 1873), p. 289.

47. D.A. Hamer, *Liberal Politics in the Age of Gladstone and Rosebery* (1972), ch. 1, esp. pp. 7, 29-33.

48. *Hansard*, vol. 253, c. 377; ibid., vol. 278, c. 1291; *Alliance News*, 29 Jan. 1876, p. 66.

49. John Bright, *Hansard*, vol. 251, c. 498; B. Samuelson, ibid., vol. 206, c. 945; F.W. Cadogan, ibid., c. 941.

50. Bruce, ibid., cc. 947-950; Samuelson, ibid., c. 945; Bright quoted in *26th Annual Report 1878*, p. 43.

51. *Alliance News*, 16 Oct. 1875, p. 660.

52. Ibid., p. 660.

Chapter 3

LIBERALS AND THE ALLIANCE

It is doubtful if a Liberal victory in 1874 would have benefitted the Alliance. It would have allowed those same MPs who had so decisively rejected Lawson's Bill in the past, to do so again. As it was, Alliance support within the shrunken parliamentary Liberal party grew somewhat from 20 per cent in 1873, to 23 per cent in the vote on the Permissive Bill in 1875. While the improvement was hardly dramatic, it suggested that the new electoral policy had made an impact because there had been a marginal change in party composition in favour of prohibition. Not all prohibitionists were satisfied with the Alliance's role in the election. Party loyalists who had objected to the electoral policy in 1872 and 1873 complained bitterly about what had happened, but Alliance leaders ignored them. Because the election had left Liberals dispirited and disunited they felt that they could push their cause more boldly. The *Annual Report* for 1874 asked

> is it possible that in any successful reconstruction of the Liberal programme, the claim to popular control of the traffic in drink can be ignored? ... To those who are Liberals (within the Alliance ranks) appeals from all quarters are addressed for union and a reconstruction of party ties. These old ties are now broken. The old impulses no longer exist. In the future Liberal party it will be the fault of the Alliance Liberals themselves if they are hampered with any of the old difficulties. Let them take care that those who have now preferred their trade interest to their party associations be not trusted again, and that any reconstructed party shall at least be pure and free from association with a trade which brutalizes the people, and dims the intelligence of those to whom Liberal politicians profess to appeal.[1]

Lawson pointed out that the Alliance could no longer be accused of smashing the Liberal party because it was 'already smashed'.[2] He was convinced that as a result, the electoral policy was less likely to meet with opposition, and therefore every effort should be made to ensure its more effective implementation.

Immediately after the general election the Executive threw more of its resources into the organisation of prohibitionist voting power in the constituencies. While it had been urging this course since 1872, the commencement of organisation in any area before 1874 had relied greatly on the existence of local initiative and enthusiasm. Now as a result of the promptings of Dr J.M. McCulloch, a pioneer of electoral organisation in Scottish constituencies, the Executive began to initiate proceedings itself by means of house-to-house canvasses.[3] Most previous pledging of votes had been done by resolutions at public meetings, now it was hoped that by visiting people in their own homes the pledges they gave would be more firmly honoured. The Alliance agent John Paton was placed in charge of this work and he initiated upward of 50 canvasses between 1874 and 1879. He was helped by regional agents, auxiliaries and by canvassers hired specifically for conducting house calls. It is difficult to gauge how successful this activity was because the membership of individual electoral associations was usually not published. Paton claimed that he was most successful in Scotland and that with further work it would be possible to organise a group of electors in every constituency powerful enough to persuade every Scottish MP to support the Permissive Bill. Other evidence suggests that he was making a considerable impact there.[4] Results in England were less spectacular, but electoral associations were gathering in enough pledged voters to tip the balance in any close contest, provided of course that all were willing to stick to their pledge. The maintenance of solidarity was crucial for effective electoral work, but last minute defections were not uncommon as we have already seen.

It was for this reason that prohibitionists in 1873 had also decided, as a second arm of the Alliance electoral strategy, to work within their local Liberal associations to ensure the selection of suitable candidates. The Executive continued to urge prohibitionists to 'permeate the councils of political organisations' and 'obtain positions of influence',[5] but the Alliance machine was not well suited to this work. Its money, pamphlets and large team of agents were designed to promote a parliamentary campaign, and could do little to start proceedings within local party organisations. If local supporters were numerous and active the best the Executive could do was to encourage them. Such efforts were indirectly aided by Alliance activity in other directions. The existence of electoral associations enabled prohibitionists to go into party rooms as representatives of a tangible and sometimes sizeable bloc of voters. Also the evidence of the general election and of by-elections where Alliance threats to abstain or support independents had been carried out, was not lost on the members of local Liberal associations.

Some progress was made. In September 1875 the Liberal association in Newcastle voted in favour of local control over licensing. Three months later the Leeds Liberal association drew up a list of reforms on which it was hoped the party would unite in future. Temperance reform was not included but, on a successful motion from the floor of the meeting, ratepayer control over the issue of licences was added to the list. A fortnight later the National Reform Union meeting in Manchester adopted 'popular control over licences' as a plank in its platform. Twelve months later the Liberal Council of Stoke Boroughs, by a vote of ten to one, decided to support the Permissive Bill as its official policy and insist that any future Liberal candidate must support it also. In some places constituency organisations favoured the Permissive Bill without publicly saying so, but when potential candidates were interviewed, temperance men were numerous or influential enough to ensure that only the right people were adopted. Nevertheless this work was not proceeding as rapidly or on as wide a front as was the formation of electoral associations.[6]

Successful infiltration of Liberal constituency organisations seems to have depended on the existence of several factors. The nature of the local party organisation was important. This varied widely in the early seventies from constituencies in which there was no discernible organisation whatever, to those where recognisably modern party machinery was being assembled. The old self-perpetuating Whig oligarchies in the counties and other seats little affected by the extension of the franchise in 1867 were outside the reach of the Alliance. In the larger provincial towns where wider and more representative forms of organisation were beginning to break down Whig domination, conditions were more favourable. Alliance supporters were most numerous in such places and if an influential and active local Alliance man was on hand to unite them, the state of flux as regards party organisation provided an opportunity to bring the Permissive Bill to the fore. Even here however prohibitionist attempts to capture local associations were hampered, most notably by the spread of the 'caucus' model of constituency organisation and the establishment in 1877 of the National Liberal Federation (NLF).

The distinctive feature of Radical activity in the late 1860s and early 1870s was its individualism and fragmentation. While individual

Radicals often personally embraced the whole spectrum of reforming activity, there remained a host of separate bodies such as the Alliance seeking always to push their own particular panaceas. Without any general principles on which all could unite, Radicalism was weak and divided. Through the NLF and the spread of the 'caucus', Joseph Chamberlain hoped to change an individualistic Radicalism, suspicious of government and concerned always to limit its authority, into a disciplined force distinguished by co-operation, and with sufficient strength to provide a Liberal government with a firm majority to be used for Radical ends.[7]

To the extent that both the NLF and the Alliance were working towards a Liberal party dominated by Radicals, their aims were identical, but the ultimate purpose for which this should be used differed. The NLF wanted effective political power, the Alliance wanted the Permissive Bill. The underlying philosophy of the Alliance was of the individualistic, anti-government kind which the NLF was seeking to displace. By acting as an open forum for all those holding Radical opinions, the NLF was designed to replace the many separate Radical organisations in existence. Questions of priority for competing reform proposals would be debated and resolved democratically within the 'caucus' and the NLF, not as hitherto by separate organisations seeking to impose their will on the Liberal party from outside. By this means, 'the whole force, strength, and resources of the Liberal Party' could be concentrated upon 'the promotion of reforms found to be generally desired'.[8] Once a decision had been reached, it was binding on everyone. Thus unity would be achieved by overriding the demands of minority groups and institutionalising the desires of the majority of Radicals. This would entail the 'sacrifice of personal claims, the surrender of some cherished crotchets, the cultivation of a due sense of the proportional importance of political questions'.[9] The Liberal Party in parliament and the constituencies would be rescued from the clutches of 'crotchet-mongers' and so also would individual MPs. Consequently, unless the Permissive Bill could become a plank in the NLF programme, this would strike at the very roots of the prohibitionist campaign.

In fact the Alliance failed to make its mark on the NLF for over a decade after 1877. In the absence of a large number of local studies of Liberal associations, the reasons for this are not clear. If, as Chamberlain and Schnadhorst always claimed, the 'caucus' system was truly democratic, it must be assumed that Permissive Bill men simply did not have the numbers to make their presence felt. But it seems that the

NLF was never as democratic as this, and therefore it is possible that prohibitionists were hampered in pushing their claims by pressures less democratic than sheer weight of numbers.[10] *The Times* as early as 1878 used the fact that the Permissive Bill was not on the programme of the Birmingham Liberal Federation, despite the existence of numerous prohibitionists in the city, as evidence of a lack of democracy in the 'caucus' system.[11] While Chamberlain certainly had no desire to see the cause of the Bill advanced within the NLF, or anywhere else for that matter, the split in Alliance ranks between party loyalists and prohibitionist extremists also hindered any attempt to win over individual 'caucuses' or the NLF itself. When loyalists such as J.S. Wright of Birmingham were prepared to toe the 'caucus' line at the expense of the Alliance, the prohibitionist vote in Birmingham was split and its influence greatly diminished. The existence of the NLF strengthened the position of moderates because they could argue that as this avenue of pushing Radical demands was available, the electoral policy pursued by the Alliance was redundant. Thus Alliance attempts to capture Liberal constituency organisations were being frustrated not only by the spread of the 'caucus' model, but also by the attitudes of some prohibitionists.[12]

Alliance attempts to infiltrate the Liberal party met with obstacles in parliament as well as in the constituencies. Liberal leaders objected to the activities of the Alliance and other pressure groups because they made the task of government more difficult. Gladstone assumed that the Liberal party was the national party in the sense that it enjoyed the support of the majority of the British people. Therefore it should govern by right and seek always to do so in the national interest. But this natural process was frustrated because many Liberal voters were prepared to give their reforming desires precedence over the interests of the party as a whole. He did not want to go back to the 'absolute uniformity' of the Tory party because a degree of individuality was healthy, but insisted that Liberals must be prepared to sacrifice sectional interests for those of the party whenever there was a likelihood of a conflict between the two. In order to govern as a national party, it was necessary to frame legislation which sought to provide a national settlement for any particular issue. If such a measure was to stand any chance of gaining widespread and lasting acceptance it must inevitably be a compromise satisfactory to all interests affected, and not just those that happened to be represented within the party. Sectional interests rendered this a difficult task in two ways. First, they could object to a compromise as being inadequate and fight it both inside and outside the party as had happened with the Education Act and the Bruce Bill of 1871. Secondly, the groups themselves tried to force the Liberal party to accept their own legislative proposals which were by definition 'sectional' and 'partial', as Gladstone pointed out. These could only form the basis for a national settlement if it could be shown that they enjoyed widespread public support.[13]

It was this aspect of the Permissive Bill that particularly worried Liberal leaders. The Alliance was attempting to press it upon the Liberal party by working through *party* channels, the constituency organisations and MPs, and the fact that it had made some progress in this way gave no indication of the public support it enjoyed. Gladstone was unsure as to just what the state of public opinion was in regard to temperance reform, but he certainly did not think that the Permissive Bill was sufficiently widely accepted to provide a lasting solution to the drink problem. He observed that

> while in some subjects we trace the mind of the country, and in the mind also of Parliament, a regular progress from the first beginnings of a conviction, along clear and definite lines, to the period of their maturity, this is a subject on which the course taken by Parliament — and, possibly, the public opinion of the country — have been attended by a marked irregularity, and even by a singular reversal.[14]

John Bright was convinced that the Permissive Bill did not enjoy wide popular support and in 1874 urged temperance men to 'leave Parliament and form public opinion'. Four years later Hartington still did not think that the Bill had 'got into the phase of practical politics' because the Alliance was too impatient in trying to run before it could walk. It must 'begin at the beginning' and convince the country of the Bill's merits before introducing it into the Commons. What worried Liberal leaders was the possibility that by bowing to sectional pressures and passing measures which did not enjoy public support, they would provoke a reaction, not only against the legislation itself, but also against the government which, because of its actions, could no longer claim to be governing in the national interest.[15]

Rank-and-file MPs of both parties were also worried about the electoral activity of the Alliance, but for different reasons. Prohibitionists considered that 'Members of Parliament were simply representatives'[16] of the people, and as such they should be prepared to fall in with the wishes of their constituency. MPs naturally resented any attempt to curtail their independence in this way. Muntz threatened to resign rather than 'consent to act the part of a mere delegate'. This he believed was contrary to the British system of representative government as it undermined the freedom of the MP in commenting on and amending legislation before parliament. Gladstone objected to attempts to pin down MPs to particular pledges, believing that the views expressed by an MP on the hustings, and his past record, should be a sufficient guide to his future action. Prohibitionists should not, he insisted, attempt to force an MP, by means of threats, to act counter to his real convictions.[17] While Alliance leaders usually treated parliamentary candidates with some consideration, rank-and-file prohibitionists were often less conciliatory. They delighted in treating candidates harshly, losing no opportunity to 'teach them a lesson'. When for example it was feared that an Alliance candidate running in the 1874 election in Birmingham might cause the defeat of John Bright, one prohibitionist observed that this 'would have been a lesson to the Liberal party in general and to the Right Honourable John Bright in particular'. Philip Muntz complained that he had received more threats concerning his vote on the Permissive Bill than on any other since becoming an MP. Colonel Makins observed that it took some courage for anyone to vote against Lawson because of the risk of being pilloried by the *Alliance News* as an 'advocate of drunkenness and drunkards'; no MP took kindly to being 'bullied and humiliated by open pressure'.[18]

While Alliance attempts to infiltrate the Liberal party were being opposed by both leaders and many rank-and-file MPs, the dominance of the Permissive Bill was also being challenged by the emergence of alternative proposals for reform originating within the Liberal party. While many private members' Bills were introduced into the Commons during the decade of the seventies, the major competitor was the Gothenburg resolution introduced by Joseph Chamberlain 1877. This advocated municipal ownership and control of the drink trade, and had been born out of the disputes within the Birmingham Liberal party between prohibition extremists and party loyalists. Chamberlain was well aware that temperance reform was an important Radical demand but he had no wish to see Radicals united in support of the Permissive Bill; it was politically contentious, and even if it got into the statute book he did not think that it would provide an effective solution to the 'drink problem'. He needed an alternative which would be acceptable to both moderates and the extremists of the Alliance. By proposing that town councils take over existing interests in the retailing of drink, reduce the number of public houses, and operate the remainder 'for the convenience and on behalf of the inhabitants', he hoped to 'put a stop to those worse results of drinking which alone justify the interference of the State'.[19]

Chamberlain expected several benefits to stem from his scheme. Most notably it would defuse temperance reform as a political issue. On the one hand it would 'get rid of the United Kingdom Alliance, and ... set free the good, earnest and able men who compromise that organisation for other philanthropic work'. He was well aware from his Birmingham experiences of the dissension prohibitionists could cause in the constituencies. With an organisation behind them they were not afraid to take an independent line and with the future forma-tion of the NLF in mind, he wished to put a stop to such divisiveness and also prevent any possibility of the Permissive Bill being accepted by the 'caucuses'. On the other hand, municipal ownership would also 'exclude from our political life the baleful influence of a gigantic vested interest'. This would benefit the Liberal party because the drink trade would have no further need to look to the Tories, nor could public houses continue to act as committee rooms for the Conservative party. Chamberlain hoped to make trade acceptance of his measure more likely, by freely admitting their right to 'fair compensation'.[20]

The importance Chamberlain placed on this question is attested to by the fact that his first major initiative after becoming an MP was to introduce the Gothenburg resolution into the House of Commons. Before doing so he approached Alliance leaders and asked them to stand aside in order to give his scheme a fair trial. He pointed out that if it failed, their more radical solution would appear more acceptable. The Executive was at a loss how to react. Chamberlain's energy and originality took it by surprise. Hitherto it had looked upon him as a valued if not entirely uncritical supporter of the principles of the Alliance, not a competitor. Lawson was given a free hand as to the tactics he wished to adopt on the forthcoming debate on the Gothen-burg proposal.[21] While the Executive tried to make up its mind, prohibitionists throughout the country took the initiative. A confer-ence of temperance reformers convened in Edinburgh in March 1877 to discuss Chamberlain's proposals was decidedly hostile to them. Prominent local Alliance men like David Lewis (whose trip to see the Gothenburg system in operation in Sweden had been financed by the Alliance) and James Begg attacked the system because it included compensation, because it would not reduce drunkenness, and because 'the profits derived [from municipal ownership] would corrupt the moral sense of the community' and leave the door open for bribery and corruption.[22] The bulk of the temperance movement rapidly fell into line and opposed municipal ownership on these grounds.

Chamberlain's resolution was debated in the Commons and defeated by 103 votes to 51. He was bitterly disappointed and took the Alliance to task for not giving him more energetic and unqualified support. Lawson was singled out because while he had voted for the resolution he had spoken against it; 'he took up the position of a candid friend, and stabbed my proposition in the back'. Chamberlain felt that 'a few years more experience of the ill success attending their efforts ... may tend to induce the Alliance party to give their favourable consideration to my proposal', meanwhile he decided to 'stand aside, to give a fair field to my competitors in the race'.[23] The Alliance had beaten off the challenge, but not without cost, for in less than two years the Permissive Bill went the way of the Gothenburg proposal, having been abandoned by Lawson and the Alliance.

Lawson introduced his Bill in the Commons for the last time in 1878. In March 1879 he substituted for it a Local Option Resolution which declared that

> inasmuch as the ancient and avowed object of licensing the sale of intoxicating liquor is to supply a supposed public want, without detriment to the public welfare, this House is of the opinion that a legal power of restraining the issue or renewal of licences should be placed in the hands of the persons most deeply interested and affected — namely, the inhabitants themselves — who are entitled to protection from the injurious consequence of the present system by some efficient measure of local option.[24]

The Alliance later gave two reasons for this transition. First, by resorting to a resolution it forced future discussion to concentrate only on the *principle* of local permissive prohibition, and not, as had hitherto happened, be sidetracked by the machinery for its implementation proposed in the Permissive Bill. Secondly, it was a compromise designed to win support from those who complained that the Permissive Bill did nothing for localities wishing to reduce but not abolish the number of licences in their area.[25] These were indeed two developments which stemmed from the change, but they hardly seem adequate to account for this sudden willingness to compromise after years of stubborn inflexibility.

In the four years since the general election, no progress had been made at Westminster but this was neither surprising nor unexpected because attempts to increase support centred on electoral activity, the results of which could only become evident after another general election. However the Executive found itself in a difficult position in 1878 and appears to have suffered a crisis of confidence in its ability to push ahead with its electoral campaign. While it had settled on a means of capturing the Liberal party, the implementation of its policy was being hampered in ways that have already been examined. Prohibitionists showed a continued willingness to form electoral associations, but the work of canvassing and organisation was becoming a serious drain on Alliance finances and manpower. For the first time a lack of finance became a major constraint on activity of all kinds.[26] Attempts to capture local Liberal associations were being frustrated by the growth of 'caucuses' and the spread of the NLF philosophy and influence. Party loyalists concerned at the damage being done to the Liberal party were refusing in many areas to stick to Alliance electoral pledges. The growth of more democratic party associations encouraged them, strengthened their resolve, and gave them a forum in which to voice their opinions. Consequently moderates grew in confidence and perhaps also in numbers.[27] This placed the Executive in a difficult position. If it continued to push ahead with its electoral campaign there was a very real danger that the party loyalists such as Handel Cossham and Thomas Whittaker would defect, taking much valuable support with them. On the other hand the Executive had long realised that its electoral campaign must be applied on a broad front if it was to succeed. If it was not, as seemed to be the case, there was a danger that the next general election would be a repetition of 1874, with a divided Liberal party kept out of office for a further term. At this rate of progress it would be many years before there were enough Permissive Bill supporters in the Commons to ensure its passage and the Executive was now unsure of its ability to keep plugging away for such a long period.

Alliance leaders were also concerned at the inability of the Permissive Bill to attract more support. While most temperance organisations accepted it, the large and influential Church of England Temperance Society (CETS) did not, and there was little prospect of it having a change of heart on the matter. In the Commons it failed dismally. When introduced in 1878 it attracted no more support than it had done nine years earlier, but opposition to it had mounted. After 1872 adverse majorities of around 200 became common as Tory and Liberal MPs attempted to vote it out of existence. Because its annual failure was predictable it excited 'neither the enthusiasm of reformers nor the fear of opponents'. As early as 1872 there had been complaints that it was introduced into the Commons 'in just the same crude, impractical condition as in former years. Its promoters seem unable either to learn or forget anything'. Bruce complained that 'the almost exclusive direction of the public mind to the Permissive Bill has a most mischievous effect'.[28] By monopolising parliamentary time and the attentions of so many temperance men it prevented reforms being aired and chosen on merit. It was largely for this reason that moderate temperance reformers such as Chamberlain and the CETS resented and criticised the Alliance. John Bright believed that the Permissive Bill was 'the main obstacle to any progress in what is called temperance legislation'. Many MPs agreed with him and some of the Liberal party loyalists within the ranks of the Alliance were coming to the same conclusion.[29]

The Executive was at a loss as to what to do. Lawson still insisted that the Bill was the best scheme that he could devise to achieve the ends both he and the Alliance were seeking. Unable to come up with any alternative, the Executive urged temperance reformers to make proposals and pledged its wholehearted support for any that included the principle of permissive prohibition, but because the Alliance had been effectively discrediting alternatives for so long it was now difficult for temperance reformers to come up with anything new. The first suggestion for a new approach came from outside the Temperance movement, in an article in the *Northern Echo* on 8 August 1878. It suggested that

if the more prominent members of the temperance party — say Mr Bright, Mr Stansfeld, Sir Wilfrid Lawson, Mr A.M. Sullivan, Mr Joseph Cowen, Mr J.W. Pease, Sir Robert Anstruther, and Mr Joseph Chamberlain — could meet to devise some broad proposals which could be laid before the constituencies as the temperance programme, effectual progress might be made towards the accomplishment of something more valuable than the repeated registration of a majority of two or three hundred against the Permissive Bill. Would it not be possible for the Temperance Reformers to draft a resolution declaring that the evils of intemperance have increased, are increasing, and ought to be diminished, that the number of public houses, being far in excess of the legitimate wants of the people, should be reduced; and that in order to deal effectively with this great and growing evil it is expedient that the control of the drink traffic should be entrusted to the rate-payers? If some such resolution were to be introduced by a leading member of the House of Commons — say, by Mr Stansfeld or Mr Bright — there are very few men who caring anything at all about temperance reform, would not vote for it, and it could be pressed upon candidates at the general election, with all the force arising from the fact that it united the whole temperance party in its support. It is true that it would be but an abstract resolution, but the Permissive Bill is practically nothing more, and it lays down general principles which, if they were once generally accepted by the electors, would supply a firm basis for subsequent legislation. The suggested resolution does not enter into details. It is elastic, and it could be accepted equally by Mr Bright, Mr Cowen, Mr Chamberlain, and Sir Wilfrid Lawson.[30]

This suggestion was featured prominently in the *Annual Report* for 1878, but the Executive remained noncommital.

In September 1878 John Bright wrote a letter in which he claimed to have 'formulated some plan of reform on this subject' but refused to discuss it publicly because 'foreign policy has filled men's minds to the exclusion of all matters of home and social interest'. Lawson wrote to him to enquire what he had in mind, assured him of the sympathetic consideration of the Alliance for any plan he might have, and asked him to meet an Alliance deputation to discuss the matter. Bright agreed to this and came to Manchester to meet the Executive on 9 October. At Bright's request no minutes were taken but he noted in his diary: 'Discussion for nearly 3 hours. Explained my objections to their Bill, and what I should recommend in place of it. Interview very friendly, and I hope not without some useful results.'[31] After this meeting Lawson offered to conclude 'a [holy?] Alliance' with Bright; he would substitute a resolution for the Permissive Bill if Bright would support it. A resolution was then drafted by Lawson and Raper and accepted by the Executive. It was sent to Bright who promised to support it, convinced that it would win a much greater degree of support in the Commons than the Permissive Bill had enjoyed.[32] The final wording of the resolution was almost identical to one of the recommendations adopted by the Convocation of the Province of Canterbury in its *Report on Intemperance and its Remedies* (1869), and closely followed the suggestion made by the *Northern Echo*. Thus the stimulus to change came from outside the Alliance and the form it took was also largely determined by outside influences. Lawson's motives for accepting the change were spelt out in letters he wrote to Bright and Gladstone. He hoped to 'succeed in welding the Liberals together and minimising friction' before the next general election in order to avoid a repetition of 1874.[33] The resolution was also 'calculated to secure a union amongst us all [in the Temperance movement], which we have not hitherto been able to secure'. The use of wording from the Convocation *Report* was specifically designed to win the backing of the CETS.[34]

The Local Option Resolution represented a change in strategy by the Alliance. It was a final admission that a private members' Bill stood no chance of success. The intention now was to get the resolution passed in the Commons and then force the government to act along the lines it set down. Thus the responsibility for developing detailed machinery was placed on the shoulders of the government. The Executive however denied that the resolution was a compromise in the sense that it had moderated its demands; it regarded local option as a 'stepping stone' to the Permissive Bill or a similar measure, which in turn was a step on the road to total prohibition. But in fact the result was a change in the emphasis of Alliance demands. The resolution gave prominence to one of the principles embodied in the Permissive Bill, that of local control, at the expense of the other, that of prohibition. One of the important effects of the agitation for the Permissive Bill had been the popularisation of the principle of local control, so much so that it became much more widely accepted than the Bill itself. The substitution of local option for the Bill took this a step further.[35]

Whatever Lawson and the Executive intended by the change, many within the Alliance saw it as an unnecessary compromise. That group which had always put the Permissive Bill above party loyalty and had supported and implemented the electoral policy from 1872 onwards saw this as a betrayal of all they had worked for. Lawson had 'lowered the Alliance flag' in order to help the Liberal party out of a tight corner. They pointed out that the Local Option Resolution and the Permissive Bill 'were two different things in the estimation of members of Parliament'. Local option was so vague a demand, and could apply to so many differing schemes of reform, that few Liberal MPs would have any difficulty in supporting it. Consequently the whole point of the electoral policy, that of bringing candidates up to the mark, was lost. Extreme prohibitionists argued that the kind of support which the resolution would attract in the Commons was not likely to be sufficiently resolute to ensure the success of the Alliance campaign. They still believed that if the Alliance had stuck to the Permissive Bill the Liberal party would have been forced to seek an accommodation with it.[36] The substance of these complaints was to be amply demonstrated from 1880 onwards, but for the moment the Executive shrugged them off. It had shifted from relying on the support of the extremists, as exemplified in the electoral policy of 1872, to a reliance on the moderates who had always been concerned that Alliance activity should not damage the Liberal party. In the years after 1872 these moderates had chafed at the extremism of the Alliance, now it was the turn of the extreme prohibitionists to complain of its moderation.

Many outside the Alliance did see in its actions a willingness to compromise and welcomed this. The CETS agreed to support local option and campaign on its behalf. Alexander Balfour, a member of both organisations, expressed the hope that 'these two most influential bodies would meet and run together as one stream to the great ocean before them'. Lawson subsequently appeared on a CETS platform for the first time, commented on 'the wedding' between the two, and expressed the view that 'it was a very good match ... one which might be looked upon with satisfaction by the friends of both parties'.[37] Even more dramatic was the change in attitude of many Liberal MPs, when local option was debated in the Commons for the first time in 1879. Although the resolution was defeated, 185 voting in its favour and 273 against, it attracted more than twice as much support as the Permissive Bill, largely because the Liberal vote more than doubled. Heyck and Klecka have estimated that the average number of Radical MPs between 1874 and 1880 was 82.[38] It was almost exclusively from among these that the Permissive Bill had attracted its customary 70 or so Liberal votes. What local option managed to do was to expand Alliance support in the Commons beyond the confines of this relatively small group. In 1879 about half of all Liberal MPs voted for Lawson and only 34 voted against. The resolution attracted the moderates for the first time and even Whigs such as Sir Harcourt Johnstone were won over; of the 110 English constituencies which voted for the measure, 19 were county seats. Support was strongest in Scotland, Wales and Ireland where a majority of all MPs voted in favour. However the majority of all those voting for the resolution came from England. In this sense the Alliance was now somewhat less reliant on the 'Celtic fringe' than it had been in the mid-seventies.

This newfound unity between the Alliance and the Liberal party necessitated a modification of Alliance electoral policy. Constituencies were now urged to persuade their MPs to vote for the resolution 'not by threatening but by entreaty'. The work of electoral canvassing ceased, the formation of new electoral associations also came to a halt and the electoral resolutions passed at the annual meeting in 1879 were far less uncompromising than they had been previously. Nevertheless it was still widely expected that the next general election would repeat the pattern of 1874. R.W. Dale confidently predicted another rash of independent candidates standing against endorsed Liberals because Liberal leaders were still unable to propound a coherent programme which appealed to Radicals. Gladstone was sufficiently worried at this possibility to point out its dangers, while Adam, the Liberal whip, singled out Alliance electoral activity for censure because he believed prohibitionists were numerous enough to affect the fortunes of the party at the polls.[39] However these fears proved unfounded. In the 1880 election there was remarkably little dissension. Candidates were still besieged with requests to pledge their support for local option, but the demand was so vague that few had any trouble complying with the request. Where they were opposed Alliance men were still prepared to take an independent course of action, but in contrast to 1874, only four constituencies suffered because Liberals stood against each other, and in only one of these, Tower Hamlets, did this result in the loss of the seat. The Liberal in Tower Hamlets was opposed to local option and therefore local prohibitionists backed the independent, Benjamin Lucraft. John Hilton, an Alliance agent, even acted as chairman of Lucraft's electoral committee. The Alliance was still prepared to exact a price for its electoral support, but many more Liberals were now prepared to pay it because they found the ambiguous Local Option Resolution much easier to stomach than the Permissive Bill.

The Liberal victory in 1880 was also a victory for the Alliance. The *Alliance News* for 17 April 1880 contained a list of 248 MPs who had pledged their support for the Local Option Resolution. Sir Wilfrid Lawson had been re-elected together with nine vice-presidents. This triumph was made all the sweeter by the downfall of many of those connected with the drink trade. Wheelhouse was defeated at Leeds together with thirteen former members who were brewers, distillers and wine merchants. The Alliance could not claim to have played a major part in the Liberal victory, local option was a minor issue in an election dominated by questions of foreign policy, nevertheless the party had benefited from the energetic help provided by prohibitionists in the contituencies. That they were able to give this help unreservedly, and augment rather than subtract themselves from the

Liberal effort, was undoubtedly due in the main to the substitution of the Local Option Resolution for the divisive Permissive Bill. But other developments also made unified action easier. The composition of the parliamentary Liberal party after the victory of 1880 was very different from what it had been before the defeat of 1874. Nonconformists and Radicals had increased in numbers at the expense of Whigs, thus enlarging that section of the party from which the Alliance was most likely to attract support. Significantly, many of the candidates proposed by the Alliance in 1874 but rejected, were returned in 1880 as official Liberals.[40] While this had been the goal of the Alliance's electoral policy, it cannot take much credit for bringing about the change. This was due to much broader shifts taking place within the Liberal party, most noticeably in its more representative character, for which the NLF and the spread of the 'caucus' system must take most of the credit.[41]

By 1880 prohibitionists had made considerable progress in their attempts to increase their influence within the various levels of the Liberal party. Both the constituencies and the bulk of the parliamentary Liberal party had been won over, at least to the principle of local option. But in its movement through the various levels of the party, the Alliance was hampered by an absence of clearly defined relationships between these levels. It was not generally accepted that the views of a local association should constrain the voting behaviour of its MP, nor had the dictates of party discipline as yet unduly circumscribed the freedom of a member to act as his own conscience dictated, particularly over temperance reform which was still widely regarded as a non-party issue. Even more important, the leadership did not consider that its programme should be dictated to it by the parliamentary party as a whole, but rather the reverse.[42] The views of the party were not binding on leaders in their choice of priorities and therefore in choosing this method of achieving its objectives, the Alliance was always likely to be frustrated along the way.

Between 1871 and 1880 Liberal leaders were either indifferent or hostile to the Alliance and its programme. Gladstone had never voted on the Permissive Bill and was not really interested in temperance reform. In the early 1870s he still favoured a free-trade policy in respect of licensing, long after this solution had been discredited in the eyes of most reformers. His views were not framed in ignorance of the ravages of drink. Gladstone was probably more familiar with the world of poverty than many well-to-do temperance reformers and if he did not read the voluminous literature sent to him by the Alliance, he was painfully aware of the contrast between the sobriety of the United States and the drunkenness of Britain. While he was not prepared to take any initiative in this area, his views were modified from the early seventies onwards. In 1876 he asked Alex Balfour of Liverpool to prepare a pamphlet on the Gothenburg system of municipal control which he believed to be 'a very happy conception', and worthy of trial. Increasingly he came to see the control of the drink trade as one where 'the action of public authority is almost necessarily involved'.[43] Prohibitionists, who found much to applaud and support in Gladstone's ideas and ideals, were puzzled by his apparent indifference to their panacea. This led them in the 1870s into attempts to either cajole or bully him into a more favourable frame of mind. In 1875, after he had relinquished leadership of the Liberal party, efforts were made to persuade him to preside at the annual meeting of the Alliance, but he refused. A further request that he meet a deputation in 1878 was turned down on the grounds that he was no longer the responsible leader of the party. When in the same year Gladstone was mooted as a parliamentary candidate for Manchester a harsher approach was adopted. A deputation from the Alliance told the Manchester Liberal Association that it would not vote for Gladstone unless he was prepared to support local option or the Permissive Bill.[44]

A similar choice was presented to Gladstone at Midlothian in 1879. Working through an auxiliary, the Scottish Permissive Bill and Temperance Association, prohibitionists presented Gladstone with memorials in favour of local option. Lawson also toured Scotland on a public speaking tour to stiffen the resolve of his local supporters. The *Edinburgh Courant* complained that he was treating Gladstone 'like an unspeakable Turk ... making a demonstration against him like that of the British fleet in going to Vourla. ' "Here we are", says Sir Wilfrid, "so many Local Optionists with votes in the county. Will you have us at our price or will you not".'[45] Gladstone refused to meet a deputation, but agreed to raise the question in one of his speeches. At Dalkeith he declared himself to be mildly in favour of the principle of local option. Local prohibitionists were pleasantly surprised by this and conveniently ignored Gladstone's refusal to pledge himself, and the qualifications with which he surrounded his statement. He probably made this gesture in an effort to maintain party unity rather than as a result of any personal faith in the efficacy of the proposed solution. His views on local option were expressed quite clearly in the last division on Lawson's resolution before the general election when he voted against it because he knew of no plan 'which fully gives effect to that principle, and which it would not be premature to submit to Parliament'.[46]

Gladstone like others of the ruling elite did not find that prohibitionists made congenial companions. His eloquence on the subject of 'that incomparable and most wholesome article which we term bitter beer' would not have been appreciated, nor would his delight in jokes revolving around drunkenness. He was ill at ease at a teetotal dinner party to which Sir Wilfrid Lawson had invited him.[47] This social and cultural gap between him and prohibitionists meant that the latter were forced always to make formal approaches to him in order to present their case. This would not have been too great a disadvantage had he been more receptive to the desires of the parliamentary Liberal party in the determination of policy, but he was not, conceiving the formation of policy and the determination of priorities as a Cabinet responsibility, which was not susceptible to outside pressures. After 1880 with most Liberals pledged to local option, this became a serious barrier which the Alliance found difficult to surmount. In Gladstone's later Ministries there were frequent complaints of his aloofness from his backbench supporters, and in retrospect he can be seen as one of the greatest obstacles in the path of the Alliance. It was he more than anyone who prevented the Liberal leadership embracing the cause of local option more wholeheartedly. The Liberal victory in 1880 was as much as anything a personal victory for Gladstone, and the enormous prestige he had built up since 1876 enabled him to bypass Radical demands and bend the party to his own will. In this sense he was, as R.T. Shannon has suggested, 'the ruin of Radicalism'.[48]

The social and ideological differences between the Marquis of Hartington and the Alliance were even more marked. It has been pointed out that misunderstanding between temperance reformers and Whig politicians could hardly have been avoided; 'the evangelical pietism, the authoritarian collectivism and the struggle for respectability' so characteristic of the temperance world were alien to the Whig aristocracy. Conversely the habits of moderation and compromise so prized by Whigs were foreign to the mind of the Alliance. Hartington seemed uninterested in temperance reform, although he regarded the problem in a typically Whig way as one demanding 'good government'. 'It is', he stated, 'essentially a question of detail, of management, and of organisation'. Hartington had always opposed the Permissive Bill, and disliked organisations such as the Alliance which interfered with the process of government. However, once he had become party leader on the temporary retirement of Gladstone it was imperative for the Alliance to arouse in him some interest in the subject. This was done by placing him on the receiving end of a vigorous and rather crude campaign of harassment and threats of electoral action in his constituency. Hartington at first resisted but was eventually persuaded to publicly declare himself in favour of local option. This alarmed publicans; the *Morning Advertiser* complained that this was 'a new departure, and that Lord Hartington is a long step on his way, with Mr. Gladstone, to swell the ranks of the Lawsonites'. Trade fears and prohibitionist congratulations were however premature. Hartington did not vote for the Local Option Resolution when Lawson introduced it in June 1880, but by now Gladstone was again in control of the Liberal Party and so Hartington's support was no longer so vital to the Alliance.[49]

The social and cultural gap between prohibitionists and Liberals such as Gladstone and Hartington was too wide to be easily bridged. An alternative was for the Alliance to seek to gain the support of those in the upper echelons of the party who had a similar background and who were therefore more likely to be sympathetic. The obvious target was John Bright. His Nonconformist origins ensured a close identification with the temperance movement. In his youth he had lectured for the Rochdale Temperance Society and later became president of the British Association for the Promotion of Temperance. He was a total abstainer until forced on medical grounds to take wine for the sake of his health. Apart from his temperance credentials, he had other attractions for the Alliance. He was a truly national figure in a way that Lawson was not, and he had about him the aura of success, for he had led the Anti-Corn Law League to victory. Furthermore, while Bright no longer inspired fear and loathing among traditionalists, he still commanded great respect among Radicals. But there were difficulties. Bright had consistently opposed the Permissive Bill from its first introduction in 1864. He preferred 'the improvement and instruction of the people' coupled with the control of licensing by town councils as the best means of promoting temperance.[50] Bright, a good friend of Lawson's, evidently regretted that he differed from many of his fellow Nonconformists on the temperance issue and hoped for a compromise which would allow them all to work in harmony, but the note of extremism often heard within temperance circles alienated him. He told a group of Birmingham publicans that he had disassociated himself from temperance organisations when still quite young, 'because I did not like to hear the language in which you were spoken of'.[51] He was at one with the other leading Liberals in disliking the activities of reformist pressure groups because they made the role of leadership more difficult. Such a complaint sounds strange coming from one who had taken a prominent role in the campaign of the most successful pressure group of the nineteenth century, but old age, a taste of government, and the need for compromise perhaps explain the change.

The importance which the Executive attached to the support of Bright can be gauged from its willingness to drop the Permissive Bill at his instigation in 1878. It hoped in return 'that we may yet have the pleasure of seeing him leading in the van of a movement in which ... are to be found the very conditions of national stability and progress'. He was asked to take the chair at the annual meeting in 1879, but he declined to do so, explaining that he was 'weary of great meetings and of platform work' and would only agree to them 'when they seem to come within the line of my accepted public duties'. His proposals for reform made public in 1883 were too timid for the Alliance. The Executive complained that 'the stalwart reformer, not to say radical, of old, was scarcely discernible'.[52] From regarding him as a potential leader, prohibitionists rapidly identified him as a barrier to further progress. Despite its willingness to compromise, the Alliance had not by 1880 won the active backing of any of the Liberal leaders that it so urgently needed.

Notes

1. *22nd Annual Report 1874*, pp. 6-7
2. *Alliance News*, 17 Oct. 1874, p. 658.
3. *Minutes*, 4 Nov. 1874, 18 Nov. 1874.
4. D.A. Hamer, *The Politics of Electoral Pressure. A Study in the History of Victorian Reform Agitations* (1977), p. 211; *Minutes*, 12 Jan. 1876.
5. *Minutes*, 12 April 1876.
6. *Alliance News*, 25 Sept. 1875, p. 611; 4 Dec. 1875, p. 776; 18 Dec. 1875, p. 816; 23 Dec. 1876, p. 832; *Minutes*, 22 Nov. 1876; 31 Jan. 1877; 1 Aug. 1877; 8 Aug. 1877.
7. D.A. Hamer, *Liberal Politics in the Age of Gladstone and Rosebery* (1972), p. 51.
8. Quoted in H.J. Hanham, *Elections and Party Management. Politics in the Time of Disraeli and Gladstone* (1959), p. 138.
9. Joseph Chamberlain, *Fortnightly Review*, vol. 24 (Nov. 1878), p. 780.
10. Hanham, *Elections and Party Management*, pp. 140-3.
11. *Times*, 31 July 1878.
12. Relationships between constituency Liberal associations and prohibitionists in Birmingham, Leeds, Scarborough and Ashton-Under-Lyne and examined in detail in A.E Dingle, 'The Agitation for Prohibition in England' (Monash University PhD, 1974), pp. 162-76, and in Birmingham and Hull in Hamer, *The Politics of Electoral Pressure*, pp. 216-22.

13. W.E. Gladstone, *Midlothian Speeches 1879* (Leicester Univ. Press, reprint 1971), pp. 181-2, 189.

14. *Hansard*, vol. 251, c. 470.

15. Bright quoted in *22nd Annual Report 1874*, p. 8; Hartington quoted in *26th Annual Report 1878*, p. 35.

16. *Alliance News*, 26 Oct. 1878, p. 678.

17. Muntz in *Hansard*, vol. 251, c. 492; Gladstone, *Midlothian Speeches*, p. 75.

18. *Alliance News*, 17 Oct. 1874, p. 660; *Hansard*, vol. 251, c. 492; ibid., vol. 262, c. 561; Joseph Chamberlain to Charles Showell, 26 Dec. 1891, *Joseph Chamberlain Papers*, 6/5/3/10. Chamberlain was pointing out to a trade representative the effects of Alliance electoral pressure on its recipients.

19. Quoted in E.E. Gulley, 'Joseph Chamberlain and English Social Politics', *Studies in History, Economics and Public Law*, vol. 123, no. 1 (Columbia University, New York, 1926), p. 61; Joseph Chamberlain, *Fortnightly Review*, vol. 27 (1877), p. 154.

20. *Hansard*, vol. 232, cc. 1864, 1873-4.

21. *Minutes*, 31 Jan. 1877; 21 Feb. 1877; 28 Feb. 1877.

22. *Alliance News*, 17 March 1877, p. 170.

23. Ibid., 1 Dec. 1877, p. 771.

24. Quoted in *27th Annual Report 1879*, p. 10.

25. W.S. Caine, Dawson Burns, and W. Hoyle, *Local Option* (1885), p. 20.

26. *Minutes*, 13 March 1878; 31 July 1878; see also ch. 8.

27. For examples of this see Hamer, *The Politics of Electoral Pressure*, pp. 202-10.

28. Francis Peek, *Contemporary Review*, vol. 29 (1876), p. 38; *Dundee Advertiser* quoted in *Alliance News*, 26 June 1875, p. 409; Bruce in ibid., 9 Nov. 1878, p. 720.

29. Bright in *Hansard*, vol. 262, c. 554; *Alliance News*, 27 Oct. 1877, p. 674.

30. *26th Annual Report 1878*, pp. 41-2.

31. Quoted in ibid., pp. 42-3; *Minutes*, 11 Sept. 1878; 9 Oct. 1878; *The Diaries of John Bright* (ed. R.A.J. Walling, 1930), p. 413.

32. Lawson to Bright, 1 Nov. 1878, *Bright Papers*, Add. MSS 43, 389, f. 300; *Diaries of John Bright*, 20 Nov. 1878; ibid., 8 Jan. 1879.

33. Lawson to Bright, 2 Jan. 1879, *Bright Papers*, Add. MSS 43,389, f. 313; Lawson to Gladstone, 11 Jan. 1879 (letter incorrectly dated 1878. Contents make it clear that it must have been the following year). *W.E. Gladstone Papers*, Add. MSS 44,456, ff. 39-41.

34. Lawson to Bright, 1 Nov. 1878, *Bright Papers*, Add. MSS 43,389, f. 301.

35. *27th Annual Report 1879*, p. 13; *Minutes*, 29 Jan. 1879. Lawson confessed that at first he did not like the change, but then came to realise that 'if we pass the head, the tail would follow'. *Alliance News*, 7 Dec. 1878, p. 785.

36. George Dodds, *Alliance News*, 25 Oct. 1879, pp. 675-8.

37. Ibid., 12 Feb. 1879. p. 115; 15 March 1879, p. 166.

38. T.W. Heyck and William Klecka, 'British Radical M.P.s, 1874-1895; New Evidence from Discriminant Analysis', *Journal of Interdisciplinary History*, vol. IV, no. 2 (1873), p. 178.

39. R.W. Dale, *Fortnightly Review*, vol. 25 (June 1879); W.E. Gladstone, *Nineteenth Century* (Nov. 1878), p. 961; *Daily News*, 30 July 1879.

40. Hugh Mason (Ashton-under-Lyne), J.S. Wright (Nottingham), Arthur Pease (Whitby), W.S. Caine (Scarborough), Prof. Thorold Rogers (Southwark), Alfred Illingworth (Bradford), Joseph Chamberlain (Birmingham), Alex McArthur (Leicester), were all returned.

41. Hanham, *Elections and Party Management*, ch. 7.

42. Hamer, *Liberal Politics*, p. 37.

43. John Vincent, *The Formation of the Liberal Party 1857-1868* (1966), p. 219; W.E. Gladstone, *Midlothian Speeches*, p. 74; *Minutes*, 2 Feb. 1876; *Hansard*, vol. 251, cc. 473-4.

44. *Minutes*, 14 July 1875; 25 Sept. 1878; 18 Dec. 1878.

45. Quoted in *Alliance News*, 15 Nov. 1879, p. 737.

46. Gladstone, *Midlothian Speeches*, p. 75; *Hansard*, vol. 251, c. 468.

47. Sydney Buxton, *Gladstone as Chancellor of the Exchequer* (1901), p. 54; Philip Magnus, *Gladstone* (1963 paperback edn), pp. 379-80; Viscount Gladstone, *After Thirty Years* (1928), p. 44.

48. R.T. Shannon, *Gladstone and the Bulgarian Agitation 1876* (1963), p. 273.

49. Brian Harrison, *Drink and the Victorians. The Temperance Question in England 1814-1872* (1971), p. 289; *Hansard*, vol. 251, c. 514; *Morning Advertiser*, 23 Feb. 1880; the campaign against Hartington is studied in more detail in Dingle, 'The Agitation for Prohibition', pp. 207-11.

50. J.E. Thorold Rogers (ed.) *Speeches on Questions of Public Policy by John Bright, M.P.* (1869) pp. 462, 467-9.

51. Quoted in Harrison, *Drink and the Victorians*, p. 139.

52. *26th Annual Report 1878*, p. 42; letter quoted in *Minutes*, 17 Sept. 1879; *31st Annual Report 1883*, pp. 36-7.

Chapter 4

THE ELUSIVE VICTORY, 1880-1887

On 18 June 1880 the Commons passed the Local Option Resolution for the first time by 245 votes to 219. The Executive, convinced that at last victory was in sight, jubilantly hailed this as 'a memorable day in the history of Temperance Legislation'.[1] The resolution was supported by 215 Liberals, 12 Conservatives and 18 Home Rulers while 40 Liberals, 167 Conservatives and 12 Home Rulers opposed it. The Alliance now had the backing of 52 per cent of the parliamentary Liberal Party, including 18 members of the new Ministry. Of those in the Cabinet, Bright, Chamberlain, Hartington, Forster and Harcourt voted in favour, but Gladstone abstained. A close look at the state of the new government, however, suggests that Alliance leaders were being unduly optimistic in assessing their chances of success.

The Liberal victory in 1880 was overwhelming but the resulting parliamentary majority deceptive. The party was in no sense unified in outlook, but consisted of a bundle of interests and electoral forces, some old and some new. Whigs, Radicals, moderate Liberals and Irish Nationalists while formally in combination, were in fact opposed to each other on many issues. Speaker Brand quickly realised that Gladstone had 'a difficult team to drive'.[2] The split of 1886 was only the climax of divisions which had been widening for some time. This lack of cohesion and homogeneity in the party was mirrored in the Cabinet. Liberal success in 1880 had owed much to Gladstone's impassioned denunciation of 'Beaconsfieldism' which so attracted Radicals throughout the country. 'The old Whigs are astonished and bewildered', wrote Frederick Harrison to Charles Dilke. 'They have not won the victory. It has been forced on them by the Radicals, almost against their will ... Gladstone must give support to the Left whether he wishes it or not.' But this was not to be. The makeup of the Cabinet did not reflect the forces of advanced liberalism which had swept the country. Gladstone, concerned to placate the Whig patricians to whom the demagogic methods which he had employed at Midlothian were extremely distasteful, gave them most of the major offices of State.

The Whig majority was thus capable of frustrating any proposals for reform which it found distasteful. Of the 14 members of Cabinet, only Chamberlain at the Board of Trade could be called a full-blown Radical. John Bright's radicalism had by this time been dimmed by age and increasing infirmity. Chamberlain observed that 'differences of opinion showed themselves from the first, and frequently threatened to break up the Government. They undoubtedly led to some vacillation of purpose and to compromises which detracted from the unity and consistency of the Government'. Even Herbert Gladstone, an apologist for the Liberal administration, was forced to admit that the Cabinet 'contained too many stars of magnitude. In temperament its members were individualist, and there were too many leaders among them'.[3]

For the Alliance, the 1880 Cabinet could not have been less promising. Gladstone himself was not greatly interested in domestic reform apart from the county franchise and felt his responsibilities were limited to those that he had incurred in attacking Disraeli's foreign policy. Ireland however was soon to preoccupy him. Of the Radicals, from whom the Alliance expected most, neither Chamberlain nor Bright gave temperance reform a high priority. Furthermore each had formulated his own proposal for reform, Chamberlain with the Gothenburg system, and Bright with municipal licensing boards, neither of which appealed to prohibitionists. Therefore the Cabinet was unlikely to be greatly moved by Alliance demands for immediate action, nor was there any guarantee that if legislation was framed, it would be along lines acceptable to prohibitionists. However support from within the Cabinet did come from a most unexpected quarter.

The Home Secretary, Sir William Harcourt, became increasingly sympathetic to Alliance demands. Personally enjoying alcohol, he had during the sixties and early seventies taken up an extreme free-trade position in regard to the sale of intoxicants which brought him into conflict with temperance reformers. He had objected to the Permissive Bill as 'Grandmotherly legislation', and attacked the 1872 Act because he believed it reversed the trend of previous Liberal policy by proposing greater restrictions. He could find nothing to admire in a 'grand-maternal Government which ties nightcaps on a grown-up nation by Act of Parliament', and was 'against putting people to bed who want to sit up'.[4] He abstained from voting in the local option division in 1879 and again in March 1880. His first vote in favour came after the election in June 1880. By 1883 he was not only prepared to take part in the local option debate and speak strongly in its favour, he also committed the government to support it in principle. This was the first time a politician of such stature allied himself so closely with the Alliance and it prompted *The Times* to remark that 'Local Option in some form will be granted; the time and manner alone remain to be determined'.[5]

Harcourt later claimed that his actions had been determined by an increasing awareness of the evils caused by drink which his tenure at the Home Office had brought home to him. Local option he felt offered the best solution to this problem. But this was not the whole story as he also became increasingly aware of the importance of temperance reformers within the party, both inside and outside parliament. In the late seventies Lawson, a friend of his, had urged him to become the leader of temperance forces, but Harcourt did not react.[6] After 1880 however, he was much more receptive to such approaches. He stayed with Lawson in Cumberland for some time in 1881, and his active support for local option dated from then. He had not long since been defeated in a by-election at Oxford necessitated by his becoming Home Secretary. His opponent, A.W. Hall, a brewer, had brought the full weight of the trade to fight against him. Hall was subsequently unseated for corrupt practices, but Harcourt had been made aware of the electoral forces publicans could muster on behalf of the Conservative party. He increasingly regarded the Alliance as a counterweight to such pressures which could be used to bolster up liberalism and so redress the political balance. Harcourt, by his awareness of the reality of pressure-group politics and his willingness to lend an ear to Alliance demands, showed himself to be an essentially 'modern' politician in contrast to the more patrician approach adopted by most of his Cabinet colleagues. For him an organisation such as the Alliance was not a nuisance to be regretted as sullying the purity of parliamentary government, but rather a positive force which could be accommodated to the benefit of the Liberal party. In retrospect it is no accident that the Alliance, given the methods it employed, attracted Harcourt more than any other member of the Cabinet. His support meant that the third stage of the Alliance campaign to infiltrate the Liberal party had now successfully commenced. A direct link with the Liberal leadership had been forged and a direct route to the legislative machinery of state had been opened up.

It was against this background that the Executive had to decide on what tactics to adopt, in what was for it the novel situation of attempting to persuade a government, pledged in principle, to take practical action. Lawson had promised in 1878 that once the Local Option

Resolution had been passed, he would then introduce a Bill embodying its principles. However he now changed his mind and decided to give the government a free hand, declaring that

> any immediate action of mine in Parliament, at the present moment, could hardly improve the prospects of sound and early legislation, but might on the other hand tend to embarrass the government in dealing satisfactorily with this vital question. Let us give them time; and for our part let us ... do all in our power to show the Government that there is a real, thorough, and earnest demand on the part of the public for that popular veto on the issue of renewal of licences, which is the sum and substance of our present demand.[7]

Mindful of the doubts expressed by Gladstone, Bright and Hartington, concerning the degree of public support for permissive prohibition, Lawson wanted the Alliance to concentrate its efforts on whipping up popular support throughout the country. The Executive agreed to do so.

Gladstone stated in 1880 that reform of the licensing laws was 'an essential part of the work and mission of the present Parliament', but added that the competing pressure of other issues must be considered. The implications of this rider became clearer in the following year. Because of 'the extraordinary and very urgent calls made upon us by the state of Ireland', he found it necessary to put temperance reform to one side. Lawson stuck to the position he had adopted in the previous year. Accepting Gladstone's promise that action would be taken as soon as possible, he felt that 'the duty of the hour is to strengthen the hands of such men'. But worse was to follow. There was no mention of licensing legislation in the Queen's speech opening the session of 1882, though the Prime Minister explained that he intended to introduce a local government measure as soon as possible, 'and that measure will have certain bearings on the question of licensing'. Lawson again accepted this and would make no further move declaring that, 'so far as I am concerned I must wait until Gladstone either introduces it, or announces its postponement'. It was eventually postponed, but by this time it was too late in the session for Lawson to introduce his Local Option Resolution once more.[8]

Subsequent sessions up to the election of 1885 were no more fruitful for the Alliance. It had been intended that the 1883 session should be devoted to social legislation for England and Wales and Harcourt urged upon Gladstone the need for 'at least one political measure from a Party point of view', and claimed that there were none but 'either Liquor or County Franchise'. He emphasised that 'if we do not give Lawson a substantial support there will be great dissatisfaction in the Party'. But the Phoenix Park murders attracted attention away from England again, and the best that could be done was for Harcourt to formally pledge government support for the Local Option Resolution which Lawson reintroduced in 1883. In the following year Harcourt wearily explained that 'if there be people outside this House who do not know why we have done nothing on this subject [i.e. temperance reform], there is no man in this House who does not perfectly know why we have not, and why we cannot legislate upon questions so deeply interesting to the community'.[9] Furthermore Bright warned Lawson that if he followed the usual procedure of following his successful resolution with a Bill embodying its principles, he should not expect the government to then take charge of it. The government already had its hands full in trying to push its own measures through and Bright pointed out the impossibility of getting 'six or twelve omnibuses abreast through Temple Bar'.[10]

The normal legislative work of the government was undoubtedly being obstructed by the problem of Ireland and the antics of Irish MPs, but this was not the only reason for inactivity on the temperance front. The seriousness of these obstructions was compounded by the division and lack of planning within the Ministry itself. Because Gladstone failed to provide over-all control and a sense of direction, very little planning was done through Cabinet meetings. The government drifted from one session to another without preparing adequate plans for the use of parliamentary time.[11] Furthermore the party was not of the same mind on the measures which were brought before it. Radicals found the coercive policy in Ireland between 1881 and 1882, and the occupation of Egypt, particularly repugnant. Whigs on the other hand found other aspects of Gladstone's Irish policy difficult to swallow. Sixty Whig peers revolted against the government over the Irish Compensation Bill in 1880, and the Land Bill of 1881 evoked a similar response. In such a situation there was little time or energy to spare for what was bound to be a controversial measure of social reform. Indeed before 1884 none of the social policies of the Radicals had been implemented, so the Alliance was not the only section to go unsatisfied.

The difficulty of embodying the principle of local option in a practical legislative measure was another reason why the government, with the exception of Harcourt, was loath to act. Chamberlain observed that the legislative work of a Liberal government was 'always decided by the maximum which the moderate section is ready to concede, and the minimum which the Advanced party will consent to accept'.[12] The government suspected that the gap could not yet be bridged sufficiently to give any legislation a chance of success. The fiasco over the Bruce Bill of 1871 was still fresh in the minds of some. Bright gave the view of the Cabinet when he pointed out that any government Bill which attempted to restrict but not suppress the drink trade was unlikely to be supported by the Alliance. There was also the thorny question of compensation to be settled. Bright realised that he stood no chance of success with a Bill unless he could rely on the unified and enthusiastic backing of the whole temperance movement to neutralise the opposition of the trade. He believed that successive debates on the Local Option Resolution would help achieve the required degree of unanimity among temperance reformers, and were therefore a necessary prelude to any attempt to legislate.[13]

This was unduly optimistic. The divisions within the temperance movement were too deep to be solved merely by parliamentary debate. One major area of disagreement was over the very matter of the detailed application of accepted principles of reform. Lawson in abandoning the Permissive Bill had shelved, but not solved, this difficulty. By 1880 he was convinced that it could best be sorted out by the government and he informed the Executive

> that it is far better for *us* to throw the responsibility of details upon the Government and not to *suggest* anything to them.
>
> As regards myself I *have* made my suggestion in the shape of the Permissive Bill. *I* cannot improve it, but the House of Commons which has adopted its principle is now bound to do so and the Government is bound to lead the House of Commons in the matter.[14]

After his experiences with the Permissive Bill, he was concerned at all costs not to provide his opponents with 'an unnecessary opening for attacking us'. Furthermore he was aware that not all Alliance men were agreed on the best means of applying local option. Lawson informed Harcourt that 'the Alliance is, really, an "anti-licensing" association. Directly a discussion arises as to the how, when and where licensing should be carried on, we find that there are about as many differences of opinion amongst us as there are members of our association.'[15] By avoiding details he also hoped to avoid dissension within the Alliance.

What Lawson and the Executive had not foreseen was that once the Permissive Bill had been withdrawn, those interested would then consider the field open for them to introduce their own measures. From the late seventies onwards the number of private Bills rose markedly. Most were of only minor significance (for example a large number of Sunday Closing Bills, many of them designed to apply to only one county, were introduced in the decade after 1880), and so had little adverse impact on the work of the Alliance. However they did indicate the lack of unanimity existing between the many Temperance organisations interested in legislative reform. It was clearly desirable to get as large a measure of agreement among the major national temperance organisations as possible. Only if all reformers spoke with one voice could the government be forced to act. The Alliance immediately set about this task, but failed to realise that other bodies might not be willing simply to declare themselves in favour of the principle of local option, without going further and spelling out in detail what legislative remedies they wanted. This was the crux of the problem it faced in seeking united action; it was entirely unprepared for the variety of interpretations which might legitimately be placed on what *The Times* called the 'somewhat elastic' phrase, local option.[16]

In June 1880, before the first flush of electoral victory had worn off, the Executive discussed the feasibility of calling a United Temperance Congress, but decided instead to make private approaches to other organisations. In view of the disagreements which emerged, this was just as well, and possibly the likelihood of just such an eventuality dictated this course of action in the first place. The first attempt at joint action was made with the Church of England Temperance Society. At a meeting between representatives from the Executive committees of both organisations, it was decided to draw up a joint memorial urging the government to act. Differences of interpretation immediately became evident. While the Alliance favoured permissive prohibition by a periodic vote of all ratepayers, and opposed compensation to dispossessed publicans, the CETS wanted existing licensing powers to be given to a specifically elected licensing board which would have the power to fix high licence fees which would be used to establish a fund to buy up and gradually diminish the number of licences. Both interpretations were included in the first draft of the joint memorial. Lawson objected to the 'cumbersome [*sic*] machinery of a Board', and to compensation. When the Alliance representative asked for the removal of the offending sections of the memorial, the CETS complained that 'any joint action which wholly ignored our own interpretation of local control, would be considered by the Members of our Society, as the surrender of our long held and cherished opinions, and a simple transfer of ourselves to the Alliance ranks'.[17] Such attitudes not only reflected divisions over policy, but also the fragmented history of the whole temperance movement; individual organisations, jealous of their independence, felt the need to justify their existence by putting forward their own distinctive programmes. Eventually two separate memorials were sent to Gladstone, each gave a different meaning to local option and each claimed that the temperance movement was united behind it.

While the CETS did not want to be swallowed up by the Alliance, prohibitionists also had to ward off takeover bids by members of the CETS. These attempts were mounted by a group of Liverpool men led by Alexander Balfour. A member of the CETS, he was also vice-president of the Alliance and president of the Liverpool Popular Control and Licensing Reform Association. As a moderate he was convinced that 'temperance reforms are only to be achieved step by step' and could not support national prohibition.[18] Balfour's aim was to use the Liverpool Popular Control and Licensing Reform Association as a unifying force within the temperance world, in the hope of persuading the Alliance and the CETS to support the same programme. He wanted both bodies to support a programme which included the immediate and national local control of licensing by specially elected bodies combined with the power of permissive prohibition to be vested in the ratepayers of any district. Balfour began his campaign to influence the Alliance when the Permissive Bill was abandoned in 1878 and continued it until 1883. At various times he directed his efforts at the Executive, at Lawson, and at rank-and-file Alliance men, but all failed.[19] The Executive did not want to lose the support of Balfour, he was a generous contributor to Alliance funds, but it was unwilling to officially support any licensing scheme for fear of alienating supporters. Nor was the CETS any more flexible. Most of its members were not prohibitionists and would not support permissive prohibition. Balfour eventually gave up. Complaining that the 'extreme teetotal section' had gained control of the Alliance he warned that 'there is such a thing as a cause suffering from the over advocacy of its friends'.[20]

Other attempts were made to promote unified action, but all foundered because each society was only prepared to act in harmony with others in the advocacy of its *own* programme. This meant that the most important attempt to achieve unity, the National Temperance Federation (NTF) founded in 1883 through the efforts of the British Temperance League, was ineffective from the start. The rules of the Federation stated that 'the basis of co-operation for the Federated Societies is that they should work together in view of legislative and other action on the points upon which they are agreed ... such common action to extend, of course, only so far as there is common agreement'. The extent of common agreement was small; while the NTF held meetings which caught the public eye, it was unable to present the government with proposals acceptable to all the societies which it represented. Even the relatively simple matter of signing a memorial in favour of Irish Sunday closing caused problems. C.H. Collyns, the secretary of the NTF wrote: 'It is difficult to hold the *cup steady*, and the contents are somewhat *explosive* in their nature, and if any portion of them were spilt into the fire, there might be a blow up!! — Now already there is jealousy among these excellent bodies — I do not mean on this point specifically, but generally ... '[21]

The inability of temperance societies to agree among themselves on what they meant by local option led to two developments. First, it forced the Alliance to articulate more clearly what it wanted, and secondly, it forced the government to arrive at its own interpretation of the phrase. The reasons for Alliance reluctance in spelling out its demands in detail have already been examined. Lawson in particular wanted to give the government room for manoeuvre, but the vigorous advocacy of popular local control by the CETS and others forced the Executive reluctantly to abandon this tactic for fear that the government might adopt this interpretation of local option rather than its own. By the beginning of 1883 it began to insist that 'nothing short of the direct popular veto will meet the claims of the Alliance'.[22] J.T. Hibbert, a minor member of the Ministry, warned the Executive of the need to come forward with 'some clear and definite scheme for carrying into practice the principles of local option'. He pointed out that three schemes had been placed prominently before the government — the transfer of licensing powers to existing local government bodies, the transfer of such powers to specially elected licensing boards, and the retention of existing licensing powers augmented by a local veto of ratepayers. The Executive, unwilling to taint its hands by coming into contact with any licensing scheme, privately favoured the last alternative, but replied that all would be acceptable if complemented by the inclusion of the direct popular veto. In 1883 Lawson belatedly suggested that the Borough Funds Act, passed by the previous government, provided a model for the kind of machinery that could be set up to operate a veto. He also claimed that any Bill could be simple and modest, and need not even upset the present licensing system. In this he was much more moderate than W.S. Caine who wished for more sweeping changes.[23]

Discordant voices within the ranks of temperance societies made it necessary for the government to arrive at its own definition of local option. All that temperance reformers were agreed upon, as was frankly pointed out by the CETS, was 'the principle ... of Local-Government'.[24] This presented no difficulty. Harcourt explained his own views on the matter in a letter to Gladstone:

The whole question appears to me to be simply a chapter in the volume of Local Government —

(1) It is admitted that the public house business is not to be a *free trade*. The licensing system involves a power of restriction and therefore a restricting authority.

(2) That authority is not governed by Statute but is left to local *discretion* ....

(3) Therefore this is a local question even on the present system determined by a local authority (even if this only at present J.P.'s) ....

(4) The only question therefore which remains is whether the present local authority is the best fitted to resolve this local question.

(5) The Cabinet determined that the whole *administrative* business of the locality both in Counties and Boroughs should be given to the representative bodies — among these affairs they determined to include the licensing of public houses. That decision I think was right and indeed inevitable. The licensing question has no judicial character (except so far as revocation of licences for misconduct is concerned) it is a social question and the needs and sentiments of the locality should prevail. That is in fact all that Lawson's resolution asserts — and one which I think we cannot contravene consistently with the decision at which we have arrived in all the branches of the Local Government question ...

P.S. I had the opportunity of discussing this letter after I had written it last night with Hartington and R. Grosvenor and they agreed with me in the opinion that the Government as a body should vote with Lawson. We are making it quite clear that we do not read the Resolution as committing us to the principle of a *plebiscite* on liquor but as favouring the control in the hands of the same *representative* body which is charged with the administration of other local affairs.[25]

Gladstone agreed that Harcourt should be allowed to argue along these lines on behalf of the government during the 1883 local option debate. Thus the agitation of the CETS in favour of local licensing boards was to no avail, and the belated insistence of the Alliance on the direct popular veto came too late. By 1883 the government had decided that drink should not be made a special issue but should be dealt with along the same lines as other areas of local responsibility. For this reason it insisted that licensing reform would come as part of a reform of local government rather than as a separate Bill. Furthermore compensation in some form was considered necessary.

The clearest indication of the government's intentions was given by Joseph Chamberlain. In 1886, as President of the Local Government Board he was busy drafting a local government measure which would establish parish, district and county councils and give to one or other of them 'the powers of the magistrates as to licensing and some control over existing licences, subject however to provision for compensation if they were taken away for other causes than abuse'.[26] The Bill was never introduced because the government was defeated on Home Rule, but it clearly would not have satisfied temperance reformers. However this proposal is of interest for the light it throws on the effectiveness of Alliance tactics. During its drafting, Alliance leaders offered no detailed suggestions to Chamberlain as to what they wanted. Consequently, while he wished to frame something acceptable to them, he was in the dark as to how to do this, despite having, at his suggestion, a private meeting with the Executive. One provision which, as a result of a speech by Raper, Chamberlain believed would be supported by the Alliance, was rejected by Dawson Burns, much to Chamberlain's surprise.[27] Thus the weakness of Lawson's tactics of leaving the drafting of detailed provisions solely to the government, was clearly exposed. Despite clear indications from as early as 1883 that the ideas of the government and the Alliance diverged markedly in several important respects, Alliance leaders had nevertheless failed to take adequate steps to make their demands known.

Lawson found the Liberal government's continued inability to tackle the temperance question regrettable but understandable. He and other Alliance leaders such as Pope and Raper, who spent most of their time in London, were familiar with the exigencies of party politics and accepted that the work of the government was being unavoidably obstructed. They continued to believe in the good faith of the government, and its often repeated promise to act as soon as it was able. Provincial prohibitionists, less familiar with parliamentary procedure, were not prepared to be as patient. They had often heard politicians echo their own words in stressing the urgency of temperance reforms, yet nothing was being done. As a result there was a growing sense of disillusionment with a Liberal government which had given promises but, apparently, made no effort to redeem them. Many rank-and-file Alliance men, convinced of the overriding importance of temperance reform, were not as willing as Lawson to accept the obstruction argument simply because the government, despite its Irish difficulties, still found time to tackle what they regarded as minor problems. An editorial in the *Alliance News* in 1882 voiced the exasperation felt by many: 'The Irish business must be dealt with, we suppose, and the year's budget necessities must be provided for; but when the Government begins to trifle into divergence into Scotch entails and corrupt practices ... it is indeed time to lift up a very earnest and a very indignant voice of remonstrance.'[28]

When Gladstone proposed in 1881 to license railway carriages for the sale of intoxicants prohibitionists found his action 'wholly unaccountable', and expressed their 'surprise, regret and alarm'. A vigorous campaign by the temperance movement killed the proposal, but the seeds of doubt had been sown. Uncompromising prohibitionists henceforth viewed Gladstone with increasing suspicion. J.G. Richardson wrote to him a year later saying he was 'strangely puzzled' at the latter's lack of action after protesting that the drink problem was so serious. At the Alliance annual meeting in 1883, T.W. Russell mounted a vigorous attack on the Prime Minister, complaining that he 'had never studied the alphabet of the question, and at his time of life he was not likely to do so', and that he had sabotaged Fry's Durham Sunday Closing Bill. There were cries of 'shame' and 'withdraw', to which Russell replied that the meeting contained a 'tolerable proportion of hero-worshippers' who, if they wished to succeed, should drop their 'deification of Mr. Gladstone and the Liberal Party'.[29] John Bright's proposals for reform, announced in 1883, caused further doubts. Lord Derby, another member of the Cabinet, exacerbated prohibitionists' discontent by arguing that as temperance reform 'mainly affects the poorest class, and affects the rural districts more than the towns ... there would be no great harm in letting it stand over till the agricultural householder also can have a voice upon it'.[30]

As scepticism about the intentions of the government grew, Lawson's waiting policy in the Commons was subjected to increasing criticism from within the Alliance. As in the 1870s, the membership began to form into two distinct groups. Moderates, following the lead given by Lawson, wished to give the government its head, while a growing and increasingly vocal advanced wing cried out for action. The Executive found itself in an increasingly difficult position as it attempted to act as a buffer between the two groups. In 1882 the Birmingham auxiliary claimed that the Executive was not doing enough and demanded that a meeting of all Alliance supporters should be convened to discuss future action. T.H. Barker the secretary replied that 'we do not see the way to assume a threatening aspect, and talk about "totally breaking up political parties" and all that .... I do not think we shall get into the threatening attitude'.[31] On the advice of Lawson, the Executive refused to call a meeting, but members of the Executive disagreed among themselves as to what they should do.[32] At the annual meeting in 1883, activists tried again and demanded a return to the stringent electoral policy of 1872-3 which had fallen into abeyance with the demise of the Permissive Bill in 1878. Moderates such as Thomas Whittaker feared this would lead to a repetition of what had happened in 1874 but extremists welcomed the possibility. William Saunders summed up their feelings by stating that it would be the fault of the Alliance if the government were not forced to act. Even Lawson was aware of the dangers of the situation, and presented himself to the meeting 'to see whether the army will follow me, and what the army wants to be done'.[33]

One thing that advanced men did want was action by Temperance MPs in parliament. While Lawson remained inactive, Benjamin Whitworth, MP and a member of the Executive, threatened in 1883 to disobey the Liberal whip, and hoped 30 to 40 temperance MPs would follow his lead, thus forcing the government to take notice of their demands. While he did not carry out this threat, indeed he appears to have made it mainly to prevent a split in Alliance ranks, temperance MPs did begin to organise themselves more effectively during the 1884 session when about thirty of them formed a temperance lobby.[34] Significantly Lawson took only a minor role in these proceedings. At the end of 1884, the Executive tried to prod him into action by urging him to take the bold step of moving the adjournment of the House 'in order to remonstrate with the Government'. This Lawson refused to do. He contented himself with privately warning Harcourt that

> unless you give assurance at the beginning of the next session [1885]
> that you intend to deal with this question, I shall endeavour to find
> a day to move a resolution affirming that there should be no further
> delay in the matter. I will be quite open with you and say that I shall
> be on very safe ground in doing so for I should indeed be surprised if
> many Liberal Members, with the new Constituency looming in the
> distance, should vote against such a resolution.[35]

This threat to use the parliamentary Liberal party as a means of bringing the government to heel opened up a new avenue worth exploring,
but promises from Harcourt that he was doing his best satisfied
Lawson who took no further action.

Outside Parliament the Executive was finally forced to adopt the
threatening attitude which it had tried for so long to avoid. By the end
of 1884 supporters were exhorted 'to refuse to support any candidates
proposing to support a Government which has failed to bring in its
promised legislation'.[36] Such advice at this time was neither useful nor
enlightening. If the Alliance men could not vote for Liberals, who in
the main favoured local option, the alternatives were to abstain or vote
for Conservatives who were opposed to it. Neither course would
further Alliance interests in the Commons. It is likely that such advice
was intended mainly for the consumption of Liberal leaders in an
endeavour to impress upon them the strength of feeling among
prohibitionists. The Executive was not so much threatening the
government that it intended taking action, as warning it that feelings
were running so high that they could no longer be contained. Steinthal
drove home this point in a letter to G.O. Trevelyan.

> I think you know there is no organised body of politicians so strong
> in the country as the U.K.A. and as a very earnest Liberal myself, I
> should be most grievously pained were its forces to be used against
> the party from which I have always hoped we should receive wise
> and judicious legislation against the traffic in drink. We, who are
> members of the Executive of the Alliance hear threats from all
> sides, that a separate temperance party is to be formed, and candi-
> dates brought forward purely on prohibition and direct veto prin-
> ciples. If this takes place in many places it will certainly lead to the
> defeat of the Liberal Candidates. Indeed the proposal has been
> seriously made to us to call the Council of the U.K.A. together in

order to call upon Temperance men to take this course.

Members of the Executive again disagreed among themselves as to what to do. Most Manchester-based members, particularly William Hoyle, wished to follow the line advocated by the advanced wing of the Alliance, but Pope, Raper and Lawson had no wish to go that far.[37]

Before these differences could be reconciled the government resigned in June 1885. This was a serious blow to the moderates as it signified the failure of their waiting policy. They complained of the resignation 'as an act, if not of suicide, yet of great willingness to be dispatched'. It played into the hands of advanced prohibitionists who, after deploring the failure of the government to live up to its promises, insisted on reviving the advanced electoral policy. Acutely conscious of the differences of interpretation to which local option had been susceptible, they feared the worst in the coming election unless they took action. One complained that

> the Liberal candidates throughout the country were conjuring with the words local option. There was the three card trick being carried on …. And so the Liberal candidates had got three cards, County Government Boards, Elective Boards, and Direct Popular Veto … but the one they almost invariably picked up was County Government Boards.

The pledge demanded of many candidates in the elections in November 1885 was not local option but the direct popular veto. This was tantamount to a return to the Permissive Bill as an election pledge. Hugh Price Hughes pointed to the way in which Chamberlain was pushing his Radical Programme as an example which could profitably be followed. Claiming that prohibitionists 'held the Liberal party in the hollow of their hands', he urged them to 'do for themselves what Mr. Chamberlain had been doing lately — put on the screw — and compel the Liberal candidates to vote for the Popular Veto'.[38]

In its attempt to swing the Liberal party behind the demand for a direct popular veto, the Alliance was moderately encouraged by the results of the elections. A total of 343 candidates were returned pledged to support local option, and of these 201 were specifically in favour of the veto. All but a handful were Liberals. But in other respects the election was a severe blow because the Alliance was deprived of its parliamentary leader. Lawson was defeated in a contest in which he could do little campaigning because of illness, and where the Alliance could not actively intervene because the Conservative candidate was also a supporter of local option. Benjamin Whitworth, a member of the Executive, three vice-presidents in W.S. Caine, Hugh Mason and Arthur Pease, were also defeated. Nor were these losses of leadership offset by any significant gains. William Saunders was elected for the first time but he was already becoming somewhat disenchanted with the Alliance. Several members of the Executive had stood as Liberal candidates, but all failed. Alexander McDougall the chairman was defeated at Perth, William Hoyle could not contest Spen Valley owing to illness, and Raper failed to get Liberal selection for the Ardwick Park division of Manchester. Thus the Alliance was forced to turn in the Commons to temperance men who were primarily associated with societies other than itself.

One quite unexpected result of the election campaign was Lord Salisbury's public declaration in favour of a measure of local option, which will be examined in more detail in the next chapter. This meant that in the new parliament the leaders of both major parties were much closer to the Alliance than they had been hitherto. Charles Dilke assured prohibitionists that they had nothing to worry about as both Conservatives and Liberals saw the need to introduce a measure of local option, consequently 'whoever has to propose legislation on local government will have to deal with it on the very same lines'.[39] It was probably the realisation of this rather than temperance pressure which finally persuaded the new Liberal government to prepare local government legislation, which was to include local option provisions, but while Chamberlain was still drafting his measure, the Home Rule controversy broke and the government was defeated.

The ensuing general election in 1886 was fought by all parties almost exclusively on the Home Rule question. Despite energetic attempts by the Alliance to keep temperance reform well to the fore, the election became virtually a plebiscite on Gladstone's Irish policy. The Executive complained bitterly of an electoral system which allowed 'the occasional cropping up of some one great over-dazzling political question which makes the electors deaf and blind to all the rest', but was forced to admit that 'strong temperance reformers — who in a normal condition of things, would have voted chiefly with reference to the temperance question', were not immune from the controversy and cast their votes largely in accordance with their views on Ireland. This led to 'the defeat of not a few candidates who supported Local Option'.[40] In the new parliament the Conservative victory meant that supporters of local option fell to 282, of whom 169 were specifically pledged to the direct popular veto. Thus the majority in the House of Commons which the Alliance had enjoyed since 1880 had been wiped out and the cause of prohibition set back considerably. The return of Lawson and W.S. Caine to the parliamentary stage was only a partial compensation.

This was the first although not ultimately the most important effect of the Home Rule split on the Alliance. Two others immediately became evident. First, it brought home to militant prohibitionists the fact that the hopes of success they had entertained since 1880 had finally been dashed. As a result the accumulated frustrations of the previous six years finally overflowed in a series of angry attacks on what was regarded as the inept leadership of the Executive. These attacks took several forms. One group, led by William Saunders, mounted a frontal assault on the position and power of the Executive itself. Saunders blamed the Executive for the lack of progress between 1880 and 1886. 'Since the Alliance adopted a waiting policy in Parliament', he claimed, 'it has been like a coach without wheels on the road of progress, a barrier to advancement.' To overcome this, he proposed that both the General Council of the Alliance, and its Executive be made 'directly representative of the various societies and individuals associated with the Alliance'. In this way he hoped to 'stimulate interest and fix responsibility'.[41] This was but the latest and most determined of several complaints along these lines. From 1881 onwards there had been growing murmurs of discontent with the 'officialism' of the Alliance, its over-centralised structure, and its tendency to generate activity through its agents rather than take the trouble to harness local prohibitionist enthusiasm. Activists claimed that if the government of the Alliance was made more representative of its rank-and-file regional supporters, local energies and finance could be harnessed more effectively, and internal conflicts would be eliminated.[42]

Other attacks on the Executive were aimed not so much at modifying its powers but forcing it to adopt new tactics and strategies. The most advanced of these demands, voiced by a small group led by Axel Gustafson, was that the Alliance should stick to the letter of its constitution and work towards the 'total and immediate suppression of the Liquor Traffic' by abandoning its demand for the veto and insisting on immediate national prohibition. Gustafson wanted the Alliance to sever its links with the Liberal party in order to become a Prohibition party running its own candidates for parliamentary seats. Most

Alliance men were not prepared to go so far and defeated the proposal, whereupon Gustafson together with a small group of supporters left the Alliance and set up a rival National Prohibition Party. This was something of a damp squib. It attracted only the most intransigent and irreconcilable of prohibitionists who squabbled among themselves as to what form their organisation should take. Nevertheless it was symptomatic of the dissatisfaction felt towards the Executive.[43] A more formidable challenge came from Alliance men who wished to see the Executive return to the methods it had employed in the early seventies. Many moderates whose patience had finally run out demanded the establishment of another guarantee fund to set Alliance finances back on their feet, a massive distribution of pamphlet literature aimed specifically at voters newly enfranchised in 1884, the drafting of a Veto Bill for England to provide 'a flag to march under', and a new drive to set up local electoral associations once again.[44]

Facing threats from several directions, the Executive's response was to appear to agree with the substance of the complaints without actually doing anything to change matters substantially. Initially the Executive was not prepared to discuss Saunders' complaints, but once the matter had been raised in public and attracted attention, it was forced to take some action. It agreed to convene a United Kingdom Convention in February 1887, open to all individuals and organisations supporting the Alliance. However delegates were invited to attend, not to discuss the constitution and structure of the Alliance as Saunders had hoped, but rather 'to suggest and agree upon the best methods of united practical action by temperance reformers and associations' to force the government to act. Despite this attempt to direct attention elsewhere, Saunders brought up the issue for discussion. The Executive however, concerned to prevent outsiders gaining control, claimed that the suggestions put forward were too vague and contradictory to be practicably utilised. Some gestures were eventually made towards the creation of a more democratic structure (these are examined in Chapter 8), but they were not substantial enough to satisfy Saunders. He finally urged those who felt like him to 'leave them [the Alliance] and devote our attention to more promising undertakings than that of whipping a horse that won't go'.[45]

The Executive had directed attention away from Saunders' complaints at the Convention by providing a forum for those who wished to see the resumption of a more active campaign. In playing off one group of dissidents against another, it was therefore forced to accept resolutions demanding the drafting of an English Direct Veto Bill, the establishment of a guarantee fund, the widespread distribution of pamphlets and a return to the advanced electoral policy of the seventies. These proposals were then considered, but at the annual meeting in October 1887, the Executive reported back that with the resources at its disposal neither the pamphlet campaign nor the guarantee fund were feasible. Nor could Lawson or Raper be persuaded to modify their waiting policy in parliament. Lawson was still convinced that a Private Members' Bill had no chance of success and he preferred to see what Salisbury's promised local government reform contained. Therefore despite the complaints, nothing was done. However one demand, for the resumption of an advanced electoral policy and the formation of what were now called Local Electoral Direct Veto Societies of temperance electors in every constituency, was not so easily dealt with. This generated the most difficult and divisive issue with which the Executive was forced to grapple, because it touched directly upon the Home Rule controversy.[46]

The Home Rule split in the Liberal party was reproduced on a smaller scale within the leadership of the Alliance. Three members of the Executive, Alexander McDougall, its chairman, Benjamin Whitworth and T.C. Raynor, became Liberal-Unionists. So also did several vice-presidents, the most influential and active of whom were three MPs, W.S. Caine, T.W. Russell and William Saunders, as well as the clerical activist R.M. Grier. The remaining Alliance leaders and the majority of rank-and-file prohibitionists remained loyal to Gladstone. The electoral position officially adopted by the Alliance in 1886, that support should be given only to those candidates favourable to the veto, or at least local option, immediately placed Liberal-Unionists within the organisation in a difficult position. As the majority of Gladstonian candidates were favourable to either local option or the veto, while most Liberal-Unionist candidates were opposed, the question of priorities immediately arose. While Gladstonian Alliance men were not forced to choose between Ireland and temperance reform, Liberal-Unionists were. If they voted for temperance, they would normally also be voting for Home Rule. It was inevitable that as they had already split from the Liberal party on the issue of Ireland, they would put that above their temperance sympathies, in contravention of the avowed policy of the Alliance.

Militant prohibitionists smarting at the diversion of attention away from temperance reform which had resulted from the Home Rule split, refused to let this issue rest. At the annual meeting in 1886 a resolution in favour of the advanced electoral policy was passed by a large majority. Those who had not adhered to it in the recent election were accused of not practising what they preached. Because he had voted against a candidate favourable to the veto, a determined effort was made to have T.C. Raynor thrown off the Executive, and the other members only narrowly prevented this from happening.[47] However after attending the meeting, T.W. Russell immediately resigned from the Alliance. He wrote to the secretary

> for several years as you know I pressed a 'forward policy' — but these two things I never dreamt of, I never proposed to attach pains and penalties to those who did not come up to my ideas — and I certainly did not think any English statesman capable of what Mr. Gladstone has shown himself equal to; and in view therefore of the position in which Irish politics stand, and my relationship thereto — and of what may be required at my hands both in and out of Parliament, I desire to be free.[48]

Caine was a much more important figure. A minor member of Gladstone's previous administration, his defection was bitterly attacked by the *Daily News* and he fought and won the Barrow by-election in the face of opposition from the Liberal whips. He then became an important Liberal-Unionist, acting as unofficial whip for Chamberlain, while still retaining high office in the temperance world. He remained as president of the National Temperance Federation as well as a vice-president of the Alliance; prior to 1886 he had come to be regarded as second only to Lawson as a parliamentary spokesman on temperance matters. Caine continued to insist that temperance was the 'most burning question of the day', but felt that Ireland must be got out of the way before any solution to the drink question could be found. He pointed out that while many temperance men could ignore all political questions other than the veto, such a position 'would be absurd, and quite untenable, for a member of Parliament'.[49] The Executive, wishing to retain his services, endeavoured to give him as free a hand as possible. Whitworth, naturally sympathetic to the dilemma in which Caine found himself, also believed that Ireland must be dealt with immediately. He drew an interesting analogy: 'suppose the question of the re-enactment of the Corn-Laws became a burning one — are the members of the Alliance to place local-option before even a measure of such vast importance to the welfare of the country?'.[50] This rare but revealing glimpse into the mind of an Alliance leader shows that while the organisation was urging its supporters to put temperance before all, its leaders were not unanimously prepared to practise what they preached.

Rank-and-file Gladstonian prohibitionists were less conciliatory than the Executive and used temperance meetings at which Caine was speaking 'for relieving their feelings as Home Rulers'. On a winter speaking tour Caine undertook on behalf of the Alliance he was continually booed, hissed and shouted down whenever he appeared. He also received anonymous threatening letters and at a meeting at Tottenham the crowd gave three cheers for Gladstone, Parnell and Ireland, and pelted him with snowballs. Immediately after this incident, Caine requested a clear statement of what membership of the Alliance involved; 'am I, as a Vice-President of the U.K.A., bound in honour to vote for any candidate, whatever his political opinions may be on other questions, who professes himself in favour of local option?'.[51] Many Alliance militants had made it quite clear that this was what they expected of him. The Executive found difficulty in agreeing among themselves on a reply. They did not wish to lose Caine as he was still a sincere and active worker for temperance. Apart from speaking on temperance platforms and acting as a link with the Conservative government, he was also attempting to get local option adopted as a part of the programme of Chamberlain's newly formed National Radical Union. Furthermore he was the focal point around which the Home Rule controversy within the temperance world revolved. If he were forced out of the Alliance, the Executive feared that 'every Conservative and Unionist Liberal will refuse to have his name retained on our list of Vice-Presidents'. If this happened the Alliance would look more than ever like a partisan organisation; it would become a 'Radical United Kingdom Alliance' and its claims to attract non-party support would be shown to be so much hot air. Perhaps more important, if Liberal-Unionists were forced out the loss of donations from men such as Whitworth and Caine would be considerable. On the other hand, rank-and-file support was likely to be lost if it was seen that a prominent Alliance man was not conforming to standards expected of everyone else. Initially the Gladstonian members of the Executive tried to force Caine into line but he refused to budge. Eventually the Executive was forced to retain him on his own terms. Whitworth wrote to Caine pointing out that 'we have never made adhesion to these [electoral] resolutions a test of membership'. He considered therefore that Caine was 'at liberty, as a member of the Alliance, to vote on any political or social question as your conscience may dictate. This is the view I take of my own position.' The correspondence was published in an attempt to take the heat out of the debate, but to no avail.[52]

Caine continued to be abused at temperance meetings by prohibitionists who refused 'to hear renegades'.[53] In an attempt to get rid of him, the Sheffield auxiliary tried to tighten up membership requirements by insisting that no person should hold any official position within the Alliance unless they were prepared to adhere strictly to the electoral policy. Pope warned that this would 'tend to lower the character and status of official connection with the Alliance', and the Executive refused to place the Sheffield proposal before the annual meeting. Nevertheless feelings were running so high that it was introduced as a resolution from the floor of the meeting by Jonathan Hargrove and Guy Haylor. They demanded to know where the Executive stood on this issue and whether or not there was a difference of opinion amongst its members. They also attacked Caine and Russell as being unfit to lead the temperance movement. Some members of the Executive replied that if the resolution was passed they would regard it as a vote of censure and threatened to resign. Interjectors responded by accusing them of merely 'seeking for office' without being sincere prohibitionists. For the first and only time the Executive lost control of the annual meeting. Hargrove refused to withdraw his resolution, but finally accepted a last minute plea to refer it to a committee before voting on it.[54] The conflict was still at this stage, with the Executive retreating uneasily and rather unsurely, when the first battle over compensation began a few months later. Fortunately for Alliance leaders this shifted attention away from internal differences and all the dissident factions showed a willingness to submerge their differences in the face of a common enemy. It also provided Caine with a more acceptable role within the temperance movement. Had Ritchie not introduced the Tory Local Government Bill at this time, however, it is likely that the rifts within the Alliance would have grown even wider, further undermining its credibility and effectiveness.

As it was the years between 1880 and 1887, which had started on such a high note, were profoundly depressing ones for prohibitionists. The Liberal government had not been forced to act, nor had the temperance movement as a whole been able to act in union. Worse still, the Alliance itself had been wracked by internal differences. The Executive, in attempting to mediate, satisfied no-one and was made to appear ineffectual. The Home Rule split made its task an impossible one. This episode undoubtedly damaged the Alliance. It lost both prestige and support, and energies absorbed by internal bickering could with advantage have been directed elsewhere. Five years later the Executive still felt the need to rebut criticisms of its lack of energy and leadership which had first been made in the 1880s. However there was also a credit side to the account. First, by attracting Harcourt, the Alliance had won support from a Liberal of the front rank for the first time. Secondly, the Home Rule split had important long-term consequences for the Alliance, although these were not immediately evident. A number of impressive figures including Dilke, Hartington and Chamberlain left the Liberal leadership in 1886. From the point of view of shaping a new liberalism capable of retaining its hold over the newly enfranchised masses, the loss of Dilke and Chamberlain was particularly serious. Both had already shown themselves capable of shaking off the sectarian demands of Nonconformity in order to direct attention to social issues which were to increasingly preoccupy politicians towards the end of the century. Those Liberal leaders who remained were more committed to Ireland, but because they were less capable of taking new initiatives outside this particular preoccupation, they were more susceptible to the influence of the Alliance and other pressure groups.

The defection of the predominantly Whig Liberal-Unionists meant that the Liberal party had been purged of most of its anti-Alliance faction. It also meant that Radicals, the vast majority of whom supported local option, greatly strengthened their position within the party. From accounting for under half the total strength of the parliamentary Liberal party before 1886, their average representation between 1886 and 1892 jumped to 66 per cent. This had the effect of strengthening the hand of the NLF within the party and it also forced Liberal leaders to pay closer attention to Radical demands. While the Irish question delayed this process, it could not halt it. Radicals were now in a position to set the pace for the party as a whole and sooner or later their demands would become official Liberal policy which leaders could not afford to ignore.[55] The Radical preoccupations of the 1892-5 Liberal government were the logical outcome of the Home Rule split of 1886. In retrospect therefore it is arguable that from the point of view of the Alliance (if not from someone desiring a practical measure of temperance reform) the lack of progress during the Liberal tenure of power between 1880-6 and the emergence of Ireland as a dominant political concern, was an advantage. It eventually helped give rise to a situation in which a Liberal government was prepared to introduce almost exactly the kind of measure the Alliance desired.

Notes

1. *28th Annual Report 1880*, p. 142.
2. Quoted in A.G. Gardiner, *Life of Sir William Harcourt* (1923), vol. 1, p. 363.
3. Joseph Chamberlain, *A Political Memoir 1880-1892* (ed. C.H.D. Howard, 1953), p. 85; Viscount Gladstone, *After Thirty Years* (1928), p. 168.
4. Gardiner, *Sir William Harcourt*, vol. 1, pp. 140, 209.
5. *Times*, 27 April 1883.
6. Gardiner, *Sir William Harcourt*, vol. 2, p. 107; *Hansard*, vol. 278, c. 1307.
7. Lawson to Thomas Burt, 22 June 1880, in *Times*, 23 June 1880.
8. *Hansard*, vol. 253, c. 365; *29th Annual Report 1881*, pp. 7-8; *30th Annual Report 1882*, p. 9; *Minutes*, 19 April 1882.
9. Gardiner, *Sir William Harcourt*, vol. 1, p. 470; *32nd Annual Report 1884*, p. 15.
10. *Hansard*, vol. 262, cc. 557, 559.
11. D.A. Hamer, *Liberal Politics in the Age of Gladstone and Rosebery* (1972), p. 84.
12. Chamberlain to W.E. Gladstone, 7 Feb. 1885, quoted in Chamberlain, *Political Memoir*, p. 116.
13. *Hansard*, vol. 262, cc. 558-9.
14. *Minutes*, 17 Nov. 1880.
15. Lawson to W.V. Harcourt, 30 Sept. 1888, *Harcourt Papers* (Box 12).
16. Quoted in *29th Annual Report 1881*, p. 47.
17. *Minutes*, 17 Nov. 1880; J.H. Ellison (Secretary of CETS) to Barker, n.d., in ibid., 24 Nov. 1880.
18. A. Balfour to Barker, 9 June 1883, in ibid., 13 June 1883.
19. These attempts are exmined in detail in A.E. Dingle, 'The Agitation for Prohibition' (Monash University PhD, 1974), pp. 234-40.
20. Balfour to Barker, 9 June 1883, in *Minutes*, 13 June 1883.
21. Ibid., 21 Nov. 1883; Collyns to Barker, n.d., in ibid., 12 Dec. 1883.
22. *Minutes*, 7 March 1883.
23. Ibid., 24 Oct. 1883; *Hansard*, vol. 278, cc. 1291, 1298.
24. *Minutes*, 5 Sept. 1883.
25. Harcourt to Gladstone, 26 April 1883, *Harcourt Papers* (original emphasis).
26. Chamberlain, *A Political Memoir*, p. 193.
27. Dawson Burns to Chamberlain, 16 March 1886, *Joseph Chamberlain Papers*, JC 6/5/3/4; Chamberlain to Dawson Burns, 18 March 1886, ibid., JC 6/5/3/5; Dawson Burns to Chamberlain, 19 March 1886, ibid., JC 6/5/3/6; *Minutes*, 3 March 1886.
28. *Alliance News*, 24 June 1882, p. 392.
29. Ibid., 4 June 1881, p. 364; 7 Oct. 1882, p. 625; 20 Oct. 1883, p. 660.
30. *31st Annual Report 1883*, p. 10.
31. Barker to Messrs. Slade and Hussey (of the Birmingham Auxiliary), 22 June 1883, loose in *Minutes*.
32. *Minutes*, 15 March 1882; 3 May 1882; 16 Aug. 1882; 20 Sept. 1882.
33. *Alliance News*, 20 Oct. 1883, pp. 657-63.
34. Ibid., p. 659; *32nd Annual Report 1884*, pp. 8-9.
35. Lawson to Harcourt, 17 Dec. 1884, copy in *Minutes*, 7 Jan. 1885; ibid., 18 Dec. 1884.
36. Ibid., 24 Sept. 1884.
37. Steinthal to G.O. Trevelyan, 11 Feb. 1885, copy in *Minutes*, 25 Feb. 1885; *Minutes*, 18 Feb. 1885; 4 March 1885.
38. *Alliance News*, 13 June 1885, p. 376; 17 Oct. 1885, p. 661-2.
39. *Alliance News*, 19 Dec. 1885, p. 818.
40. Ibid., 16 June 1886, p. 392; *34th Annual Report 1886*, p. 31.

41. Saunders to Barker, 7 Feb. 1888, in *Minutes*, 8 Feb. 1888.

42. *Alliance News*, 22 Oct. 1881, p. 674; 21 Oct. 1882, p. 658; 16 Oct. 1886, p. 661; 13 Nov. 1886, p. 736; 2 April 1887, p. 224.

43. Ibid., 16 Oct. 1886, pp. 662-3; 13 Nov. 1886, p. 736; 4 June 1887, p. 371; 6 Aug. 1887, p. 512, 10 Dec. 1887, pp. 816-17.

44. *35th Annual Report 1887*, pp. 10-16; *Alliance News*, 15 Oct. 1887, p. 688.

45. *35th Annual Report 1887*, pp. 8, 15; *Minutes*, 7 Sept. 1887, 1 Aug. 1888.

46. *35th Annual Report 1887*, pp. 16-19. The vigorous but sometimes confused efforts to revitalise local electoral associations during this period are dealt with in D.A. Hamer, *The Politics of Electoral Pressure. A Study in the History of Victorian Reform Agitations* (1977), ch. 12.

47. *Alliance News*, 16 Oct. 1886, pp. 659-62. Raynor resigned soon after to take up an appointment in Africa.

48. Russell to Barker, 14 Oct. 1886, in *Minutes*, 20 Oct. 1886.

49. John Newton, *W.S. Caine M.P. A Biography* (1907), pp. 80, 179-82.

50. Whitworth to Barker, n.d., in *Minutes*, 30 March 1887.

51. Newton, *W.S. Caine*, pp. 177-82; *Alliance News*, 5 March 1887, p. 157; 26 March 1887, p. 212; Caine to Barker, 17 March 1887, in *Minutes*, 23 March 1887.

52. Whitworth to Barker, n.d., in *Minutes*, 30 March 1887; *Alliance News*, 16 Oct. 1886, pp. 659-60; 9 April 1887, p. 241.

53. Ibid., 9 July 1887, p. 453.

54. *Minutes*, 20 July 1887; Pope to Barker, 2 Sept. 1887, in ibid., 7 Sept. 1887; *Alliance News*, 15 Oct. 1887, pp. 683-90.

55. T.W. Heyck and William Klecka, 'British Radical M.P.s, 1874-1895: New Evidence from Discriminant Analysis', *Journal of Interdisciplinary History*, vol. IV, no. 2 (1873), pp. 178-82.

Chapter 5

CONSERVATIVES AND COMPENSATION, 1888-1890

During a speech at Newport in October 1885, Lord Salisbury declared his support for the principle of local option. An astonished and jubilant editorialist on the *Alliance News* declared: 'Saul *is* among the prophets. Lord Salisbury *has* become a local Optionist'.[1] Two years later, Lord Randolph Churchill followed Salisbury's lead. While prohibitionists were taken completely by surprise, these moves were not without precedent. Although the Tory party had adopted a very different approach to temperance reform than that favoured by the Alliance, from the 1860s onwards the party always contained a minority of sincere temperance reformers. While most of them disliked the Permissive Bill, they also objected to the centralisation of the Cross Act and in the 1870s became increasingly willing to give ratepayers some say in the issue of licences.[2]

Salisbury, for long an arch opponent of restrictive measures of any kind, was not a temperance convert. He was convinced that attacks on the liquor traffic 'only exist in a particular strata of society' which was not at all representative of the views of the public at large. Nor did he personally like local option. Upon hearing that the Welsh Local Veto Bill had passed its second reading in the Commons in 1891 he assumed that Tory MPs were counting on 'a good drunken majority in the House of Lords to throw it out'.[3] However by supporting the catchphrase local option, something to which all temperance reformers subscribed, he realised that there was political capital to be made. His support would hearten Tory temperance men, particularly those in the influential CETS, and perhaps even more important it would lessen the hostility of temperance men, particularly prohibitionists, towards Conservative candidates at elections. If Conservative candidates were willing to pledge their support for local option, Alliance men could not then throw all their weight behind the Liberal. Significantly he announced his support for local option during an election campaign. Like Chamberlain almost a decade earlier, Salisbury hoped to defuse temperance as a political issue. However if he was to succeed in this, he had to devise a scheme which would be acceptable to the moderates within his party and the drink trade.

Salisbury proposed that local authorities should be given the power to reduce the number of licences but if they did, dispossessed publicans would be compensated for their losses. As a safeguard against wholesale closures he also suggested that ratepayers should pay most of the costs of compensation, convinced that 'the terror of having to provide ... fair compensation would furnish no inconsiderable motive to induce the local authority to observe a wise and cautious moderation in the exercise of this important duty'. Churchill also wanted safeguards against the wholesale expropriation of trade pro-perty. His scheme was similar to that of Salisbury except that he wanted to make revenue from liquor licences an important source of local government revenue. If this happened, local authorities 'would not hastily or impulsively or fanatically deprive themselves of a useful source of revenue'. When asked if he would give local authorities the power of prohibition Churchill replied: 'I would and I wouldn't. I would in theory but in practice I would not.' He believed that 'a properly devised check which affects the pocket would check fanati-cism with regard to the abolition of the sale of liquor'.[4]

Alliance leaders were so bemused by these professions of support that they neglected to study the qualifications with which they had been surrounded; 'full of ardent and hopeful anticipation', they looked forward to the unveiling of the Conservative Local Government Bill. The Executive, 'wearied and disgusted by the delay of Liberal Governments', and battered by internal conflicts, was predisposed to find in the Bill 'something that would shame the Liberal Party', and quieten its dissident troops. It publicly expressed its willingness to accept 'as an instalment of an overdue debt, though not as full pay-ment of the debt, any measure based on sound principle which, although far short of their demands, would ... have supplied a basis for future development in the right direction'.[5]

Ritchie introduced the Local Government Bill on 19 March 1888. A spirit of goodwill and conciliation prevailed. Both parties had long recognised the need for local government reform and the Conservative Bill differed from previous Liberal draft reforms only in detail. It was expected that it would be treated in a non-party spirit as Gladstone had pledged his aid in easing its passage. Both Ritchie and Gladstone agreed that 'there was not any great force of public opinion behind this question to help us deal with it', but they felt this would be advantageous as it would allow discussion in a 'spirit of calmness'.[6] The press, both Liberal and Conservative echoed the view of *The Times* that it was a 'comprehensive scheme of reform, which ... will begin a great work of safe and moderate decentralisation'. The only clouds on the horizon came from a few Tory MPs, disgruntled that the role of the country squire was to be diminished by the transfer of functions from magistrates to local authorities, some concern that London was to be included, and a warning by the *Daily Telegraph* that the licensing question was too dangerous to tackle and should therefore be left out. The *Pall Mall Gazette* also struck a slightly discordant but prophetic note when it pointed out that 'the new Bill is as big as Noah's Ark, and the menagerie inside is almost as large and varied .... It is a stupendous scheme: merely to look at it is enough to take away one's breath. To pass it is utterly and absolutely out of the question.'[7]

The general proposals of the Bill are well known, but those relating to licensing and compensation need outlining briefly in order to set the ensuing debate in its context. While Ritchie had been advised by many not to touch the 'thorny question' of licensing, he felt he had to do so if the transfer of function from magistrates to local authorities was to be effective and comprehensive. Licensing authority was to be transferred to the newly constituted County Councils who would divide their areas into licensing divisions. A licensing committee for each division would consist of the elected County Council members for that division, together with other selected members of the Council. The powers of these licensing committees were to be twofold. They could refuse to renew licences if they wished to see a reduction in the number of licensed houses and they also had the power to close public houses on Sundays, Good Friday and Christmas Day. However if licences were not renewed for any reason other than misconduct, compensation would have to be paid. The level of compensation to be awarded was to be calculated by an arbitrator and the burden of payment was to be 'thrown primarily upon the ratepayers of the district in which the licence has been refused'.[8] County Councils were also given the power to increase licence fees by up to 20 per cent. This it was calculated would provide an extra £300,000 per year throughout the whole country and would go to the Councils as revenue. In addition to this, all existing revenues from drink licences would go to the County Councils and would constitute almost half their proposed total revenue. Initially the £300,000 from increased licence fees was not earmarked for any special purpose but during the second reading of the

Bill Chamberlain suggested that the Councils should use this to compensate dispossessed publicans. Ritchie accepted this. Thus the licensing clauses closely followed the proposals first outlined by Salisbury and Churchill some years earlier.

Successive governments had continually shied away from attempts at licensing reform because they were aware that neither temperance reformers nor brewers and publicans placed much faith in the art of compromise. The fate of the Bruce Bill was still fresh in the minds of many. Ritchie therefore took a risk in attempting to frame a compromise, but must have been heartened in doing so by the conciliatory noises that the Alliance had recently been making. His scheme involved 'very substantial concessions' to the temperance movement and he hoped that they would be recognised as such. He argued that in return temperance reformers must be prepared to accept the need for compensation. He felt that parliamentary opinion was overwhelmingly in favour of financial compensation and it would be a 'gross injustice' if it were not paid. Indeed the government warned that if it was not accepted all the licensing clauses of the Bill would be dropped. Publicans and brewers on the other hand had to accept the need for some reduction in the number of licences and they also had to pay more for them. In return their position would be made more secure than at present. Existing licence holders would be given a vested interest in their licences and the right to compensation in the event of non-renewal.[9]

As soon as these details were announced the conciliatory attitude of the Alliance evaporated and it denounced the Bill as a 'mockery and a snare ... a most specious production'. Not only was it 'a skilfully devised measure for securing the impregnability and permanence of the liquor traffic' and a 'deliberately devised plan to hoodwink and rob the nation', it was also regarded as a personal affront to the Alliance. Lawson and the Executive were furious at having been taken in by Tory promises and Lawson claimed that 'the measure was so constructed as if its sole object had been to baffle and befool the Local Option party'. This was somewhat unfair to Salisbury and Churchill who had never made any secret of their intentions. Nevertheless the concession of local option, on which the Tories had placed so much emphasis, was a far cry from the popular participation in decision making which the Alliance wanted. Even the CETS, for long favourably disposed to licensing boards rather than periodic referenda, felt the Bill 'did not make popular control as efficient or as strong as it ought to be'.[10]

Many temperance men were critical of Ritchie for 'wedging a Licensing Bill into a Local Government Bill' because it prevented the drink question from being raised and discussed on its own merits. Cardinal Manning for example, sincerely welcomed local government reform because he thought it would revitalise provincial life, but the benefits he hoped would flow from decentralisation were 'rudely destroyed by the clauses which place the great drink traffic at the very outset of the Bill, as if it were the palladium of our liberties'. He reluctantly concluded that 'the drink trade, like the shirt of Nessus, so clings to the Bill as to be identified with it; and if it be not fatal to the Bill, it will be fatal to the moral and domestic life of the people'.[11] Conservatives as well as Liberals were also worried that once local authorities were responsible for licensing, County Council elections would be dominated by this issue. The partisan candidates subsequently elected would not be the people best fitted to carry on the general work of local government. There was also the danger that licensing would become 'mixed up with all sorts of heterogeneous matters, so that the Temperance issue would always be confused with other issues'. Temperance reformers thought it likely that in such circumstances the new local authorities would be no more effective or responsive to the wishes of the locality than the magistrates had been. There were other criticisms. Some complained that giving drink revenue to local authorities implicated them in the drink trade and morally corrupted them. Others pointed out that the least sober areas, which contained most pubs, would gain the largest revenues, while those with few pubs would be penalised financially for their sobriety.[12]

It was the compensation clauses in the Bill which excited the most violent reaction from prohibitionists. Throughout the nineteenth century almost all attempts at licensing reform aimed at some reduction in the number of licensed houses. *The Times* noted in 1872 that 'practically speaking "confiscation" and nothing else, is the direct object of every licensing reformer, whether reasonable or not'.[13] The compensation question revolved around the right of publicans, dispossessed of their licences for reasons other than misconduct, to claim some form of compensation for their loss. Publicans claimed they had a legal right to compensation because the law recognised that they had a vested interest in their licence, furthermore, because the loss of a licence would mean a loss of livelihood, they claimed it should also be given on equity grounds. Prohibitionists disputed both claims. They insisted that no vested interest could exist because licences were only issued for a period of one year and magistrates could refuse to renew them if they wished. While the legal position of licence holders was unclear, several court cases during the 1880s tended to support the Alliance interpretation. Nevertheless public opinion favoured compensation and so also did the leaders of both political parties. For most of the seventies and eighties the matter was not much discussed because, after Bruce's failure in 1871, no licensing Bill made sufficient headway to pose any real threat to the trade. Nevertheless it remained a vital question for both sides. It was fundamental to publicans and brewers because it determined the extent to which they would be hurt by any reform, and also to the Alliance because compensation could make prohibition so expensive as to be impracticable.[14]

Prohibitionists were alarmed by the compensation clauses of Ritchie's Bill because they feared that if they were passed, they would make future attempts at reform impossibly expensive. W.S. Caine estimated that the granting of a statutory vested interest would put the capital value of the assets of the trade at a little less than £250,000,000. He employed two firms of chartered accountants to get valuations of public houses under the terms laid down by the Bill, in order to gauge the amounts of compensation payable if licences were not renewed. It was found that the average sum payable would be £1,800 in the country, £8,000 in suburban areas, and £32,000 for city gin palaces. Therefore government claims that the publican would pay for compensation through the £300,000 fund especially earmarked for the purpose was alleged to be fallacious as this sum would be inadequate to diminish noticeably the number of licences. T.R. Reid claimed it was not enough to compensate twelve licensed houses in London that he knew of. Therefore if any considerable reduction was to be achieved, local ratepayers would have to foot most of the bill. This of course had always been the government's intention but temperance reformers now branded it as a cynical appeal to man's baser instincts. Experience had already shown that many parishes had refused to stand the additional rate of even a halfpenny in the pound in order to establish public libraries. What hope then was there that ratepayers would be willing to pay for a significant reduction in the number of licences? Lawson claimed that compensation of the kind proposed was an 'attempt to fine local communities for efforts to purify themselves'. Indeed there was an incentive to increase the number of licences because this would increase county council revenue and could perhaps lead to a reduction in rates. Temperance reformers insisted that the people had not previously been given any say in the multiplication of licences, therefore they should not now be asked to bear the cost of any reductions.[15]

Another major objection raised by temperance men, one that they used extensively in the ensuing agitation, was that compensation when granted would not in most cases go to licence holders who were 'the poor drudges of the monopolist brewers'. Most would find its way into the pockets of the 'beer kings', the 'millionaire brewers' and distillers who had already grown fat on the monopoly granted them by the state and on whose behalf the legislation had been introduced. There was much truth in the first part of this claim. The tied-house system had been widely adopted throughout the country and gained new impetus when the 'brewery boom' began in 1886. Guinness went public in that year and many other concerns rapidly followed. As breweries with increased funds at their disposal sought to capture retail outlets for their own exclusive use, they bid up the price of licensed property and therefore increased the compensation payable. Caine calculated that about two-thirds of all public houses and beerhouses were owned by brewers and distillers. Temperance reformers were also concerned that the financial stake in alcohol, through public share issues, was being spread more widely throughout the community. Lawson unsuccessfully attempted to get a list of MPs with a financial interest in joint stock breweries, hoping to get them disqualified from voting on the Local Government Bill on the grounds that they had a direct pecuniary interest in the outcome.[16]

The Alliance was not in 1888 in a good position to mount a strong and sustained campaign because internal splits and a deepening financial crisis had weakened its unity and effectiveness. Furthermore there was initial uncertainty within the Executive as to what strategy to adopt. While it was clearly necessary to oppose the compensation proposals, it was by no means so clear that all the licensing provisions should be condemned. Aware that these were a concession to the Alliance and had been very favourably received throughout the country, some members of the Executive were worried that they might lose the support of moderates if they did so. After a few days' hesitation the risk was taken and the decision made to oppose both compensation and licensing clauses, but the main target was compensation. The National Temperance Federation agreed to join in the campaign with the Alliance and the two bodies co-ordinated their plans. This was an important move because it allowed W.S. Caine, the President of the NTF, to work closely with the Alliance. He soon became the leading figure in the campaign.

The strategy adopted was a two-pronged one of rousing public opinion throughout the country and working with politicians inside the Commons. For the first part, the Alliance machine clicked smoothly into gear. An 'Agitation Superintendence Committee' consisting of six members of the Executive was formed to meet daily and direct the campaign. W.S. Caine asked for 'at least ten thousand petitions from temperance societies, and half a million letters from constituencies to their members, protesting against these clauses'. Alliance agents were told to drop all their other work to concentrate on this 'supremely momentous crisis of our Movement'. They were to organise protest meetings, persuade friends and supporters to write letters of protest to their MPs, provide the Executive with the names of able and influential men in their districts who were 'capable of dealing in conversation' with MPs, and encourage press communication of any kind. They were urged to be 'active and aggressive'.[17]

This part of the campaign went well. The Executive was unable to subsidise meetings because of its shortage of funds but deputations, pamphlet literature and petition forms were all widely distributed. The only setbacks occurred in Manchester where the Lord Mayor initially refused to hold a town meeting and at Oldham where publicans turned up in force and almost managed to carry a resolution in favour of compensation. Elsewhere a large number of protest meetings were held without complication. Persons of influence were bombarded with letters; one member of the Executive had personally written 180 such letters by the beginning of May. An initial batch of 125,000 tracts was distributed and more printed subsequently. These made great use of Caine's investigations into the likely costs of compensation and the extent of the 'tied house' system. The press freely opened its columns to letters on the compensation question and agents and others availed themselves of this opportunity. A petition movement was also mounted, the first for many years. Printed petition forms were sent free of charge to anyone who requested them: a total of 12,000 were eventually sent out, of which 5,000 were distributed by Joseph Malins through the Good Templar Lodges. W.S. Caine was the most active of the temperance leaders, both inside and outside parliament. During the first few weeks of the campaign he personally spoke to a large number of protest meetings and spent over £600 out of his own pocket on meetings and literature.[18]

The campaign in the Commons got underway much more slowly because the Executive appeared to be unsure of the best way of going about it. However, it possessed an advantage never previously enjoyed in fighting a Conservative government for it had some active supporters in the heart of the enemy camp, the most important of whom was W.S. Caine. His differences with the Liberal Party over Ireland had not dampened his temperance enthusiasm and he immediately began lobbying Tory leaders and relaying their views to the Executive. He rapidly became convinced that the government was firm in its intention to proceed with the licensing clauses and that it would be supported not only by Conservatives but also some Gladstonians, Liberal Unionists and Irish Nationalists. This gave scant comfort to the Executive but the position adopted by Caine persuaded it to try and win over other Liberal-Unionists, and it began by making a private approach to Chamberlain. The result was discouraging. Chamberlain liked the Bill very much and believed the Alliance should support it but he did concede that temperance men could put up a good fight and promised to talk to Ritchie about the possibility of dropping the licensing clauses. He added that in order to secure this, temperance men must put up a strong showing during the second reading. Chamberlain perhaps already dimly perceived that these clauses could cause problems between the Tories and their Liberal-Unionist partners.[19]

Despite Caine's conviction that the Bill would attract support from among all parties, it was generally assumed before the second reading that party lines would not be unduly disturbed. Liberal-Unionists were expected to unite behind the government, if only to prevent any chance of a defeat which might allow Gladstone to return to office and implement Home Rule.[20] With a strong majority behind it the government looked set to sweep aside the protests of prohibitionists, particularly as Liberal leaders had initially given the Bill a favourable reception. Most of the early Liberal speakers, Stansfeld, H.H. Fowler, Rathbone, Broadhurst and T.E. Ellis failed to mention the licensing clauses and presumably therefore found little to object to in them. Some Conservatives made passing reference, mainly in relation to the legal status of licensed victuallers. Only on the third night of debate did the licensing and compensation clauses come suddenly to the fore. Joseph Chamberlain spoke strongly in their favour and urged temperance reformers to accept what he regarded as a generous compromise. He also insisted that 'there is an undoubted vested interest in a licence'. Lawson replied with a bitter attack on the government and its clauses, and particularly the notion that a vested interest did exist. He called on the Liberal party to oppose the measure to the last 'if there be a spark of Liberalism left'. The following evening, W.S. Caine joined the fray with an attack on compensation, the legal position, and the speech of Chamberlain. Pledging his 'uncompromising opposition' he threatened Ritchie that

> It will be the duty of the Temperance Reformers to move a considerable number of Amendments in an endeavour to improve that Licensing Bill, and he must expect a considerable number of evenings to be devoted to discussion on a question which a large number of Members believe to be of paramount importance to the welfare of the country ... [21]

From this point on, the debate in a poorly attended House became dominated by licensing and compensation, to the exclusion of other aspects of the Bill, so much so that there were complaints that proceedings had degenerated into a discussion on licensing.

This was a reflection of the heat being generated throughout the country, but the government did not heed the warning signs. Instead of trying to win over temperance men the Solicitor General, Sir Edward Clarke, mounted an all out attack on them, and on the Alliance in particular. He argued that the House of Commons was not the proper place for temperance men and he seriously underestimated the strength of those there by claiming that 'temperance advocates in this House have never defeated anything except a Liberal Government'.[22] In his enthusiasm he went further and brought up once again the thorny issue of vested interests. While replying to Lawson's speech, Clarke insisted that 'the Acts, properly read, do give to the licensed victualler a vested interest in the continuous enjoyment of his licence'. He went further and pointed out that Lawson's claim, that no vested interest existed, was based on a supposed utterance of Mr Justice Field during the Over Darwen case of 1882 that 'the legislature recognised no vested interest at all in any holder of the licence'. Clarke had gone through the judgement on this case, failed to find the sentence and implied that the Alliance had fabricated it. However the phrase had in fact been used during the *argument* on the case, as the Alliance quickly pointed out. The view that no vested interest existed had also been expressed by legal minds in the House during the debate, especially by Harcourt. The Alliance was quick to point out a discrepancy between the opinions of Clarke and Ritchie. While the former believed a vested interest existed, the latter presumably did not, as he was actively trying to pass legislation which would create one. W.S. Caine asked the obvious question. If Clarke was right why was there a clause in the Bill to create that which already existed?[23]

Clarke's bungling did little to advance the government's cause but when the protracted second reading debate ended on 20 April, the prospects for passing the licensing clauses intact still looked good. The fire of the 'temperance fanatics' had been drawn and it seemed unlikely that Lawson could find anything new to say when the Bill went into the Committee stage. Temperance morale was at a low ebb. D.R. Daniel, the Alliance agent lobbying Welsh MPs, reported that most were prepared to back Lawson but 'the general opinion among them was, that the Government will beat us on the general principle, and that the best they can expect to do is driving a hard bargain on the details'. This seems to have been the prevailing mood. Lawson in a letter to the ailing T.H. Barker was hardly optimistic in telling him 'not to despair of beating Compensation even in this'. Harcourt later told John Morley of 'the trouble I have had in screwing up the G.O.M. [he believed in the Solicitor General] and (low it be spoken) even Wilfrid Lawson to the sticking point of no surrender'.[24]

Nevertheless the Alliance-inspired campaign was gaining momentum, so much so that Ritchie had to emphasise that the government would proceed with the licensing clauses despite manifestations of public opposition to them. One prominent Liberal, Harcourt, had been tempted into the arena by the legal wrangles and the chance of attacking Chamberlain, one of his favourite targets. Henceforth he took a leading part in the campaign against compensation. The Alliance received a great boost on 30 April when the Court of the Queen's Bench found, in the case of *Sharpe* versus *Wakefield*, that 'the licensing justices have absolute discretion as regards renewing or refusing to renew an inn-keeper's licence',[25] in other words, no vested interest existed. The advice provided by Clarke was now shown to have been incorrect. The government remained outwardly unmoved and claimed that the decision would be reversed by the House of Lords on appeal. Ritchie refused to modify the compensation clauses and pointed out that there were still claims of equity to be considered. However the government case had been damaged and the press, which up to now had largely accepted that a vested interest existed, changed tack somewhat. *The Times* believed the government should now be prepared to compromise and fix compensation on a 'lower scale'.[26]

Now that their interpretation of the legal status of licences had been vindicated, temperance men became somewhat more optimistic of their chances of success. The Temperance Parliamentary Committee under the leadership of Caine was busy drafting amendments to the offending clauses while the campaign throughout the country gathered strength. As *The Times* later noted, the licensing clauses 'lend themselves with great facility to partisan misrepresentation in the constituencies' and, irrespective of their merits, were proving 'much more useful to the attack than to the defence.'[27] Meanwhile the government was not benefitting from any campaign on behalf of the Bill. Manchester brewers were opposed to it, and while London and Burton brewers were prepared to accept it, they did not like it overmuch and hoped to amend its provisions in Committee. No section of the drink trade was prepared to mount a campaign in its favour that might offset temperance opposition.

The weakness of the government's position was clearly exposed for the first time in a by-election at Southampton at the beginning of June. In a contest dominated by the compensation issue, the result was a victory for the Gladstonian, T.H. Evans, over his Unionist opponent, A.E. Guest, by nearly 900 votes. This reversed a Unionist majority of over 300 in 1886. It came as a complete surprise to most that 'Imperial issues', particularly Ireland, were pushed into the background by the 'frivolous question' of compensation. The Conservative press, furious about this, accused Liberals of deliberately forcing Home Rule into the background in order to make a 'double appeal to the pockets of the ratepayers and the bigotry of the total abstainers'. Evans it was felt had 'conciliated opposition and won votes by a surrender at discretion to every fad and crochet which raised its head against him'; he had accepted 'the main articles of the Socialist creed'.[28] However this interpretation of events ignores the fact that the government had seriously miscalculated in not realising that compensation would prove a good rallying cry for the Liberals. The Tories initially set down the conditions under which the election would be fought, even to the extent of selecting a time for the contest when they knew the Gladstonian candidate would be absent on a trans-Atlantic trip. Furthermore the previous history of representation in the borough indicated that drink would indeed be a good rallying cry. This being so, a Liberal victory was all the more remarkable and demonstrated the extent to which the Alliance-inspired agitation had attracted wide public support. The temperance electoral campaign in the town had been led by Canon Basil Wilberforce, an Alliance vice-president and local resident, and the local Alliance agent. The Executive sent a deputation including J.H. Raper to help, but the effort was mainly a local one, drawing upon the resources of the sizeable Nonconformist community in the town, with additional support from 'a few injudicious ladies' and, it was claimed, some members of the Primrose League.[29]

The highlight of the Alliance campaign in the country came immediately after the Southampton election, in the form of a mass rally in Hyde Park on 2 June. Estimates of the numbers attending varied around 60,000 (*Pall Mall Gazette*).The Alliance had taken care to emphasise that the demonstration was neither exclusively Liberal nor temperance, but rather 'a demonstration of ratepayers who are most deeply interested in the compensation question'. Members of the various organisations taking part wore their own emblems and marched under their own banners. The procession was led by Lawson and W.S. Caine and, once in Hyde Park, the meeting was addressed by many speakers, some of whom were Conservatives. Twelve MPs spoke. The national press, while mainly unsympathetic to the aims of the meeting and to this method of agitation, was nevertheless impressed by its size and reported it at length. The *Saturday Review* was incensed that 'the authority of the Legislature should be superseded by a promiscuous audience excited by the declamation of irresponsible agitators' but admitted that the proceedings were 'more respectable' than was usual for this kind of gathering: 'Knots of blue riband are less objectionable than hop-holes'. Elsewhere it was seen as 'a splendid popular pageant'. Even trade organs admitted it was 'artistically arranged'. Coming immediately after the Southampton election, the Hyde Park meeting was regarded by some as a confirmation of the decision arrived at in Southampton. The *Daily News* concluded that 'as the present Government is nothing if not amenable to popular pressure, Saturday's proceedings may fairly be regarded as the death-blow of an unrighteous job'.[30]

The position of W.S. Caine became increasingly important as the campaign proceeded. The success he enjoyed in leading attacks on compensation was a measure of the damage he was inflicting upon the Unionist and Tory coalition of which he was a part. The Executive had been quick to realise this and see the importance of exploiting differences of opinion within Liberal-Unionist ranks. It therefore did all it could to neutralise the attempts being made by Chamberlain to persuade temperance reformers to accept the Bill. The Birmingham auxiliary worked strenuously to win over Liberal-Unionists in Birmingham, and agents throughout the country were instructed to bring pressure to bear on Liberal-Unionists to join in the campaign.[31] The first evidence of a split in the coalition came during the Southampton by-election. Just before the poll was taken local Liberal-

Unionist leaders released their supporters from the necessity of supporting the government on compensation. They evidently feared the secession of some of their supporters to the ranks of the Gladstonians unless they made this concession. Lord Wolmer attempted to plaster over the cracks by agreeing with the Conservative candidate, Guest, that the latter would not declare in favour of compensation at the expense of the ratepayers, but only if it were provided out of premiums on existing licences. This was not enough to snatch victory, nor was it likely to have been authorised by the government as it went against a promise formally made by Ritchie in the House.[32]

Caine was the instigator of the split and effectively the leader of dissident Liberal-Unionists. He had already attacked Chamberlain and the government in the Commons during the second reading and he now went further. In a letter to *The Times* he declared

> I am a Liberal Unionist; but if I stood tamely by and sacrificed the temperance movement to the fetish of party, and consented to the creation and endowment of a new vested interest, I should withdraw the word 'Liberal' ... Persistence in these compensation proposals will inevitably throw the whole strength of the temperance party into the ranks of the Gladstonian Liberals.

He added that 'some of us Liberal Unionists think that it is about time for the Conservatives to make some sacrifices on behalf of the Union'.[33] Liberal-Unionist leaders were particularly susceptible to this kind of pressure because a by-election was pending in Ayr Burghs and they feared a repetition of what had happened at Southampton. Compensation was again becoming the major issue. The Liberal-Unionist candidate, the Hon. Evelyn Ashley, found himself compelled to throw overboard the compensation clauses. By promising to vote against them he hoped to pick up support from temperance men of both Liberal persuasions but once again the gesture came too late. While the poll was not held until after the government had decided to drop the licensing clauses, the largest Liberal-Unionist majority in Scotland of nearly 1,200 in 1886, had been converted into a Gladstonian victory by 63 votes in 1888. Meanwhile, before the clauses had been dropped, Hartington, concerned to heal the split that was opening in his party, called a meeting at which it was decided that no Liberal-Unionist should feel himself bound by the clauses as the government had never declared that they were vital to the Bill. So the temperance agitation had gained a powerful albeit unwilling ally.[34]

Even within the Conservative party opposition to the clauses was growing. Because they had become so controversial they endangered the rest of the Bill and it was expected that a few Tory MPs belonging to the CETS would follow the lead of Sir William Houldsworth and vote against them. The threat of defection became more serious when twenty-six Metropolitan MPs demanded that they be withdrawn. By the beginning of June it was freely rumoured that the government would drop the licensing provisions but the decision was not finally taken until after the Cabinet meeting on 12 June. The delay gave temperance reformers the chance to inflict one last humiliation on the government. On the evening of 11 June, W.H. Smith, the government leader in the Commons, was asked if he intended proceeding with the clauses, to which he replied 'Certainly, Sir'. This answer was greeted with dismay among Tory and Liberal-Unionist supporters involved in the Ayr Burghs by-election and they remonstrated that the clauses must be dropped if they were to win. This was done the next day, thus making Smith's performance look foolish and inept.[35]

Ritchie explained that he had dropped the licensing clauses because they had met with 'strenuous opposition'. There were 200 amendments on the Notice Paper and as there were only two months to go before the end of the session, the retention of the clauses would have endangered the rest of the Local Government Bill. These proposed amendments, as Caine had threatened, were largely the work of temperance men in the Commons, but whether they could have effectively held up the rest of the Bill is debatable. Some were of the opinion that if the government had chosen to go ahead it could have overcome this obstacle but the costs involved would not have been worthwhile as many Liberal-Unionists would 'resent being compelled to give effect to their convictions'.[36] It was the threat of revolt among some Liberal-Unionists and the possibility of more electoral disasters like Southampton which weighed most heavily upon the government. However the Alliance can take credit for this because the political manoeuvering by both Unionists and Gladstonians would not have been possible without the creation and mobilisation of public opinion against compensation. Southampton, Ayr and the Hyde Park demonstration were evidence of this feeling; these provided avenues by which political pressure could be brought to bear on the Ministry by Gladstonians, Liberal Unionists and some Conservatives.

The role of Liberal leaders in this affair is a curious one and worthy of closer examination. In 1886 one of the fundamental differences between them and the Alliance was that they accepted the need to include compensation in any licensing reform, whereas the Alliance did not. This was still their position at the beginning of 1888; even after the Local Government Bill had been introduced the Liberal committee of ex-ministers examining its provisions were still in favour of compensation.[37] By May 1888 however Harcourt was beginning to see that the compensation clauses might be a useful weapon for the Liberal party. He had already taken a stand on the legal question of a vested interest during the second reading, and his arguments had been vindicated soon afterwards by the *Sharpe* versus *Wakefield* decision. He was also aware of the temperance campaign and the groundswell of opposition to compensation among provincial Liberals which was expressed through an NTF resolution condemning the Bill. He therefore tried to swing Gladstone into formal opposition to compensation.

Harcourt took the Southampton result as a clear indication of the fighting capabilities of temperance men. The successful local alliance between Gladstonians and dissident Liberal-Unionists delighted him. In a letter to John Morley he claimed, 'I believe in the truth of what I maintain, that Temperance is the backbone of the Liberal Party *vice* Nonconformity retired'.[38] Gladstone was also impressed and immediately showed his hand. Attributing the Liberal victory to the licensing clauses, he objected to 'the principle of converting a licence into an estate', came out strongly against compensation, and implied that any future Liberal government would repeal these clauses. Convinced that licensing was one matter on which real divisions of opinion existed within Unionist ranks, Gladstone shrewdly exploited the situation. He simply outlined the alternatives open to the government. If they made the issue a question of confidence Liberal-Unionists, fearing the defeat of the Tory government and its replacement by Gladstone and the Home Rulers, would forget their temperance principles and toe the line. In the words of Gladstone, 'if England is doomed to be saddled with these licensing clauses ... it will be lest Ireland should obtain the benefits of Home Rule'.[39] But this course, as Caine feared, would drive many Liberal-Unionists back to the Gladstonian ranks and open the way for more debacles like Southampton. If on the other hand the government did not make the issue a question of confidence, defecting Liberal-Unionists were likely to swing the balance sufficiently to defeat the government in Committee. Either way, the government could only do itself harm. The only way out was simply to drop the clauses. This would preserve the unity of the coalition, the Alliance would be satisfied, the rest of the Bill could be pushed through and the Liberals would come away empty handed. All that would be involved would be some loss of face. This was the course adopted, and the bulk of the Local Government Bill passed relatively easily.

The position taken up by Gladstone, Harcourt and Morley was dictated largely by political considerations. They had done a complete about turn on the question of compensation and the trade and the government were not slow to point this out and condemn such opportunism. It was enough to persuade the brewer, Lord Burton, to leave the Liberal Party. Caine was also furious at the 'opportunist opposition which has been imported into the struggle when victory appeared probable'; Liberals had muscled in on a fight which he believed had been fought and won by the temperance movement.[40] Nevertheless Liberal leaders thereafter consistently claimed that the victory was theirs. Harcourt's essentially political motives are clearly revealed in the letter he wrote to Morley immediately before the clauses were dropped. 'The row', he wrote, 'will be when the Government move to omit the clauses. We must then smote them hip and thigh in their retreat.' He also considered fighting for the retention of the ninth clause on Sunday closing because 'it would bother them and be a good position for us'.[41] Harcourt was concerned to make political capital at the expense of the government and the compensation clauses happened to be the best ammunition available. However the Liberal leaders had paid a price in taking this opportunist course because they had been forced to accept the Alliance stand on compensation.

Prohibitionists were justified in regarding the episode as a major victory. They had been instrumental in defeating a reform which they disliked, and which, had it been enacted, would have prevented the effective implementation of their own alternative. Further benefits had accrued. The Liberal party had been impressed by the unity and fighting spirit displayed by temperance men and surprised by the degree of popular support they had achieved. Now that Liberal leaders had rejected the principle of compensation, one great difference between them and the Alliance had been removed. The presence of Harcourt at the Alliance annual meeting in October 1888 was at once evidence of this harmony, and a measure of the extent to which the Alliance had risen in the estimation of Liberal leaders.

It rapidly became clear however that the new alignments which had achieved victory were as yet tenuous and easily upset. The new-found fighting efficiency of the Alliance was endangered in the following year by another bout of internal faction fighting similar to that of 1886 and 1887.[42] The stringency of electoral pledges again became a bone of contention as militant prohibitionists once more attacked the actions of their leaders. This time Lawson himself was the main target. He had been relatively inactive during the campaign against compensation, allowing W.S. Caine to shoulder most of the burden and subsequent proddings by the Executive failed to arouse him to more active leadership. He continually refused to address important Alliance gatherings while still finding time to speak at Liberal meetings. This was the subject of much unfavourable comment among prohibitionists and forced the Executive to remonstrate with him about it. Lawson also refused to do anything in the Commons to push the Alliance case except to promise half-heartedly to reintroduce a Local Option Resolution. This was not sufficient for the Executive who reluctantly threw their support behind other MPs who were introducing separate Direct Veto Bills for Ireland, Wales, England and Scotland. Lawson further alienated many Alliance men by supporting the candidature of the Liberal distiller Mark Beaufoy at Kennington, even though Beaufoy was not pledged to the veto. This was taken by many to mean that Lawson did not adhere to the advanced electoral policy. A few months later Francis Amos resigned from the Executive and cancelled his subscription to the Alliance because it had 'become much too decidedly "party" political (thanks to its president)'.[43]

Even before this, the compensation victory was soured by another squabble. When Ritchie proposed to drop all licensing clauses, there were attempts to retain Clause 9 which gave County Councils the right to institute Sunday closing if they wished. Harcourt wanted it retained, but Caine wished to see it dropped. In a bitter debate between the two Harcourt insisted that Caine had advised him to work for the retention of the clause, but Caine denied this. He claimed that Harcourt had 'never given a shilling of his money or an hour of his time to the temperance movement' but had simply 'picked up the 9th clause as a stick good enough to beat the Tory dog with'. In fact Caine had changed his mind, having originally supported retention at a meeting of the Temperance Parliamentary Committee. Lawson had also wanted the retention of the clause, and in the Commons used the phrase '*cave canem*', thus bringing a burst of anger from the recipient. Caine's about turn and his attack on Harcourt angered and alienated most other members of the Committee, causing its virtual demise.[44] Once more temperance MPs had failed to agree among themselves and were again left without effective organisation and direction in the Commons.

As the dropping of the ninth clause was being contested, it was necessary to put it to a vote in the Commons. Liberal Unionists met under Hartington and decided to support the government. For once Caine was in a position where no conflict existed between party requirements and his temperance principles. He wanted the clauses dropped because he favoured Sunday closing by national enactment not local option. In this he was supported by the Central Sunday Closing Association. The government, in order to retain its Liberal-Unionist support, had already promised to find a day for the discussion of Stephenson's Sunday Closing Bill. When the vote was taken it proceeded along normal party lines and the clause was dropped. So already the temporary alliance which had defeated compensation had split back into its constituent parts. It was not so much the licensing question as a whole which had originally created it, but the specific threat of compensation; Liberal-Unionists were particularly aware of this, hence Caine's often expressed wish that the government should not again attempt to deal with this question. However two years later the government did just this and once again tried to push through a measure of licensing reform and compensation.

The new proposal differed somewhat from that which had failed in 1888. It was, in the words of Sir Edward Hamilton, 'an ingenious way of dealing with the vexed licensing question by a side door'.[45] Out of an increase in duty of 3d on a barrel of beer, and 6d per gallon on spirits, a sum of £1,304,000 was to be raised each year and turned over to county councils who could use up to £438,000 of it annually to buy up excess licences. Councils were also empowered to borrow up to three times their annual share if they wished to hasten the reduction of licences. Henceforth no new licences were to be issued except in exceptional circumstances and the practice of transferring old licences to new premises was to be discontinued. The campaign which ensued resembles that of 1888 so closely that it can be discussed rather more briefly.

With the events of 1888 still fresh in their minds some Conservative leaders expected stiff opposition, particularly from the drink trade. Even before the proposals had been made public W.H. Smith was 'beginning to funk'. However Goschen was determined to press on and introduced the scheme in his budget speech of 17 April 1890. Initial reactions were more favourable than anticipated. Trade interests grumbled somewhat, but with doubt being thrown on their security of tenure by the *Sharpe* versus *Wakefield* decision, they decided to accept the security it offered them. Conservatives offered no objections and within the Liberal party Rosebery particularly liked this part of the budget, while Gladstone had no important criticisms to offer. Moderate temperance reformers, including many in the CETS, saw much of value in the scheme and only the Alliance and the National Temperance Federation declared their opposition. It was expected therefore that the clauses would have little trouble in passing.[46]

As in 1888 the debate began quietly but as Liberal MPs saw the Alliance campaign in the country picking up they stiffened their opposition in the commons. Harcourt was instrumental in promoting this. Early in May he was already 'pegging away at the "Compensation clauses" ' and working to see that Gladstone was 'up to the mark'. He was as yet unsure as to 'how much *real grit* there is in the Teetotal Party' but was already convinced that 'if they are determined they ought to be able to wear out the Bill'. Gladstone now came out and denounced the proposals and debate on the Budget Bill dragged on through May, opposition centering almost exclusively on the licensing clauses. The government majority held firm as very few Tories and Liberal-Unionists defaulted but many began to 'wince considerably and growl at having had this awkward question sprung upon them unexpectedly'. The government was determined to press on but already this was 'becoming a very nasty question' and the prospects of the Session began to look 'decidedly gloomy'.[47]

Alliance opposition was based on two points. First, the plan would create a vested interest in the renewal of licences which did not until then exist and, secondly, it would place enormous obstacles in the way of the free exercise of the direct veto power of local inhabitants. Prohibitionists were convinced that the government intended to create a new national debt 'of at least one hundred and fifty millions, at the expense of the people for the benefit of the brewers and publicans'.[48] Much of the debate in the Commons revolved around the existing legal situation of publicans. Liberals and the Alliance stuck to the *Sharpe* versus *Wakefield* decision and insisted that no vested interest existed and therefore local Justices could exercise complete discretion as regards the number of licences they issued. The government argued that because probate duty and income tax were assessed on the current value of licences the holder of an annual licence had a vested interest in it beyond the term for which it was granted. The government claimed that it was simply recognising that licences possessed a current market value as a result of the goodwill attached to them and it was giving local authorities the means to purchase what someone else wished to sell on the open market. It persistently denied that it was giving compensation; all that was involved was a normal commercial transaction. It seemed to assume that Justices would not exercise their right to cancel licences (a right confirmed by the *Sharpe* versus *Wakefield* decision) because an alternative method of reduction was now being made available. This was a curious argument because the government had sold the scheme to the trade on the grounds that it did recognise a vested interest and therefore offered a financial recompense if this was to be taken away. Despite this smokescreen, all interested parties, temperance reformers, the trade, as well as the national press, recognised that compensation was being offered.[49]

Despite vigorous opposition the Commons passed the third reading of the Supply Bill by a majority of 74 on 23 May. Meanwhile it had agreed to the second reading of the Local Taxation (Custom and Excise) Duties Bill, which contained the licensing and repurchase provisions of the government scheme, on 13 May by a majority of 70. While it was delayed somewhat before going into its Committee stage, the Alliance agitation culminated in a massive procession and rally in Hyde Park. Attendance was estimated to be even larger than in 1888 and once again there was clear evidence of a great deal of public opposition to compensation. The Bill finally went into Committee on 10 June and the government majority almost immediately fell to 32 on an amendment to the first clause. Opposition to the measure was building up within the Tory party. Sir Richard Temple complained that the Bill was a blunder and had been sprung upon the party without warning. He blamed W.H. Smith for this. Chamberlain was also convinced that the government was 'ill-judged' in bringing up the licensing question once more. The role of W.S. Caine was again critical. At the outset of the campaign he had urged everyone to 'oppose the present measure tooth and nail, without the slightest regard to other issues or the conditions of Parliamentary Government'.[50]

On the day that the Bill went into Committee, Caine met with the Alliance Executive to examine ways in which Liberal-Unionist hostility to compensation could be brought home to the government. It was decided to draw up a petition in the name of W.S. Caine to be signed by Liberal-Unionists. This read in part:

> We deem it our duty to inform you, as leader of our party, that if these clauses are passed, it will inevitably lead to serious dissension in our ranks. We have so far been able to make our general Liberal principles subservient to Irish questions, and should greatly regret any circumstances which compelled us to deviate from this line of

action. But we cannot accept, without emphatic protest, what appears to us to be a new departure on the part of the Government, whom we consider pledged not to bring forward in the present Parliament acute questions on which any large section of the Liberal Unionist party feel strongly.

.... we respectfully urge upon your Lordship to use the great and legitimate influence you possess as leader of our party, to get these clauses withdrawn in Committee.[51]

The Alliance secretly distributed this to influential Liberal-Unionists throughout the country who were known to be opposed to compensation. Once they had been signed and collected, Caine triumphantly presented a batch of them to Liberal-Unionist leaders. Hartington remained unmoved and refused to act.[52]

On 16 and 17 June, at the beginning of Ascot week, further amendments to the first clause of the Bill were defeated by majorities of only 33 and 35. The annoyance of backbench Tories and the defection of Liberal-Unionists was beginning to make an impact. There was 'a good deal of demoralisation and discontent' within the Unionist party, particularly as a compromise to limit compensation to ten years, which was attractive to the CETS and may have won over some of the recalcitrant Liberal-Unionists, was rejected by the trade. Worse was to follow on 19 June when a motion to reject the whole of clause one was defeated by only four votes. This division came as a surprise to the government, having been cleverly engineered by the Liberals and it was won only when four Unionists and Liberal-Unionists dashed into the chamber at the last moment. One of these was Hartington, 'hurrying at a pace unprecedented in his Parliamentary history', but with his hand still firmly in his pocket.[53] Liberals were jubilant at this turn of events; Harcourt told his son that the strategy was succeeding: 'It is just like the parallels of a well managed siege, and the garrison are being defeated yard by yard'.[54]

While it was freely rumoured that the clauses would be dropped, the government was not yet ready to admit defeat and insisted that it intended to press on with them. Hartington, who had made repeated efforts to persuade Liberal-Unionists to support the government, made one last effort to rally his party by telling them that Goschen and Ritchie had threatened to resign rather than drop the clauses and it was doubtful if Salisbury would accept their resignations. W.H. Smith even proposed to invite Liberal-Unionists as well as Conservatives to a meeting on the question, but Chamberlain vetoed this. However before the loyalty of Liberal-Unionists could be put to the test, W.H. Smith was forced on 23 June to concede that 'it is practically impossible in the present state of public business to pass the Bill in its entirety without calling on the House to submit to sacrifices the Government do not feel justified in proposing'. He therefore proposed to withdraw the compensation clauses until the next Session when they would be reintroduced.[55] In the meantime the taxes on liquor, already passed in the Budget Bill would be allowed to accumulate until next year. T.M. Healy asked the Speaker for a ruling on whether it was constitutional to allow money to lie unappropriated from one session to another, and was told that it was not. The government was therefore forced to abandon the clause altogether and, on a suggestion by Arthur Acland, the unappropriated money went to technical education.

The Alliance had again succeeded in humbling a powerful and apparently united government and brought it almost to its knees entirely on the question of compensation. Hamilton noted that, 'the licensing cargo having gone overboard, the Government ship is already labouring under far less difficulty than it was'.[56] Prohibitionists had been given another opportunity to demonstrate their political muscle and had seized it with both hands. The campaign of 1890 confirmed the advances won by the Alliance in 1888. The Liberal party had been given another chance to appreciate the strength and political usefulness of prohibitionists and had become more appreciative of such a valuable ally. Following in the footsteps of Harcourt in 1888, John Morley presided over the annual meeting of the Alliance in 1891. During the campaign Liberal leaders had been forced to commit themselves more firmly to Alliance views on compensation. They were now much more aware of exactly what kind of reform would be acceptable to prohibitionists. Harcourt claimed that the defeat of compensation and the *Sharpe* versus *Wakefield* decision had 'cleared the field' and the battle for acceptable reform was already half won.[57] However as the Alliance became more closely aligned with the Liberal party, its perennial assertions of political neutrality sounded increasingly hollow. After its actions in 1888 and 1890, its claim to speak on behalf of all serious temperance reformers increasingly alienated moderate temperance men, particularly those with Conservative affiliations. J.R.D. West, a Tory member of the Alliance, pointed out that 'the time ... has come when temperance workers on other lines shall not be misrepresented by men who are Radicals first and always, and who make temperance and teetotalism (these Radicals themselves not being perforce teetotallers) stink in the nostrils of sensible men, by their one-sided bigotry and bitterness'.[58] Such complaints did not worry the Alliance unduly because it had long ago abandoned the attempt to persuade popular opinion of the rightness of its cause; it was hoping to achieve success by working through party-political channels and in this direction its actions in 1888 and 1890 had done it a great deal of good.

As in 1888 however, the compensation victory was soured by an unpleasant episode involving Lawson and Caine. As a result of his opposition to the government Caine had been forced to resign as Whip to the Liberal-Unionist party. He also resigned his seat at Barrow and then immediately offered himself for re-election as a means of testing the feeling of his constituency over his recent actions. He did not expect to be opposed but found to his surprise that both a Tory and a Gladstonian were going to contest the seat. The Executive gave him literature, the use of an agent and two clerks for campaigning and urged local electors to support him. It also tried to get the Liberal candidate withdrawn, as did Harcourt, but the local Liberal association refused to back down. Caine's chances were fatally damaged when Lawson refused to speak on his behalf, giving as his reason the fact that the Liberal candidate was also pledged for the veto and he could not therefore run counter to the wishes of the local Liberal association. Caine was furious about this but despite entreaties by the Executive, Lawson refused to change his mind.[59] Caine came bottom of the poll.

This episode further damaged the credibility of Lawson as leader of the Alliance. Many prohibitionists wished to record their dissatisfaction with his conduct and the Executive had great difficulty in suppressing hostile resolutions intended for the forthcoming annual meeting. It could not prevent some agents at the meeting voicing opinions hostile to Lawson, which were later inserted in the *Alliance News*. However the episode eventually turned out well for the Alliance as it was instrumental in persuading Caine to return to the Liberal party. As a result, the divisiveness of the Home Rule issue within Alliance ranks virtually disappeared. Caine later returned to the Commons after winning a by-election as a Liberal in East Bradford in 1891.[60]

Notes

1. *Alliance News*, 24 October 1885, p. 688.

2. Paul Smith, *Disraelian Conservatism and Social Reform* (1967), pp. 208-11, 290-3.

3. *Alliance News*, 19 July 1889, p. 590; John Morley, *Recollections* (1917), vol. 1, p. 269.

4. Quoted in *36th Annual Report 1888*, p. 7.

5. Ibid., pp. 5-6.

6. *Hansard*, vol. 323, cc. 1641-2.

7. *Times*, 20 March 1888; *Alliance News*, 20 March 1888, p. 170; *Pall Mall Gazette*, 20 March 1888.

8. *Hansard*, vol. 323, cc. 1665-70.

9. Ibid., cc. 1832, 1669-70.

10. *36th Annual Report 1888*, p. 6.; *Hansard*, vol. 324, cc. 1420, 1382.

11. Ibid., c. 1512; H.E. Manning, *Fortnightly Review*, vol. XLIX (1888), p. 790.

12. *Hansard*, vol. 324, cc. 1382, 1501, 1796; F.W. Farrer, *Fortnightly Review*, vol. XLIX (1888), p. 796.

13. *Times*, 13 April 1872.

14. For more on compensation see A.E. Dingle, 'The Agitation for Prohibition', (Monash University PhD, 1974), pp. 87-105.

15. *Hansard*, vol. 325, cc. 1366, 1407, 1502-3; *Times*, 11 June 1888; F.W. Farrer, *Fortnightly Review*, vol. XLIX (1888) pp. 797-9.

16. *Times*, 25 June 1888, p. 15; *Hansard*, vol. 325, cc. 1537-8.

17. Caine to James Whyte, 10 April 1888, in John Newton, *W.S. Caine M.P. A Biography* (1907), p. 192; Circular letter to all agents, 29 March 1888, in *Minutes*, 4 April 1888.

18. Ibid., 11 April 1888; 9 May 1888; Newton, *W.S. Caine*, pp. 191-3. The Solicitor General refused to present some Alliance petitions, much to the fury of prohibitionists, see *36th Annual Report 1888*, pp. 12-14.

19. Newton, *W.S. Caine*, p. 192; *Minutes*, 11 April 1888.

20. *Saturday Review*, 24 March 1888, p. 336.

21. *Hansard*, vol. 324, cc. 1357-67, 1407-23, 1512.

22. Ibid., cc. 1520-2.

23. Ibid., cc. 1505, 1514, 1516; ibid., vol. 325, c. 115; *36th Annual Report 1888*, pp. 18-20.

24. *Minutes*, 25 April 1888; 2 May 1888; Harcourt to Morley, 10 June 1888, *Harcourt Papers*, Box 10.

25. *36th Annual Report 1888*, p. 16. The case of *Sharpe* versus *Wakefield* stemmed from a decision by Kendal magistrates in 1887 to refuse to renew the licence of a moorland public house. Quarter sessions upheld this decision on appeal because the pub was too remote to be adequately supervised by police and because it was not needed. A group of northern brewers then financed an appeal to the Queen's bench. The case was later taken to the Lords.

26. *Times*, 1 May 1888, p. 9; 2nd June 1888, p. 13.

27. Ibid., 9 June 1888.

28. *Saturday Review*, 26 May 1888, p. 612; *Standard*, 24 May 1888; *Birmingham Daily Post*, 24 May 1888.

29. *Saturday Review*, 26 May 1888, p. 612; *Alliance News*, 30 October 1891, p. 717.

30. *Saturday Review*, 9 June 1888, p. 676; *Daily Chronicle*, 4 June 1888; *Morning Advertiser*, 4 June 1888; *Daily News*, 4 June 1888.

31. *Minutes*, 9 May 1888; 18 May 1888.

32. *Saturday Review*, 26 May 1888, p. 612.

33. *Times*, 11 June 1888.

34. Newton, *W.S. Caine*, p. 196.

35. *Alliance News*, 2 June 1888, p. 435; Sir Edward Hamilton's Diary, 7 and 9 June 1888, *Sir Edward Hamilton Papers*, Add. MSS. 48,648, pp. 116, 119; Harcourt to John

Morley, 10 June 1888, *Harcourt Papers*, Box 10.
36. *Times*, 9 June 1888.
37. Harcourt to Morley, 10 June 1888, *Harcourt Papers*, Box 10.
38. Ibid.
39. *Alliance News*, 2 June 1888, p. 437.
40. *Hansard*, vol. 325, cc. 119-20; *Times*, 11 June 1888.
41. Harcourt to Morley, 10 June 1888, *Harcourt Papers*, Box 10.
42. *Minutes*, 20 February 1889; 10 April 1889; 31 October 1889.
43. Ibid., 31 October 1889.
44. Newton, *W.S. Caine*, pp. 200-2; *Times*, 27 June 1888; *Minutes*, 19 November 1890.
45. Sir Edward Hamilton Diaries, 25 March 1890, *Sir Edward Hamilton Papers*, Add. MSS, 48,652, p. 100.
46. Ibid., 9 April 1890, p. 109; 17-19 April 1890, pp. 117-21; B.L. Crapster, 'Our Trade, Our Politics. A Study of the Political Activity of the British Liquor Industry, 1868-1910' (Harvard University PhD 1949), p. 339.
47. W.V. Harcourt to Lewis Harcourt, 14 May 1890, *Harcourt Papers*; Sir Edward Hamilton Diaries, 6-20 May 1890, pp. 5, 9, 13, 15.
48. *Minutes*, 22 April 1890; 6 May 1890.
49. *38th Annual Report 1890*, pp. 13-14, 16-29; Crapster, 'Our Trade, Our Politics', p. 340.
50. Viscount Chilston, *W.H. Smith* (1965), p. 324; Sir Edward Hamilton Diaries, 15 June 1890, p. 37; Newton, *W.S. Caine*, pp. 214-15.
51. *Minutes*, 11 June 1890.
52. Newton, *W.S. Caine*, pp. 218-19.
53. Sir Edward Hamilton Diaries, 17 June 1890, p. 41; Crapster, 'Our Trade, Our Politics', p. 341; H.W. Lucy, *A Diary of the Salisbury Parliament 1886-1892* (1892), pp. 282-4.
54. W.V. Harcourt to Lewis Harcourt, 21 June 1890, *Harcourt Papers*.
55. Arthur D. Elliot, *The Life of George Joachim Goschen First Viscount Goschen 1831-1907* (1911), vol. 2, p. 167; *Hansard*, vol. 345, c. 1652.
56. Sir Edward Hamilton Diaries, 27 June 1890, p. 55.
57. *Alliance News*, 2 October 1891, p. 638.
58. Letter in *Minutes*, 19 November 1890.
59. Details of elections in *Minutes*, 26 June to 2 July 1890.
60. Ibid., 9 July 1890; 29 October 1890; W.S. Caine to W.E. Gladstone, 3 July 1890, Gladstone to Caine, 4 July 1890, *W.E. Gladstone Papers*, Add MSS. 45, 510. ff. 132-7; Harcourt to W.S. Caine, 3 July 1890, *Harcourt Papers*, Box 11.

Chapter 6

THE FIRST VETO BILL

By 1886 the extent of Alliance influence upon the Liberal party was clear. The principle of local option had been accepted by Liberal leaders but they believed that it could best be implemented by using the existing local bodies as licensing authorities. They also recognised the need to give dispossessed publicans financial compensation for their loss. Both proposals were unacceptable to the Alliance. During the next six years however the views of leading Liberals changed dramatically. By 1893 Harcourt was prepared to introduce a Bill which not only included the Direct Popular Veto but also denied publicans the right to financial compensation. Why did Liberal leaders, who for so long had endeavoured to keep prohibitionists at arms length, suddenly and wholeheartedly accept the Alliance programme *and* act on it? The reasons for their change of heart on compensation have already been examined in the previous chapter. Conversion to the veto stemmed from changes taking place in the party at both parliamentary and constituency levels during these years, changes which the Alliance was able to exploit to its benefit.

There was little in the events of 1886 to give the Alliance any cause for optimism. The Liberal party had split in two over Home Rule. Purged and reconstructed, and with Gladstone at its head, it was now even more firmly committed to the solution of Irish problems. Most leading Liberals welcomed this; Harcourt appears to have been the only one who expressed doubts about this return to what D.A. Hamer has termed 'single question' Liberalism.[1] Even the NLF was prepared to accept that Ireland must be cleared out of the way before the ordinary work of the Liberal party could continue. More surprising still, some of the reformist groups which were being shouldered aside were also prepared to wait. In 1887 the Alliance Executive accepted that Ireland still blocked the way and urged prohibitionists to be patient because the situation was 'altogether abnormal and must be transitory'.[2]

It was not until the Parnell divorce case broke that the Liberal party was forced to take a greater interest in domestic reform. Harcourt was convinced that Parnell had 'fatally checked our *positive advance* in the direction of *Home Rule*', leaving him in a stronger position to urge a greater concentration on English questions. Even Gladstone felt that some expansion of policy might be advisable in order to preserve party unity and give it 'reparative strength'.[3] Deciding upon a wider programme involved choosing between the competing claims of the special interest groups within the party and outside it. J.S. Spender claimed that it was the 'unofficial members of the party in and out of Parliament' rather than the leaders who formulated policy between 1886 and 1892.[4] Nevertheless leaders still had to decide on priorities. During these years various 'advanced' groups offered comprehensive programmes of domestic reform. The London progressives put forward their 'London Programme', while the Fabians through Sidney Webb argued for a programme more heavily weighted towards labour questions. A third alternative was the 'omnibus resolution' of the NLF which had been approved at Manchester in 1889 and passed again at Sheffield in 1890 and Newcastle in 1891. This last, which embodied the claims of provincial Radicalism and Nonconformity, proved most attractive to leading Liberals. This was a realistic approach to the maintenance of party unity because the bulk of the interest groups which made up the party were represented on the NLF and voiced their demands through it. In terms of electoral and parliamentary support such groups were much stronger than either the Fabians or the London progressives. However in turning to the NLF for a programme Liberal leaders were confronted not with their own interpretation of local option but with the Alliance demand for a direct popular veto.

It had taken a little more than a decade for the NLF, a body founded by Chamberlain to rescue Liberalism from its factions, to succumb to the demands of the Alliance. The success of prohibitionists in this area owed much to their own exertions, but they were helped by the way in which constituency organisations developed in the 1880s. From the start there had been an inherent conflict between the style of popular democracy favoured by the caucus model and the supporters who possessed both the time and the means to give effect to it.[5] Because local associations could not afford a fulltime secretary, local men with both the time and enthusiasm to devote to party affairs, usually businessmen and Nonconformists, took on the task. Initially the enthusiasm for popular participation had been so widespread that these local activists had been unable to dominate proceedings, but by 1883 Blanchard Jerrold was complaining that the caucuses were 'losing their hold on the electorate ... because they are the offspring of cliques and are elected sometimes by an infinitesimal proportion of the contituencies they appear to dominate.'[6] The resulting indifference and apathy of constituency politics worried the *Westminster Review* which complained in 1887 that

> too much power has remained in the hands of the few ... Many associations have become more or less closed bodies, representative of a few, and out of touch with the bulk of the Liberal party. It has been so common as to be almost a rule, in ordinary times, for small ward meetings to elect more members to the association than there have been persons present at the meetings. Selected lists of names have been put to the meeting, and carried as a matter of the commonest routine. ... There exist only vague and superficial relations between the associations and the electors; the central body takes little or no trouble to ascertain the opinions of the masses ... the association in effect represents ... no one at all but the members themselves.[7]

In the early years of caucus formation Alliance men had often been shouldered aside, but as associations ossified in the late 1880s, local temperance enthusiasts could begin to dominate them. Ostrogorski noted with some regret that 'the partisans of temperance have attempted to "capture" the caucuses, and they have been successful in a great many cases'.[8] There was now no need to generate mass support for the veto (nor should NLF advocacy of the measure be taken to imply that such support existed). Because the pressure for reform from below was so slight, local prohibitionists could insist that the veto was a more pressing concern than specifically labour demands without fear of contradiction. Prohibitionist ascendancy in the caucuses provided a springboard for an attack on the NLF itself. The process of conversion within the NLF can be traced through the resolutions passed at its annual conferences. Before 1885 temperance reform was not mentioned, but in that year alderman Tatham of Leeds successfully moved an amendment in favour of local control over licensing. In 1886 the third item of an omnibus resolution demanded 'the right of popular control over the granting and transfer of licences'. In the following year Lawson was successful with a resolution calling for 'Local Option' and this was passed a second time in 1888.[9]

Before the NLF conference in Manchester in December 1889, Schnadhorst had informed the Alliance Executive that there would be no problem about submitting a resolution on temperance reform to the meeting. The Executive then drafted a resolution incorporating the direct veto and sent it to Lawson for his approval. He thought it too extreme and offered a more moderate one of his own requesting 'the popular control of the liquor traffic'.[10] In a letter to the Alliance secretary he likened the Liberal party to a large salmon.

> We, the Prohibitionists have hooked him, and are now 'playing' with the object of landing him as soon as possible. If we make a clumsy attempt to 'gaff' him before the right moment he may get off the line altogether, and leave us to fish for him again.[11]

The Executive did not agree. It felt that the Liberals had not yet completely taken the bait and the hook needed driving home hard. Mindful of past disappointments it took a firm line. If the organisers of the NLF meeting refused to include the direct popular veto, Lawson was instructed to move it as an amendment to any alternative, or leave the meeting as a mark of protest. This he refused to do, but raised no objection to anyone else doing it. Lloyd George was prepared to do so on behalf of the Alliance and the fact was well publicised. It was also generally assumed that if he was forced to move an amendment, it would succeed. To make sure, the Executive sent a memorial to all representatives at the meeting explaining just what kind of reform it wanted. As a result of 'determined action' by Lloyd George the omnibus resolution moved by Lawson included the demand for a direct popular veto.[12]

After this initial breakthrough prohibitionists found it much easier to keep their demands to the fore. Lloyd George, rapidly becoming an important figure in the temperance movement, promised to ensure that the direct veto was placed on the agenda of the NLF meeting at Sheffield in the following year, either as an original resolution or, if necessary, as an amendment. This he duly did. At the end of 1890, the Manchester Executive felt confident enough to discuss with Lawson, Lloyd George and G.O. Trevelyan the possibility of sending a deputation to Harcourt and Morley to urge that the veto be given a 'foremost' place in the Liberal programme. It had already asked the party to consider the possibility of introducing a joint Home Rule, Local Veto Bill, once it was returned to office. Local Liberal associations were also asked by the Executive to write to Schnadhorst to demand that the veto be given a more prominent place in the NLF programme.[13] While the veto was still only one item in the omnibus resolution at Newcastle in

1891, this mattered little because the question was widely discussed. By now the Reform Union and the Women's Liberal Federation, as well as the NLF, were all firmly committed to the veto.

The NLF did not dictate official policy to the parliamentary Liberal party but in their choice of priorities for any programme of social reform Liberal leaders were influenced by developments both inside and outside parliament. Harcourt's qualified support for the Alliance in the early 1880s has already been discussed. The compensation battles then convinced him that the Alliance had become a sufficiently powerful section within the party to be important for its continued survival. Prohibitionists were also able to demonstrate that the veto could attract considerable support in the House of Commons. A Direct Veto Bill for Scotland passed its second reading in 1888, and in 1891 a Welsh Veto Bill got through its second reading by a majority of seven in a House dominated by Tories. The majority consisted of 158 Gladstonians, 7 Tories, 7 Nationalists and, most significantly, 15 Liberal-Unionists. Here then was an issue that was politically successful and also capable of bringing some Liberal-Unionists back to the fold, at least temporarily. A further reason for Harcourt's strengthened support of the Alliance suggests itself. He had obviously enjoyed the compensation battles immensely and fought with great verve and gusto. It has been suggested that his aggressive personality led him to pick a position for its 'combative possibilities'.[14] If this was so, he could not have chosen more wisely. The Nonconformists of the Alliance were experts at the combative approach to politics and loved nothing more than a good fight. Significantly it was during the compensation battles that Harcourt first appeared on an Alliance platform after having refused to do so earlier in the eighties.

John Morley's espousal of the cause was less predictable and came more rapidly. Concerned always to push forward one great rallying cry which the party could embrace, he began after 1886 to cast around for an alternative which could act as a focus for political action once the Irish question was out of the way. He began tentatively to explore temperance reform as just such an issue. While declaring himself personally in favour of local control in some form, he was doubtful if public opinion was yet ready to accept it. However after witnessing the outcome of the first compensation struggle in 1888 many of his doubts dissolved. A year later he told the NLF that temperance was perhaps the most important cause of all, and that he was 'fervently convinced of its urgency and its necessity'. In a list of various reforms which he drew up and presented to Gladstone immediately afterwards, temperance headed the list. But it was significant that he included not simply local option, but the Alliance proposal for a direct popular veto. Morley's conversion, like Harcourt's, would seem to have been prompted largely by political considerations. Prohibitionists had shown their teeth in 1888 and 1890 and Morley was sensible of the need to satisfy them: 'They are, no doubt, on our side, as it is. But the Irish business will chill them, and they need to be stirred up by warm and active interest in their own question'. He clearly demonstrated his own interest by giving a major speech during the second reading of the Welsh Direct Veto Bill. Later in 1891 he appeared for the first time on an Alliance platform and at its annual meeting publicly declared that one of the 'main objects' of his future parliamentary life would be to work for a measure of direct local control.[15] Lesser figures were also publicly declaring their conversion to the veto. G.O. Trevelyan, Arnold Morley and Herbert Gladstone all supported it for the first time in 1888 and 1889.[16]

The NLF meeting at Newcastle in 1891 provided the setting for a clear and public declaration of support for the veto by Liberal leaders. Both Morley and Harcourt pledged their support and stressed their sense of urgency about the need to act. Gladstone's role in regard to the Newcastle programme has been obscured somewhat by the claims of Herbert Gladstone who denied that his father ever adopted the programme as his own.

> Mr. Schnadhorst ... pressed it on my father through the usual channels as something essential for party interests. In promulgating that policy my father gave pretty clear indications that it was for the future and others rather than for the present and himself.[17]

This explanation must be viewed with some scepticism as after 1895 Herbert Gladstone blamed many of the ills which had befallen the Liberals onto the Newcastle programme and the encouragement it had given to the various interest groups within the party. This represented a complete change of heart on his part, for in 1889 he had declared that the next Liberal goverment must concentrate on Home Rule, local option and registration, and added 'Local Optionists have been patient almost to the damage of their cause, and ... they have a right to insist that the paramount importance of the Irish question shall not put their just claims out of the way of speedy settlement'.[18] At this time he could no more resist the momentum generated by the Alliance than any other Liberal. Most of those at the NLF meeting, including Harcourt, believed that W.E. Gladstone had pledged his support to the programme. The Alliance certainly put this interpretation on his speeches. He had placed the veto 'in the first rank of reform for the whole of the United Kingdom' and declared that 'to that cause the Liberal party are deeply pledged, and are prepared to take the consequences'.[19]

It is in the changing views of Liberal leaders such as Morley and Harcourt that we find the answer to changing Liberal policy on local representative bodies versus the direct popular veto and compensation versus no compensation. In the eighties the Liberal party was concerned to formulate a measure of *social* reform which would gain wide acceptance and be practicable, but in the years after 1886 temperance reform was increasingly seen as a *political* measure, as a way of satisfying a vocal section of the party in order to preserve party unity. It naturally followed that if this was the prime motive behind the introduction of legislation, then legislation could only take the form advocated by the Alliance. Had it not done so, no political advantage would have been gained.

However this did not mean that the parliamentary Liberty party was united in placing temperance reform at the head of its list of priorities. Gladstone and Morley were still primarily concerned with Ireland, despite their public utterances to the contrary, and other interest groups were concerned that their particular demands should receive priority. While the veto featured prominently in the election campaign of 1892, Sidney Webb regarded it and its bedfellows collected together under the auspices of the NLF, as 'political Dead Sea fruit'. Likewise Francis Channing regretted that a more pronounced Labour policy had not been put forward in 1892 instead of 'the stereotyped but rather hackneyed list of disestablishment, local option, registration and taxation, each appealing only to special groups'.[20] Such straws in the wind were not in themselves damaging to Alliance prospects but they did presage a much more determined opposition to the Liberal commitment to the veto. The split in 1886 had purged many of the anti-Alliance elements within the party but in the nineties their place was to be taken by others.

The Executive professed itself well satisfied with the results of the 1892 election. Of the 567 English, Scottish and Welsh MPs elected, 286 were pledged to the veto. Almost as many MPs had given their support after the elections of 1880 and 1885, but then their pledge had been to support local option. Now there was no ambiguity. While most support came from Liberals, a handful of Liberal-Unionists and

Conservatives were also favourable. Of course this picture omits the Irish members who were numerous enough to tip the balance either way. The Executive refused to state how many of them would vote for the veto but believed that the majority of them would. However the over-all majority in favour was likely to be very slender and, as with much else in the 1892 parliament, the 81 Irish Nationalists could tip the balance either way.

Alliance confidence was not based solely on head-counting. Its long campaign to capture the Liberal party reached its peak in 1892. Now all but five of the Liberal MPs had pledged their support and the Liberal leaders had also been won over. Prohibitionists had helped elect a government which they believed they could trust and were convinced that 'after long years of strenuous labour, success is in full view'. Lawson congratulated Herbert Gladstone on becoming a member of 'the best administration ... which we have ever seen', and added: 'You may do great things if you have pluck.'[21] However the Alliance had now identified itself almost completely with the Liberal government and henceforth its independence was necessarily circumscribed. It could prompt, push and threaten and endeavour to ensure that whatever measure was introduced would meet its wishes, but ultimately it was in the hands of the Cabinet. It was from here that the final initiative must come and the Alliance could only hope that its past work was effective and its support at this level sufficiently resolute to see it through to final victory.

Most Liberals were disappointed with the results of the election. Expecting to sweep the country they found themselves instead without an independent majority and in need of Irish support. Many believed that the hostility of the trade had led to the defeat of some Gladstonian candidates and that this hostility had been aroused by the pledges extracted by prohibitionists. The *Speaker* blamed the Alliance for the poor showing of the Liberals and accused it of being an obstacle to realistic temperance reform. It urged Liberals to sever their links with 'frantic abolitionists'. 'Why', it asked, 'should we persist in making all reform impossible by longer following the Alliance along the line of most resistance?'[22] Even Harcourt was dissatisfied. He placed little faith in the list of MPs pledged to the veto and complained of a 'want of activity and zeal' by prohibitionists during the election.[23] The Executive found some difficulty in answering these attacks. While it claimed that other Liberal policies had also cost votes it was on much stronger ground when it simply pointed out that the Liberal party was stuck with the Alliance whether it liked it or not. Any attempt by Liberals to sever the links between them and the prohibitionists would be electorally disastrous because 'the trade is now predominantly Tory, if not from conviction then from prejudice. Its atmosphere and associations are Tory, and have been becoming increasingly so since the passage of Bruce's Act in 1872.' In other words Liberals could not expect to escape trade hostility simply by ditching the Alliance.[24]

Liberal ministers in 1892 faced the dilemma typical of all minority governments. They could refrain from tackling anything beyond what the prevailing circumstances, especially their reliance on the Irish, made practicable, or they could go ahead boldly with a full programme and if defeated appeal to the electorate for a further mandate. The differing interpretations placed on the election by Liberal leaders led them to differ as to what they believed was the right policy to pursue so far as legislation was concerned. Given Gladstone's previous preoccupation with Ireland and his reliance on the Irish to maintain his majority, it was to be expected that for him Home Rule must be the major issue but, initially at least, he remained surprisingly receptive to the need for other reform. He realised that 'Ireland herself has by her incidents a good deal damaged herself and us' and the emphasis on British questions during the election probably won him the contest. He was therefore searching for legislation 'which shall be at once concise and drastic, to help the British part of the bill of fare'. Harcourt encouraged Gladstone in this and tried to push him still further away from any concentration on Ireland. Convinced that 'the only chance of holding together our majority such as it is will consist in giving satisfaction at once to the various sections of which it consists', he believed that an attempt must be made to legislate on the main items in the 'Newcastle Programme'. John Morley was horrified by this. Wishing to see Home Rule retain first priority, he tried to prevent Gladstone committing himself to any wider programme because he believed 'the Irish are our masters and we had better realise it at once'. The Radical sections of the party would have to wait until this obstruction was out of the way.[25]

The differences between Harcourt and Morley were fundamental. Morley believed 'we have moved much too fast and too far towards the Extreme left in every subject at once — and quiet sensible folk don't like it'. Harcourt replied that this was in the nature of the Liberal party: 'When the Whigs left the Liberal party they forced the pace and it will go on with accumulated ferocity.' He was convinced that the party was too committed to its sections to have any option but to do its best to satisfy them: 'In a big storm safety is sometimes to be found only

in "cracking on" and we must "run" the ship, she can't "lay to".'
Harcourt felt so strongly about this that he threatened not to serve as
Gladstone's second-in-command in the House of Commons unless a
full British programme was promised.[26]

While Gladstone reiterated his support for the idea that a full programme was required, in practice he soon began to concentrate on his
Home Rule Bill and increasingly regarded all other legislation as
subservient to this. After several months Harcourt found the situation
intolerable. He invited Arnold Morley, Bryce, Fowler, G.O.
Trevelyan and Acland to dinner in order to discuss matters. They all
objected to Gladstone's concentration on Ireland and demanded a full
domestic programme including most of the Newcastle items. This had
the desired effect, for Gladstone immediately accepted all proposals,
and a few days later a committee of Cabinet was set up to consider and
draft a Direct Veto Bill. Harcourt was chairman of this committee
which also included Lords Spencer and Herschell, Thomas Burt, J.T.
Hibbert, G.O. Trevelyan and Arnold Morley.[27]

From the outset the committee was concerned above all to frame a
measure which was acceptable to prohibitionists and therefore the
veto had to be included. However because the Alliance had consistently refused to commit itself publicly on anything other than the
principle of the veto, it was necessary to cast around for detailed
machinery which would receive the widest possible public support
consistent with keeping prohibitionists on their side. It was immediately decided not to attempt any comprehensive reform of existing
licensing laws as there was insufficient time available during the session, but even a concentration on the veto did not dispose of the thorny
problem of compensation to dispossessed publicans. While the
Alliance officially opposed compensation in any form, most other
reform proposals included it. The committee looked particularly at
the plans of the 'Manchester Committee', to which several prominent
Alliance men belonged, which advocated 'time' compensation. It also
considered the 'Westminster Scheme', the brainchild of Liberal
Unionists and the CETS, which offered financial compensation. Not
surprisingly the latter was rejected as impracticable but the committee
was not in principle opposed to 'time' compensation provided prohibitionists would accept it. Harcourt seems to have believed that this
might enable him to retain prohibitionist support and also win over
many moderates, particularly those in the CETS.[28]

Interested parties were canvassed as to their views. Harcourt told
W.S. Caine that he was 'much besieged in different quarters to settle

the Temperance Question on the basis of a *five years term* to allow the publicans to "get out" '. Caine was prepared to accept some 'time' compensation provided it led to effective veto powers after the time limit had expired but he adopted a negative role in negotiations with Harcourt and refused to make any suggestions which might have helped the committee.[29] Lawson was even less helpful. A civil servant involved in drafting the Bill had approached Dawson Burns in an attempt to find out what the Alliance wanted. Burns was disturbed that the government had no clear idea of Alliance views and suggested that Lawson should try to work closely with Harcourt in determining the acceptability of various proposals. Lawson however was still obsessed with the need to leave the entire responsibility for what was produced on the shoulders of the government and refused to cooperate in any way. In fact he objected strongly to Caine's acceptance of 'time' compensation, thinking it 'an abominable proposal', but he did not inform Harcourt of this until after the Bill had been tabled.[30]

The Alliance Executive found itself in an awkward situation. It wished to be informed of what draft proposals were being considered but Lawson, its normal mouthpiece, had retired from the fray and was consequently of no use. Caine could not be used in quite the same way because he also represented other organisations and did not always see eye to eye with the Executive over matters of detail. No other confidential channels of communication were available. It was therefore forced to resort to the device of sending a memorial to Fowler reiterating its opposition to compensation, but this did not truly reflect its views. In order to save a Bill which included the veto it was, in the last resort, prepared to accept 'time' compensation for a period not exceeding three years. The other issue to worry the Executive was the majority required before a local veto could become operative. It wanted a bare majority and was worried that the Welsh Direct Veto Bill, which it had supported, stipulated a two-thirds majority. It was worried lest Harcourt might therefore assume that it approved of this. In fact if pushed the Executive was prepared to accept a two-thirds majority, but once again there was no way of transmitting these views to Harcourt.[31]

At a time when the Executive should have been working as hard as it could behind the scenes, it found itself unable to do so. On the other hand it still had to cope with the more impatient and enthusiastic prohibitionists who, not knowing if the government was taking any action, wished to force the pace. At the end of 1892 the London auxiliary attempted to get the veto introduced as a separate resolution at the forthcoming meeting of the NLF, rather than as part of an 'omnibus' resolution as formerly. Lloyd George was prepared to move an amendment to this effect if the Executive wished it, but Hilton, the Alliance parliamentary agent, pointed out that, 'if an effort to get more from the Federation were to raise a discussion and show disunion it would injure us immensely in the House, while any alteration could not give us more than we have got'. Lawson, convinced that whatever happened at the Federation meeting was unimportant, agreed, adding that, 'the *Country* passed the resolution last July, and now the Government have to carry it out or else we shall "know the reason why" '. The Executive only managed to head off the London auxiliary with great difficulty.[32]

Meanwhile Harcourt attempted to win over the CETS as he realised that a favourable response from this quarter would greatly improve the prospects of his Bill. If he succeeded he would have many moderate reformers and the Church establishment behind him. Many were Conservatives and in a position to influence the line taken by the opposition. However the CETS remained firm in its support for some form of financial compensation. Immediately after the introduction of his Bill, Harcourt made one last half-hearted and rather impatient bid for its support. Emphasising that his object was to introduce 'a moderate Bill which will have a chance of passing and of working' he added that if the CETS would not moderate its position, 'you may bid a long farewell to any Temperance Legislation in this generation'.[33] The difference between the Alliance and the CETS was a major stumbling block to any reform and Harcourt was in no position (or mood) to attempt to effect a reconciliation. Nor it seems were the two bodies themselves; they had lived fairly amicably side by side for so long that neither of them could see any reason for merging their endeavours. However a determined attempt to do this came from an unexpected quarter. A.F. Hills, a Conservative and 'earnest temperance worker', had refused hitherto to contribute to Alliance funds but Cowley, an Alliance agent, had been cultivating him assiduously. Hills realised, as Alexander Balfour had done some years earlier, that the 'great obstacle' to reform was the lack of agreement between the CETS and the Alliance, especially over compensation. In an attempt to break the deadlock he offered to arrange a conference between the two with the aim of coming to a common agreement. If this was done, he offered to give the Alliance a lump sum of £1,000 and an annual subscription of £250. The bait was too tempting to resist. After careful preparation, representatives of all the major temperance bodies met, but failed to resolve outstanding differences.[34]

The defensive and unhelpful attitude which temperance organisations took towards the government measure, as well as the differences of opinion between them, removed much of Harcourt's enthusiasm for their fighting qualities which had so impressed him in 1888 and 1890. In December 1892 he wrote to Lord Herschell, the Lord Chancellor, 'I am very much disposed to agree with you as to the forces which the Temperance Party will bring into the field when the battle is engaged, but we are too deeply pledged not to fight. It may turn out like a French duel'. Two days before introducing his measure into the Commons he confided in his son: 'I am not in much spirits about the Local Veto Bill. The Temperance Party will I expect behave as they have always done.'[35] In fact the most realistic and constructive advice Harcourt received during the drafting of his Bill came from E.N. Buxton, the Liberal brewer, but Harcourt was too preoccupied with placating prohibitionists to give Buxton's ideas serious consideration.[36]

On the 27 February, 1893, the Liquor Traffic (Local Control) Bill was introduced into the Commons. It provided that upon a requisition of one-tenth of the ratepayers of a locality, a poll of ratepayers could be held to determine whether all licences in that area should be prohibited. If a two-thirds majority of those voting were in favour of prohibition then it would come into force after a period of grace of three years and remain in operation for at least three years before a further poll on the question could reverse the decision. There was no option to reduce the number of licences, the alternatives being either prohibition or the *status quo*. The localities chosen were the smallest feasible administrative units, parishes in rural areas, wards in boroughs, or the borough itself if it were not subdivided, and in London the sanitary districts set up under the 1891 Public Health (London) Act. Sunday closing in England was also dealt with (Wales and Scotland already had Sunday closing) along the same lines. A vote by a bare majority could determine whether or not it would be instituted. The Bill was aimed almost exclusively at public houses and beerhouses, liquor producers would be exempted from the veto and so would refreshment rooms at railway stations, inns or hotels for the accommodation of travellers or lodgers, restaurants and other eating houses. Harcourt emphasised that he did not 'desire to put down the use and the consumption of liquor by persons in their own houses, or, if they have no house of their own, the place where they reside or take their meals'. He believed that any attempt to do more would only result in a 'violent reaction'. The restrictions were designed to curb 'tippling', not the 'ordinary habits of the people'.[37]

In his introductory speech Harcourt took care to emphasise that his Bill would face 'a determined and well-organised resistance' both from the trade and the Tories. He therefore urged temperance reformers to unite 'without distinction of Party, and without distinction of sections', in order to ensure victory. The response to his appeal was hardly encouraging. Lawson reacted before the Bill was formally introduced. In a letter to Harcourt he objected to the list of exemptions: 'there will be trouble over that. Very likely from our good fellows. Certainly from the lot who *want* to make trouble.' Nor did he think the time limit would be liked by prohibitionists because, 'there is the danger of the Tories coming in and repealing the whole thing before the three years are up'. He also thought that the Sunday closing clauses should have been omitted, but then concluded by saying that he had 'nothing but praise' for the Bill. He later called it 'the greatest measure that had been introduced into Parliament since the attack upon Slavery'. The Alliance Executive was less equivocal. Realising that the Bill had been framed largely with prohibitionists in mind, it quickly realised that its 'obvious defects and shortcomings' could be eliminated either in committee or in a later Bill and threw its whole weight into whipping up support for it throughout the country.[38]

Not all prohibitionists were prepared to follow this lead. Alfred Ecroyd, a member of the Alliance Consultative Council, complained that the Bill was no good because it 'is *not* a Bill to give the people power to veto the issue and reissue of all licences. ... It is a mere regulation measure ... based upon the [false] theory that it is the abuse and not the use [of drink] that is wrong'. He also objected to the partisan approach of the Executive:

> The Alliance opposed a bad Bill brought in by the late Government and rightly opposed, and Conservative temperance men who also opposed the late Government are asking why does not the Alliance oppose an equally bad Bill when brought in by a *Liberal* Government? What answer can an absolutely non-party man like myself give to such a question as that?[39]

It is difficult to determine how many Alliance men felt as Ecroyd did but it is likely that the few Tories and some of the more uncompromising prohibitionists agreed with him. He was certainly exhibiting many of the characteristics of the prohibitionist mentality in an extreme form, but although Ecroyd publicly spoke out against the Bill, such isolated gestures are unlikely to have had more than local impact.

A much more serious threat was posed by the lack of parliamentary discipline of many MPs pledged to support the Veto. Welsh members, despite the introduction of the government measure, went ahead with their own Welsh Local Veto Bill. Lawson was 'much annoyed' at this because it distracted attention from Harcourt's Bill and was 'a very bad device if we can carry it at all'. He found it strange that those who professed to support the government should take this 'most inconvenient and irritating course'.[40] His attempts to stop them failed so he tried to get T.E. Ellis to dissuade them. This also failed and the Welsh Bill passed its second reading by a majority of 35 on 15 March 1893. There were several reasons why Welsh MPs pursued this course. They were a section within the party in their own right, and prepared to take determined action to ensure that Welsh measures such as disestablishment were given priority in the Liberal programme. They were Welsh representatives first and foremost and for most of them temperance came second; by promoting a specifically Welsh measure they were able to satisfy both their desire to assert a distinct national identity and also their desire for temperance reform. It was also a salutory corrective to what some Welsh temperance men considered was the excessive English bias of the Alliance. There was another reason. The growing unpopularity of Harcourt's Bill and the possibility that it might be quietly dropped convinced some that the government might then be prepared to take up and push through the Welsh Bill instead. This was symptomatic of an approach which temperance men had developed in earlier years when governments had not looked so kindly on their demands. In the 1870s and 1880s, when over a dozen private temperance Bills had often been introduced each year, it had been assumed that if enough bullets were fired, one might reach its target. Such habits were difficult to eradicate. As early as December 1892, W.S. Caine had urged Harcourt to give government assistance to get the Scottish Veto Bill through if the government measure was not going well.[41] This was two months before the latter had even been introduced!

Those temperance reformers in the Commons not firmly committed to the Alliance saw no reason to sacrifice their own particular panacea in favour of the government's measure. Sunday closers were the most vocal in their disappointment. They had always advocated universal Sunday closing and now Harcourt was prepared only to allow closing by local option. He had done this because he believed there was a danger of legislation out-running public opinion if compulsory universal Sunday closing was enacted but if local opinion was allowed to decide the issue, there would be no problem. Both he and Lawson urged the Sunday closers to accept this, but they refused.[42] The CETS also went its own way and the Bishop of London introduced its Bill into the House of Lords on 24 March 1893. This was the 'Westminster Scheme' which proposed locally elected licensing boards and a reduction in licences coupled with financial compensation to be drawn from within the trade. Only a few days after Harcourt's Bill had been given its first reading yet another temperance Bill was introduced into the Lords by the Bishop of Chester. Supported by Lord Thring, the Duke of Westminster and the Archbishop of Canterbury, he sought to implement the recommendations of the 1878 *Lords Committee on Intemperance* in a modified version of the Gothenburg system championed by Chamberlain almost twenty years previously. These two measures made little headway but they were again symptomatic of the lack of unity among temperance men. As he had expected Harcourt faced the hostility of the trade and the Conservatives but also, as he had feared, a lack of unity among temperance reformers.

In the country a straight fight developed between the trade and prohibitionists. The trade immediately pledged its complete opposition to the Bill and worked to get it defeated with great single-mindedness. Temperance reformers were somewhat slower to get down to business. Indecision among many of them as to the real merits of the measure somewhat delayed the start of their campaign, but most of them eventually decided to work with the Alliance.[43] In the meantime the trade had gained the initiative in determining the course which the campaign should take and this they managed to retain. Their aim was to demonstrate the existence of overwhelming popular antipathy to the Veto and they chose to do this by means of petitions and mass meetings. They chose their ground well; the 150,000 public houses throughout the country were an ideal base from which to mount a petition movement and the vast financial resources at their command made the cost of mass demonstrations easier to bear.

The Alliance originally discouraged a petition movement, preferring the promotion of memorials and private letters to MPs, but the flood of publican petitions forced a change of mind. The Press had begun to interpret this as evidence that there was no popular support for the Bill, so the Alliance began promoting rival petitions and battle was joined. House-to-house canvasses were undertaken in many towns in search of signatories and even Lady Henry Somerset was pressed into action in an attempt to persuade the Salvation Army to take up the task. After three months, opponents of the Bill were still well ahead having submitted 5,706 petitions containing 1,103,666 signatures, as against 7,546 petitions with only 369,585 signatures from its supporters. Thereafter temperance men made up some ground, but at the end of the campaign they had failed to match the effort mounted by the publicans. There were 6,132 petitions signed by 1,163,259 people against the Bill, as against 10,088 petitions with 610,769 signatures in its favour. The smaller size of *individual* petitions for the Bill indicated their source. They came largely from the small temperance communities and Good Templar lodges in towns throughout the country.[44]

A similar situation developed in regard to mass demonstrations. Temperance men held 4,940 meetings during the course of the campaign, as against 302 by the trade. While many of the former were small local meetings of the faithful, no different from routine weekly gatherings, most of those held by the trade attracted substantial audiences. Both sides occasionally disrupted the meetings of their opponents. The trade did so at Nottingham and Liverpool and prohibitionists did the same in London. This last, in which the Alliance Executive was not directly involved, cast the temperance cause into some disrepute for a time. A demonstration against the Bill in Trafalgar Square organised by the London United Workingmen's Committee was broken up by supporters of the Bill; fights broke out and resolutions in favour of the Bill were carried. The Alliance Executive tried to dismiss the incident as of no consequence but disinterested observers felt differently. When a request was made to use the Manchester racecourse for a mass demonstration, it was refused because, 'after the ruffianly conduct of your temperance associates in Trafalgar Square the Racecourse Co. cannot afford to run the risk of a breach of the peace on their grounds'. However one Alliance meeting was an undeniable success. This was a demonstration in Hyde Park which was quiet, orderly and, according to police estimates, the largest demonstration ever held there.[45]

While the Alliance claimed that it had demonstrated overwhelming popular support for the veto, the Press considered that the trade had emerged clear winners. The Executive attempted to denigrate trade efforts, arguing that they owed everything to money and nothing to popular support, other than from the 'loafing classes'. It maintained that 'in those methods of agitation in which money is the main factor, as, for instance, in the purchase of sham sentiment, in the organisation of bogus demonstrations, and in the manufacture of "shoddy" petitions, it would be futile for the Alliance even to attempt to compete with the trade'.[46] This of course is just what the Alliance did attempt to do and thus it was guilty of a serious tactical error. It could never hope to match the finances which the trade could draw upon, indeed a shortage of cash severely curtailed its efforts. As it was, it ended the campaign with a £3,000 overdraft. One further factor working to the disadvantage of the Alliance was the parallel campaign being mounted on behalf of Gladstone's Home Rule Bill. While trade interests seem to have been remarkably single minded in their opposition to the veto, many prohibitionists divided their time and energies between support for Home Rule and the veto.

Harcourt meanwhile was being made aware of opposition much nearer home. The party managers had always been lukewarm about the Bill and some Liberal MPs began to voice concern about the effect it might have on their electoral prospects, particularly in London. Mark Beaufoy and Frye, both of whom had metropolitan constituencies, felt particularly threatened. Liberal workers in the constituencies were also worried. John A. Crawley, a London Radical, was convinced that the Bill would 'bring discord into the ranks of the Radical Party' in his constituency. He objected particularly to Sunday closing 'by a bare majority of ratepayers *going to the poll*' and pointed out that this 'practically disenfranchises the ordinary working man voter on a concern which affects him principally and primarily'. London working men had always objected to Sunday closing and the 'Liberal and Radical Anti-Sunday-Closing Union' was formed to fight the offending clause. The North Herefordshire Liberal Association also believed that the Bill smacked of class legislation and would lead to 'a lot of ill-feeling on the part of the working classes, who feel that their privileges [so called] are being taken from them in a sense whilst the drinking privileges of the wealthy classes are left untouched'.[47]

From the moment it was introduced, it was widely assumed that the government had no intention of pressing on with the Bill. The circulation of such rumours in the Press seriously worried Alliance men and they did their best to scotch them. Both Dawson Burns and Lawson urged Harcourt to declare publicly his intention to proceed. This he did in a letter to *The Times*, but to no avail. Joseph Chamberlain even went so far as to claim that there was collusion between Harcourt and Lawson.

I do not believe that it is a serious measure ... I think we might picture to ourselves an interview between Sir Wilfrid Lawson and Sir William Harcourt. I can understand Sir Wilfrid Lawson saying, 'Come now Sir William, you have been doing a little for everybody. You have not thought of your teetotal friends, who are a very important body; why not give us a Local Option Bill?' Then I can understand Sir William ... explaining to Sir Wilfrid Lawson that a Bill such as he suggested had been already disposed of by the admirable arguments which he [Sir William] himself used at Oxford some time ago ... On that occasion it was that he invented the term ... 'grand-motherly legislation' to which he would never be a party .... I can understand Sir Wilfrid Lawson saying, 'I see your difficulty, but this is an electoral question, we must do something to please our followers. Now let us come to an understanding. You bring in the Bill and you need not carry it'; and upon a liberal offer of that kind I can well understand the two gentlemen at once came to an agreement, and like the augurs of Roman history, they must have laughed in each other's faces before they parted company.[48]

While this account was altogether too fanciful, designed more to sow seeds of doubt in temperance ranks than to illustrate the truth of what took place, the fact remains that Harcourt had no encouragement to press on. He faced trade and Tory hostility, a crowded legislative timetable with the Home Rule Bill in course of passage, divisions among temperance men, and the possibility that Nationalist MPs might not give their support. An Irish Member had already told Hilton, the Alliance parliamentary agent, that he and others would oppose the Veto because 'it stands in the way of Home Rule and the Government ought not to have introduced it'.[49] Given these obstacles, it was hardly surprising that the Bill was withdrawn before its second reading. T.E. Ellis later explained that the lack of progress was the fault of temperance men themselves. Their lack of unity left the government in a position where any attempt to proceed would have left it open to defeat.[50]

Prohibitionists had finally brought a Liberal government to the point of action but when the cards were down they had failed to provide it with enough backing to ensure success. Their campaign in the country paled in comparison with that mounted by the trade and in their dealings with the government they had been guilty of blunder after blunder. Because of Lawson's refusal to transfer the views of the Executive to him, Harcourt had been forced to frame his Bill without accurate knowledge of Alliance thinking and, even more important, he was unaware of the Executive's willingness to compromise on compensation. Lawson's parliamentary tactics of lying low and avoiding backroom discussions had been learnt in the seventies, but they were inappropriate to the changed circumstances of the nineties.

Notes

1. D.A. Hamer, 'The Irish Question and Liberal Politics, 1886-1894', *Historical Journal*, vol. 12 (1969), p. 517.
2. *35th Annual Report 1887*, p. 5; cf. the attitudes of other groups discussed in D.A. Hamer, *Liberal Politics in the Age of Gladstone and Rosebery* (1972), pp. 131-3.
3. Quoted in D.A. Hamer, *John Morley: Liberal Intellectual in Politics* (1968), p. 265.
4. J.A. Spender, *Sir Robert Hudson : A Memoir* (1930), p. 19.
5. H. Emy, 'The Liberal Party and the Social Problem 1891-1914' (London University, PhD, 1969), pp. 474-8.
6. Blanchard Jerrold, *Nineteenth Century* (1883), p. 1085.
7. *Westminster Review*, vol. 128 (1887), pp. 394-5.
8. M. Ostrogorski, *Democracy and the Organisation of Political Parties* (abridged edn 1964), vol. 1, p. 276.
9. National Liberal Federation, *9th Annual Report 1886*, p. 7 and *10th Annual Report 1887*, pp. 19-20.
10. *Minutes*, 30 October 1889; 6 November 1889.
11. Lawson to Whyte, 26 November 1889, in *Minutes*, 27 November 1889.
12. Ibid., 20 November 1889; 4 December 1889; *Alliance News*, 13 December 1889, p. 998.
13. *Minutes*, 12 November 1890; 3 December 1890; 11 December 1890; 21 January 1891.
14. P.Stansky, *Ambitions and Strategies* (1964), p. xv.
15. Hamer, *Morley*, pp. 244-5, 265; *40th Annual Report 1892*, p. 25.
16. *Alliance News*, 28 April 1888, p. 330; 1 December 1888, p. 958; 2 March 1889, p. 171.
17. *Herbert Gladstone Papers*, Add. MSS 46,020, 9 and 10 March 1898.
18. *Alliance News*, 2 March 1889, p. 171; C. Mallett, *Herbert Gladstone: A Memoir* (1932), p. 156.
19. *39th Annual Report 1891*, p. 11.
20. *Wanted : A Programme* (1888), p. 12; F.A. Channing, *Memoirs of Midland Politics 1885-1910* (1918), p. 117.
21. *40th Annual Report 1892*, p. 6; Lawson to Herbert Gladstone, 20 August 1892, Add. MSS 46053, f. 237, *Viscount Gladstone Papers*.
22. *Speaker*, 3 September 1892.
23. Harcourt to Caine, 1 August 1892, *Harcourt Papers* (Box 11).
24. *40th Annual Report 1892*, pp. 22-3, 31-3; Canon E.L. Hicks to Herbert Gladstone, 21 July 1892, Add. MSS. 46,053, ff. 222p4, *Viscount Gladstone Papers*.
25. W.E. Gladstone to W.V. Harcourt, 14 July 1892, *Harcourt Papers* (Box 9); Harcourt to Gladstone, 15 and 16 July 1892, in ibid.; Lewis Harcourt Journal, 29 July 1892, p. 25, in ibid.
26. Morley to Harcourt, 14 July 1892, in ibid. (Box 10); Harcourt to Morley, 15 July 1892, in ibid; Lewis Harcourt Journal, 29 July 1892, pp. 284-5, in ibid.
27. Lewis Harcourt Journal, 27 October 1892, 2 November 1892, pp. 336, 342, in ibid.

28. Cabinet Committee on Direct Veto, *Minutes*, 28 November 1892, in ibid. (Box 4).

29. Harcourt to Caine, 28 November 1892; Caine to Harcourt, 30 November 1892; Asquith to Harcourt, 23 December 1892, in ibid.

30. Dawson Burns to Whyte, 9 November 1892, in *Minutes*, 16 November 1892; Lawson to Whyte, 13 November 1892; 30 November 1892, in ibid.

31. *Minutes*, 30 November 1892; 1 February 1893; 8 February 1893.

32. Hilton to Whyte, 6 January 1893; Lawson to Whyte, n.d., in ibid., 11 January 1893.

33. Harcourt to Canon Farrer (of the CETS), 1 March 1893, *Harcourt Papers* (Box 4).

34. *Minutes*, 19 October 1892; *41st Annual Report 1893*, pp. 57-8.

35. Harcourt to Herschell, 24 December 1892, *Harcourt Papers* (Box 4); W.V. Harcourt to Lewis Harcourt, 25 February 1893, in ibid.

36. Buxton to Harcourt, 23 November 1892; 29 November 1892; 7 December 1892, in ibid.

37. *Parliament Debates*, vol. XXII, p. 529.

38. Ibid., pp. 531, 534; Lawson to Harcourt, 25 February 1893, *Harcourt Papers* (Box 4); *41st Annual Report 1893*, pp. 6-8.

39. A.R. Ecroyd to James Whyte, 2 March 1893, in *Minutes*, 8 March 1893.

40. Lawson to Harcourt, 8 March 1893, *Harcourt Papers* (Box 4).

41. *Annual Register*, 1893, p. 59; Caine to Harcourt, 9 December 1892, *Harcourt Papers* (Box 4).

42. *Parliament Debates*, vol. XXII, pp. 530-3, 537; Lewis Harcourt Journal, 17 January 1895, p. 922, *Harcourt Papers*.

43. *41st Annual Report 1893*, p. 6.

44. Ibid., pp. 12-13; *Minutes*, 8-29 March 1893; 12 June 1893.

45. Ibid., 18 April 1893; 21 April 1893; *41st Annual Report 1893*, pp. 16-17.

46. Ibid., pp. 11-17.

47. Beaufoy to Harcourt, 6 March 1893; Crawley to Harcourt, 21 March 1893; 12 August 1893; W.D. Fening to Harcourt, 27 March 1893, *Harcourt Papers* (Box 4).

48. Quoted in *42nd Annual Report 1894*, p. 22.

49. John Hilton to Justin McCarthy, John Redmond and 'all Nationalist and Parnellite M.P.s', 15 July 1893, *Harcourt Papers* (Box 4).

50. T.E. Ellis to Harcourt, 27 October 1894, in ibid.

Chapter 7

THE SECOND VETO BILL
AND AFTER

Initially the Alliance was not unduly concerned by the withdrawal of the Veto Bill. It assumed that there would be an autumn session and that it would be reintroduced then. Lawson's approach to Harcourt followed what had become a standard pattern. Aware that the government would choose those sectional measures which were most likely to succeed, he insisted that the Bill had attracted more popular support than any other government measure and expressed the hope that Ireland would not push temperance out of the way. He considered his conduct had been extremely moderate when compared with that of other sections and therefore worthy of reward.

> The eager hands have frequently urged me to do what is called 'put pressure on the Govt' — in the kind of way I suppose which the Welsh Liberals adopt.

> But I have steadily resisted any recommendation thus to harass the Govt. I always told our friends that they might safely rely on you, and that for my part I was unwilling even to assent to the possibility of the Bill being withdrawn.[1]

Lawson asked that this letter be shown to Gladstone before the priorities for the autumn session were decided upon, but this had no effect. The Queen's Speech did not mention the veto.

The Executive was furious and realised that it would have to mobilise all its resources in order to ensure the Bill had first place in the Government programme for 1894. T.P. Whittaker claimed that 'those who made the loudest demand would be attended to first' and advocated a more vigorous approach than that being pursued by Lawson. The Executive agreed and set out to demonstrate that the veto should be given priority. During the agitation for the Bill early in 1893 it had been aware of the need to win genuine labour backing for its cause. Most of those supporting the measure had clearly been

153

temperance men so there was a need to widen the basis of support by winning over those not directly associated with temperance in the public mind. Consequently at the TUC meeting in Belfast in September 1893, a determined effort was made to get trade union and labour support. The result was a document urging the government to push on with the Veto Bill in the interests of the working classes. It was signed by 172 trade union officials including the labour MPs John Burns, John Wilson, Havelock Wilson, Keir Hardie, Charles Fenwick, William Abraham, J.A. Murray McDonald, Samuel Woods and Joseph Arch, as well as Ben Tillet of the London County Council. The document stated that:

> The control of the liquor traffic (a matter closely concerning the domestic, social, financial and political well-being of the working classes) has hitherto been in the hands of the classes. The Government propose to make the masses the masters of the situation. The control of the Liquor traffic by the classes has hitherto resulted in the impoverishment of and degradation of the working people and the enrichment of the already rich property owners and great liquor monopolists. We do not suggest that the capitalists who have drawn their wealth from the demoralisation of the people had a deliberate design of injuring the people, but certainly no more effectual means could have been used for the purpose. ... The opponents of the Veto Bill profess to be intensely interested in protection of the *liberties of the working classes*. It is a fraudulent profession. The liberty which most of them really desire to maintain is the *liberty of privileged monopolists to exploit the working classes*.[2]

This was valuable propaganda but it demonstrates the problem the Executive faced whenever it attempted to widen its support. The document used language and expressed sentiments which had hitherto been alien to the Alliance, and while the Executive had been careful not to connect itself publicly with the declaration, George Livesey, a prominent Alliance man for forty years, discovered that it had initiated the preparation and signing of the document. He was profoundly disturbed by talk of 'classes' and 'masses' and complained that 'the Alliance, untrue to its name of *United* is doing its best to promote disunion and separate one class from the other'. He pointed out that it relied on the 'classes'; 'it was founded by them ... and if they withdrew their support it would fall to pieces in a week'.[3]

In November 1893 Harcourt privately reassured Lawson of the

good faith of the government, but the Executive was already busy organising a national conference of prominent temperance men from all societies to bring further pressure to bear on Liberal leaders. Gladstone and Harcourt, concerned that prohibitionists should not adopt too independent a line, agreed to see a deputation from the conference. They reiterated that the government was firmly and irrevocably pledged to reintroduce the Veto Bill and push it along as quickly as they were able. Harcourt however resurrected the obstruction theory to account for their inactivity in the autumn session of Parliament. 'We are fighting our way in the House of Commons, with unrelenting energy', he declared, 'like an explorer in Central Africa, through a forest of amendments and through swamps of talk and against the javelins of the pigmies'. Satisfied with this, the Executive assumed that a Bill would be introduced in 1894 and redoubled its campaign throughout the country.[4]

Throughout February and March 1894, Alliance hopes were kept alive by promises of action. The appointment of Lord Rosebery as Prime Minister initially appeared to make no difference to the government's attitude. Although the Alliance would have preferred Harcourt, it could not complain while Rosebery was prepared to 'make every effort to proceed with the Bill during the present session'.[5] But it did not appear and Harcourt refused to give any indication as to when he might have a chance of introducing it. In fact he was at the time preoccupied with the budget. Matters came to a head in the middle of April. Lawson again wrote to Harcourt on behalf of the Parliamentary Temperance Committee complaining of the delay. He pointed out that 'our Temperance supporters out of doors, who do not and cannot know the obstacles in the way of the Government, are getting uneasy at the non appearance of the Bill'. This was too much for Harcourt who exploded into one of his periodic fits of temper. He flatly stated that his main aim was to push through the budget and everything else must wait.

> If my Budget proposals have not satisfied the Temperance Party that I am prepared to fight and do battle with the Brewers Distillers and all their crew, I can only say that they are even more unreasonable than I supposed them to be, and that is saying a good deal …

> If the Temperance people are not satisfied of the good faith of the Govt. in desiring to promote the Local Veto Bill as soon as possible, the remedy is in their own hands and they can as soon as they please find another Govt. in whom they have more confidence.

I am dead sick myself of all this constant distrust and menace on the part of rival sections, and the sooner I find myself delivered from the odious and impossible task of reconciling and satisfying them the better I shall be pleased.

Harcourt saw that temperance men were up to their old tricks again and was infuriated by them.

I observe a report today that a body called the Temperance Parliament under the Patronage of Caine, Stafford Howard, Snape, Hugh Price Hughes, and others from whom the Govt. might have expected a reasonable support have launched a Bill of their own athwart the hawse of the Govt. Bill, which must have the effect of greatly weakening our hands.

I think on the whole perhaps the best thing would be that the Temperance Parliament should take on themselves the responsibility of legislation and relieve me from it. There is really no use in trying to help people who make it impossible to help them. If the Temperance Party choose to trust me I will do what I can for them. If they think they can do better for themselves, I shall be delighted to make my bow and leave the field clear for them. It is no sort of use menacing me with the defeat of the Govt. as that is a catastrophe which I should welcome with perfect equanimity.[6]

Lawson was at a loss to know what to do. He recognised that there were 'uncomfortable elements at work', but had no idea as to how they might be combated. He attempted to justify his actions to the Executive: 'My line all along has been to leave all the responsibility with the Govt. which they voluntarily assumed. I have therefore been careful to say or do nothing which would enable them to say that I in any way hampered them.' While hoping that Harcourt would still make a 'brave effort to hold the fort', he could see no way in which the Alliance could expedite matters. Telling the Executive to take what initiatives it thought necessary he refused to offer any advice.[7] For the rest of 1894 he was content to extract pledges of good intent from Harcourt identical to those he had received over the previous two years. The failure of Lawson's leadership was clearly exposed. Now, as in 1892/3, he virtually abdicated from his responsibilities as a leader and left the Executive to fend for itself during a period of crisis.

Immediately after Harcourt's outburst, Rosebery told Caine that there was no chance of a Bill being introduced during 1894. While it looked for a moment as if it would be introduced after all at the beginning of June, having been put down on the Notice Paper then, prohibitionist hopes were dashed when Harcourt made no move. Herbert Gladstone explained that the government was not pressing on with the Bill because they feared that although they would get a majority for the second reading, 'many of their men were so unsound that, haivng satisfied their conscience by voting for the principle, they would vote wrong in Committee, and that the Government felt *sure* they would be defeated on the Committee stage of the measure'. He had already become lukewarm about the veto for other reasons. The united opposition of the Tories and the trade, which Harcourt's Bill would face, was likely to slow down business in the Commons thus delaying the passage of other important but less controversial measures. Furthermore, if it got through the Commons it would certainly be thrown out by the House of Lords and therefore too much exertion on its behalf hardly seemed worthwhile. It was considerations such as these that made many Liberal MPs 'not altogether sound on the subject'. If, against all the odds, the Veto did become law, Herbert Gladstone was also concerned at the impact this might have on the Liberal party. The Alliance would be disbanded but the trade would remain unfettered and consequently there would be a situation of serious political imbalance which would disadvantage Liberals through their loss of Alliance support.[8]

There were also other factors at work. The Liberal sections were competing with each other for priority and temporarily at least the moderate approach adopted by the Alliance failed to ensure it the premier position. For much of 1894 Welsh claims, in the form of disestablishment, held the centre of the stage and the veto was forced into the background. Liberal leaders, faced with a flood of sectional demands now that Gladstone and Ireland were out of the way, struggled to impose some kind of order on their undisciplined followers. There was an attempt to escape from the Newcastle programme by finding another rallying cry like Ireland which would submerge sectional demands and bring all factions together to work for a common purpose. Reform of the House of Lords seemed to offer such possibilities; it could be argued that only when this institution was reformed would the individual items in the programme stand any chance of success. The Lords question became increasingly prominent in 1894 because Rosebery chose it as his concentrating issue. This was a return to the politics of obstruction, of the single great issue, which had been so dominant in the history of the party from the early 1880s. Even some of the sectional leaders were prepared to acquiesce as they had done over Ireland in 1886; Lloyd George stated that 'Wales was prepared to forego for a time even the question of Disestablishment to join in the pursuit and lynching of this culprit'. Lawson also, more in despair than anything else, accepted the need to remove the Lords obstruction. He complained to Harcourt that 'we shall get nothing done about anything until you have tackled these Lords. Do you suppose they are drunk?'.[9]

Government inactivity placed the Alliance Executive in an awkward position. Militant prohibitionists, angry and frustrated at the delay, were only kept in check with increasing difficulty. On the other hand the few Conservative and Liberal-Unionist prohibitionists who had voted Liberal in 1892 were becoming disillusioned and drifting back to their former party allegiances. A Tory member of the Executive, the Reverend Robert Catterall, had voted for Liberal candidates because of their support for the veto, but while it was not forthcoming, other measures, which he as a Conservative did not like, were. With the introduction of the Welsh Disestablishment Bill he found himself unable to continue to support the Liberal party and so 'with great sorrow' resigned his position on the Executive. Meanwhile critics pointed out that because it continued to support a government which refused to introduce a Bill that was already in existence, the Alliance was showing itself in its true colours as nothing more than a Radical wing of the Liberal party.[10]

The Executive was forced to censure the government for not pushing the Veto Bill harder but defended it by claiming that the government was not 'solely or even chiefly responsible for that delay. The persistent obstruction — sometimes open, but oftener disguised — is the main cause of the disappointment of the legitimate hopes and expectations of Temperance reformers.' Those who accused the government of hypocrisy on the issue did so only in the hope that it would provoke a quarrel between prohibitionists and the government. The Executive pointed out that the Liberal party had won the temperance vote only at the cost of losing 'the support of about one half of the great drink interest', many public houses formerly used as Liberal committee rooms and 'at least four-fifths of the *residuum* vote'. It was scarcely credible therefore that the government would now squander temperance votes by not bringing in a Bill; 'the manifest fact is that the Government has much to gain and nothing to lose, by going forward.' It also sought to discredit the belief that as most temperance men were

Liberals the government would still retain their support even without a Veto Bill; 'it is impossible to believe that they could have been so exceedingly foolish as to seek to secure the support of the Temperance party at such a price, if, as the theory implies, they believed they could have it for nothing.'[11]

This theory of obstruction and conspiracy propounded by Alliance leaders to pacify their followers shows remarkable similarities to similar obstruction theories put forward by Liberal leaders to achieve the same ends.[12] In an attempt to channel the energies of its supporters the Executive began a policy of attacking alternative proposals for licensing reform and working hard in those constituencies where the MP was hostile to the veto but only enjoyed a small majority. In this way they were effectively strengthening Harcourt's hand in working as an electoral arm of the Liberal party. Late in 1894 prohibitionists in the constituencies also became increasingly aware that they were competing with other sections within the Liberal party and pushed their own claims more aggressively. At a meeting of the Midland Liberal Federation in December they were present in sufficient numbers to force through an amendment to a resolution demanding the immediate introduction of the Welsh Disestablishment Bill. This campaign was taken a stage further at the National Liberal Federation meeting in the following January. Snape argued that Welsh disestablishment would be given priority over the veto only because 30 Welsh MPs had threatened to withdraw from the Liberal party if it were not and asserted that 'ten Welsh parsons were not likely to do as much harm as one publican'.[13]

The Alliance assumed that when the government did decide to push on with temperance legislation it would reintroduce the 1893 Bill unchanged. This measure had not altogether pleased them and they tried to get it modified somewhat. Lawson asked Harcourt to drop the exemptions as they had displeased temperance men without pleasing the trade. Harking back to his Permissive Bill he really wanted a 'short simple, straightforward Bill' which would not be open to much amendment. Harcourt however was not interested in making any changes and pointed out that 'when once you have hoisted a fighting flag, it is not a good thing to haul it down in order to add a few stars or stripes to it'.[14] Lawson was quite satisfied with this, but others were not. Rosebery did not like the old Bill. Believing it to be an electoral liability he felt that if it were proceeded with it should be modified in such a way as to widen its electoral appeal. He proposed that it should include provision for an option to reduce licences as the privately introduced Welsh and Scotch Bills had done. Convinced that if a Veto Bill had to be introduced it should be 'framed not only in the interests of the extreme temperance party but on the broad principle of giving all the power to exercise an option', many Liberal MPs agreed with him. T.E. Ellis was of this opinion and so were 'scores and scores' of Liberal MPs to whom he had spoken. Welsh members were particularly strong on this point.[15]

Initially the Alliance took no heed of such criticisms, secure in the belief that Harcourt would not accept any change, but became concerned when at its annual meeting in October 1894 T.E. Ellis implied that the Bill would be greatly improved were it to include regulatory provisions. Lawson noted that Asquith also had 'been talking a little in that direction', and remonstrated with Harcourt. He was convinced that such tactics were designed to wreck the Bill and would tend to 'disconcert those who are so earnestly supporting you in the country'. Surprised that 'members of a Government should go about "crabbing" a Goverment Bill', he implored Harcourt to put a stop to it because 'these sort of deliverances are endangering both your Bill and the Government itself'.[16]

At this stage Harcourt does not appear to have had any intention of modifying his old Bill. He had decided at the end of October to insist on the Veto Bill having a prominent place in the programme for the next session but doubted if 'anything can be done before or after the House of Lords Resolution — if it can ever be drawn'. He made the introduction of a Veto Bill the condition of his continued membership of the government and Cabinet agreed to give priority to four measures at the beginning of next session, a Welsh Disestablishment Bill, Irish Land Bill, Registration Bill and a Veto Bill. From this point onwards however a formidable new force entered the field. His son, Lewis Harcourt, declared himself 'strongly in favour of a larger Bill than last year's which will establish Licensing Boards and give powers to close a portion of the licensed houses'. He believed this would secure 'a much greater force of popular support than there is for the present Bill and take very little longer to pass'. Lewis discovered that Fowler, a member of the Cabinet committee on the Bill, was of the same opinion but he was unsure of his ability to convert his father to his point of view. Harcourt himself, concerned mainly with the reaction any changes might provoke among prohibitionists after Lawson's warning, believed that any alterations would be 'difficult if not impossible'.[17]

Nevertheless Lewis Harcourt continued to press his father and within a fortnight he noted that the Cabinet committee had come up with 'a very drastic Bill' but one which 'quite meets my views'. While much drafting remained to be done, it had been agreed in principle to include an option to reduce the number of licences. This was largely a result of the promptings of Lewis Harcourt and the Bill which subsequently took shape was very much the joint creation of him and his father. He wrote in his diary,

> W.V.H. and I sat till nearly 3 this morning looking out various plans of local option. We devised many of great ingenuity for a popular vote on reduction of licences and found conclusive and unanswerable arguments against each — after which we went to bed, W.V.H. saying that I was the only person he knew who might be able to devise a solution, but I don't feel like it.

Once again, temperance men were of little help. Lewis Harcourt reported on an interview he and his father had with Dodge, a visiting American temperance reformer, who was 'quite devoid of useful information. He did nothing but dilate on abstract principles at interminable length and we only got rid of him with difficulty.'[18]

When Lawson called on the Harcourts and was told of the changes he was 'rather staggered' and 'not much inclined to approve'. However as in 1893 he behaved in an inconsistent way during a crucial period. He subsequently wrote a letter to Harcourt which began by objecting to the changes and ended by welcoming them. Rosebery when arguing for a wider measure had claimed that the 1893 Bill was essentially an Alliance product and had been widely recognised as such. Lawson denied this, telling Harcourt that it was 'your own production accepted by the Alliance ... as a practical and worthy measure'. Nevertheless he realised that 'certain persons and influences are driving you to the conviction that, for tactical purposes, it will be wise and prudent to make certain alterations', and assumed that 'after Rosebery's approbation of the Scotch Bill ... you feel yourself driven to adopt it'. At this point Lawson suddenly began to think that something akin to the Scottish Bill would have 'compensating advantages' because it gave the veto power to a bare majority and contained no exemptions. 'The "wise men" could not blame you', he concluded, 'for taking up the Scotch Bill after what Rosebery said' and then went on to pledge the support of all prohibitionists for such a change. His motives for doing this bore little relationship to those which had been exercising the minds of Harcourt and his son. He declared:

I must say that I ... rather maliciously look forward with pleasure to seeing the engineers hoist with their own petard.

The more I think of it the better I like the idea. All these people who for the last year and a half have been perpetually jabbering about the beauty and practicability of the 'diminution veto' really desiring to wreck your Bill, would be in a most awful hole.[19]

But Lawson was not consistent. He did not wish actively to aid Harcourt in drafting the Bill, claiming, 'I am better not mixed up in this thing'.[20] He made no attempt to prepare the Executive or prohibitionists in general for what was coming, nor did he take any steps to ensure that they would support it, despite having assured Harcourt of their enthusiastic backing. It appears that he did not even notify members of the Executive of what he had found out from Harcourt; they discovered what was going on from another source. At the National Liberal Federation meeting in January 1895, he asked Spence Watson if Harcourt intended modifying his old Bill, while knowing all the time that this was the case. The Direct Veto Resolution at the meeting had been modified from previous years to give ratepayers 'the power of deciding how many, if any' licences should be suppressed. This had been done to fall into line with the wider range of options Harcourt was drafting, but it upset Lawson. He asked that the phrase 'how many' be omitted but his request was turned down. He then launched into an attack on those Liberals who had been criticising Harcourt's 1893 Bill up and down the country, arguing that experts such as Harcourt and himself knew best and that a simple Bill was the thing.[21]

After what had happened in 1893 this must have appeared distressingly familiar to Harcourt but he was now too heavily committed to draw back. By early January 1895, drafting had been completed and he was pleased with the results. Lewis Harcourt believed it to be 'a very good Bill and [it] ought to command the support of all extreme *and* moderate Temperance people'.[22] This it did. The inclusion of the option to reduce as well as prohibit was enough to win the backing of the Church of England Temperance Society, although it reserved the right to try and include compensation in the Committee stage. The Alliance also threw its whole weight behind the measure, as did the National Temperance Federation.

While Harcourt could take heart from these signs of fighting spirit, he faced serious problems from other quarters. There were rival proposals in the field, as there had been in 1893, but this time they were pushed with more energy and authority. The Bishop of Chester had revived his plans for the introduction of a modified Gothenberg system of licensing and public control. The Public House Reform Association was set up in the middle of 1894 to push this proposal and it attracted the support of the Duke of Westminster, Lords Wemyss and Thring, and Joseph Chamberlain. Once Chamberlain gave it his backing, Temperance organisations were forced to sit up and take note and they began to denounce the scheme. However worse was to follow. Lord Thring wrote to W.E. Gladstone asking him to join the Association, and Gladstone replied that 'in principle you are working on the only lines either promising or tenable'. He added that local option could never be more than 'a partial and occasional remedy'. This was a serious matter; the Gothenburg proposal now had the backing of Chamberlain, Gladstone and the Bishop of Chester, 'three eminent men whose age and experience entitle their utterances to the thoughtful consideration of social reformers'.[23]

The result was a flurry of activity as temperance organisations and newspapers sent their representative to Gothenburg to assess the merits of its licensing system. *The Times* reporter concluded that Gothenburg was the most drunken city he had seen. Joseph Malins, a vice-president of the Alliance and head of the Good Templars, prepared a detailed report of the system and provided Harcourt with a copy. The attack mounted by temperance men and the ammunition which they gave Harcourt was enough to head off the threat of legislation but this was not the end of the matter. Gladstone's letter was taken by many as evidence that he had systematically misled prohibitionists by publicly pledging himself and his governments from 1883 onwards to local option, while in reality favouring some form of municipal control. Chamberlain believed that many Liberals who had pledged themselves to local option would now consider themselves freed from that pledge in consequence of Gladstone's statement. Harcourt was furious with Gladstone for his inconsistency and accused him of making a mess of the whole subject because 'at heart he abhors temperance'. This episode stiffened Harcourt's resolve to stand or fall by his Bill and John Morley agreed with him that he had been badly treated.[24]

Meanwhile opposition to the veto was growing among Liberals at all levels in the party. This was based mainly on the belief that it was a serious electoral liability. Joseph Rowntree attempted to measure the cost to Liberal electoral chances of the political hostility of the trade and his calculations indicated that this hostility would be a major and possibly fatal blow. Spence Watson, concerned by this, passed on the results to Harcourt who however was unimpressed. Like the Alliance, he was convinced that the brewers and publicans had done their worst in 1892 and had no more reserves to bring up.[25] Many Liberals were not as optimistic. At a time when Liberal fortunes were at a low ebb, local associations faced with by-elections were prepared to go to any lengths to ensure success. It had long been realised that active political intervention by the trade was not automatically directed against Liberal candidates because they were Liberals, but only in cases where they supported the veto. It was their support of the veto not their Liberalism which called it forth. The solution was simple. By fielding candidates who were neutral or prepared to oppose the veto, publican hostility could be avoided. Liberals in Grantham, faced with a by-election in 1894, went one step further. By selecting a maltster as a candidate they ensured they would have the support of the trade and 'his maltster's gold will save their pockets'. The candidate, Earp, was naturally not prepared to pledge his support for Harcourt's Bill, promising only to be neutral. The Alliance immediately set about bringing together the temperance voters in the constituency to oppose him. To its horror it found that

> The leading men in the Dissenting Churches, in the Liberal Executive, and in the Temperance League have thrown every other consideration to the winds, save that of *Party* ... Their fears are excited and they will throw every possible hindrance in our way.[26]

Despite the expenditure of a great deal of time and effort in the constituency, the Alliance failed to keep temperance men together in opposition, nor could it persuade T.E. Ellis, the chief whip, to intervene in order to persuade Earp either to support the veto or get a new candidate.

This was not an isolated example. Mark Beaufoy, who had been in trouble over the veto in 1893, was re-elected as a candidate for Kensington only on condition that he oppose Harcourt's Bill and declare for compensation. Beaufoy believed it was better that a Liberal retain the seat and be loyal on all questions other than this, rather than let the Tories in as would happen with a veto candidate. W.S. Caine tried to intervene on behalf of the Alliance, but once again without success. The Executive became increasingly aware of the unsympathetic reception given to its deputations by Liberal workers at by-elections. When Ellis was tackled about this he claimed that he always advised candidates to 'Tackle the Veto boldly and stick to it' but admitted that he was powerless to influence those who were opposed. 'It is', he said, 'one out of a thousand indications which have reached me that to push through the prohibitive Veto alone will smash a *far* larger majority than ours.' Lawson was horrified at this. 'Tom Ellis's letter is *rotten*', he complained: 'I am getting to believe that there are traitors in the Government. H. Gladstone too, is abominable.'[27]

The conspiracy theory mentioned earlier had now undergone a significant transformation. Instead of depicting Liberal leaders as the victims of outside obstruction, as they had done previously, Alliance leaders now believed that some were themselves conspiring to defeat the veto. This became a constant theme in Alliance literature during the next few years. However it is misleading to view this as a 'conspiracy', for while it was certainly true that some leading Liberals opposed the veto, they were not alone in their views as opposition was also growing outside parliament and leaders were simply reflecting this. Having initially embraced the veto for political reasons they were eager to be rid of it once it looked like becoming an electoral liability.

Harcourt was presumably aware of increasing hostility in the constituencies and he certainly knew that many Liberal MPs viewed his Bill with great trepidation. H.S. Leon warned him that it was of 'vital importance to some of our seats and I for one will stand to win or lose by such a bill'. It was 'from an electioneering point of view out and out the most important one of the session'. Beaufoy was even more forthright: 'Local veto is not popular, I know by the confidences various members have made to me that a large number of our own side are desperately afraid of it. If we could shake off the Prohibition Party we should be ten times as strong as we are now.'[28] There was even less support for Harcourt within the Cabinet. As early as November 1894 all the other members were convinced that the Bill would not get a majority on its second reading because of the difficulty in getting Irish MPs to vote. Rosebery, still convinced that even the modified veto was an electoral liability, believed 'Harcourt's views about temperance and the Local Veto Bill are shared by no other member of the Government unless it be John Morley'.[29]

Despite this formidable opposition, Harcourt was determined to proceed with his Bill. By the beginning of 1895 it was completed to his satisfaction and he sought the earliest opportunity to give it a first reading. However the lack of enthusiasm displayed by his Cabinet colleagues delayed him somewhat. He and Morley could not agree whether the veto or the Irish Land Bill should be given precedence. Tom Ellis was also holding back. Convinced that the opposition would force a division on the introduction of the Bill, he feared a defeat at this early stage, and wanted to introduce it at about the same time as the second reading of the Welsh Disestablishment Bill in order to ensure a good turnout of Members who were there for the Welsh measure. Finally, by the end of March, Ellis was confident of 'a majority for us of 8 to 10 on the introduction of the Local Veto Bill if the Tories divide on it'. Some Liberals were expected to oppose or abstain, but they would be partially offset by the support of a few Conservatives and Liberal-Unionists.[30]

Its introduction on 8 April sparked off a lively campaign throughout the country by both prohibitionists and the trade. Generally this followed a similar pattern to that of 1893, with both sides seeking to demonstrate the depth of support for or against the Bill. The Alliance was more than usually handicapped by a shortage of cash; a fighting fund was opened but the response was disappointing. In one respect the Alliance campaign in 1895 did differ somewhat from that of 1893. It realised at last that instead of indiscriminately whipping up manifestations of popular support, it must also actively aid the Liberals in ensuring a parliamentary majority for the veto. For the first time the Executive was prepared to work closely with the Liberal whip Ellis in using its agency network as a means of bringing constituency pressure to bear on the few Liberal MPs unfavourable to the veto.

Meanwhile Harcourt was endeavouring to get a second reading for his Bill. He once more became embroiled with other members of the Cabinet by insisting that it should take precedence over the Committee stages of the Irish Land Bill and the Welsh Disestablishment Bill. Sir Edward Hamilton summed up the feeling of Cabinet thus: 'The fact is nobody wants and still less likes his Bill.' Despite this, Harcourt was still intent on continuing to the extent of being more concerned with his Bill than with the budget.[31]

Why was a shrewd politician like Harcourt so insistent, almost obsessively insistent it seemed, on pressing ahead with the veto despite the opposition arrayed against him? He had after all been prepared to drop it in 1893 because he felt it stood little chance of success, and the prospects now looked even poorer, as even he must have realised. If the Bill reached its second reading it was calculated that one Liberal would abstain, twelve were doubtful, and five would definitely vote against. In addition, the Nationalists were still a largely unknown quantity. To be offset against this it was expected that only four

Unionists would offer their support and even this could not be counted upon.[32] The majority was likely to be very small indeed and once this hurdle had been surmounted the Committee stage posed further problems. Some support was likely to melt away as Members considered they had already fulfilled their electoral pledges to prohibitionist constituents. Those who supported the CETS were prepared to move an amendment for the inclusion of financial compensation, while T.W. Russell, a temperance Liberal-Unionist sitting for an Irish seat, objected to the exclusion of Ireland from the Bill. He saw this as a sop to win Parnellite support and while his temperance sympathies forced him to vote for a second reading, he threatened to move an amendment in Committee for the inclusion of Ireland. This he believed would get Unionist backing and if the British Temperance party opposed this, he in turn would oppose a third reading.[33] The likelihood then was that the Bill would absorb a great deal of time, and risk being mutilated or even defeated during Committee. Even if it passed a third reading the House of Lords was unlikely to receive it favourably. Given that it could only have scraped through its final stage in the Commons by a small majority, the Lords would presumably have felt little compunction in throwing it out.

At first sight Harcourt's actions seemed to be completely divorced from political realities. He professed himself 'now to be ready to make any sacrifices in order that he may promote the great object of his life — the lessening of the curse of drink'. Dilke believed that Harcourt was 'a genuine convert to the principle — a curious intellectual phenomenon, this development of a belated conviction in a mind hitherto essentially opportunistic'. However his attitude must be seen in the light of the position of the government in 1895. It was staggering along, bankrupt of enthusiasm and expecting defeat at any moment. The rift between Harcourt and Rosebery was now virtually complete. Several Liberal leaders had become increasingly fatalistic, positively welcoming defeat and a release from office. As early as February Harcourt was being rude to his colleagues and talking loudly while in the House about the coming downfall of the government. Hamilton thought he was pushing on with the Local Veto Bill in order to 'ride for a fall'.[34] Others were adopting the same approach. John Morley declared that 'popular or not we stand by that measure ... I am not in favour of going about with a thermometer and a wind gauge ... to set the sails to every passing breeze'.[35] But Harcourt's actions were less negative than they seemed, as some of his colleagues slowly realised. Rosebery believed 'Harcourt, *as at present minded*, is really bent on trying to bring the government or himself, or both, to grief over this Local Veto Bill.' Hamilton also gained the same impression.

> He [Harcourt] told me he had just received what he considered an important notification, which was that the Church Temperance party had decided to support his Bill. But the importance he attaches to this announcement was not very consistent with his subsequent professions of a longing to fall upon it. I said I could not conceive a worse thing upon which to fall. He told me I knew nothing about it: he was convinced that temperance was the only question which really interested the electors. I am afraid I was not really convinced — for all the temperance people or the bulk of them, as it is vote Liberal. He went on to say that what would suit him better still would be if the Cabinet declined to let him proceed with the Bill.

Harcourt could then resign and go into opposition where he could dominate the party more effectively.[36]

It is not absolutely clear what Harcourt meant by this. He may have thought that by breaking away from the government he would bring about its downfall. Hamilton assumed that is what he intended, but doubted that this would be the outcome because, 'even if Harcourt did break away, R. would hold on with Campbell-Bannerman as leader of the House of Commons'.[37] What Harcourt expected to follow is even less clear. Did he think that he could win any ensuing election with the help of temperance votes, or did he contemplate going into opposition as leader of the Liberals? What is reasonably beyond doubt is that he was using the Local Veto Bill to serve his own political ends, at least in the short run and saw in it a way of displacing Rosebery from the party leadership. At the basis of his whole strategy lay the belief that the veto was *the* burning issue in the constituencies, in contrast to the House of Lords question which he considered a 'dead-letter'. Alliance propaganda had convinced him of this. He may have envisaged himself as leader, after an election, of a compact opposition united on the veto, with Rosebery, who had refused to espouse the cause, thrown to one side. If this was the case, Hamilton was certainly mistaken in thinking Harcourt inconsistent over the question of support from the Church of England Temperance party, because this assured the unity of the whole temperance movement behind the Liberal cause. His subsequent action in making the veto the main issue in his 1895 electoral campaign certainly demonstrated his belief in its potency in the constituencies and its importance in his eyes for the future of the Liberal party.

However one interprets Harcourt's motives, the Alliance was to be disappointed once again. The Local Veto Bill never reached a second reading because the government was defeated on the 'cordite' vote and hastily used this as a pretext for resigning. Salisbury promptly dissolved Parliament. Prohibitionists at the time regarded this as just one more temporary setback on the road to ultimate success but in retrospect 1895 can be seen as a watershed. The Alliance was never again able to exert such an influence over the Liberal Party and its leaders as it had between 1892 and 1895. In future Liberals, while still desirous of a measure of temperance reform, looked with increasing scepticism upon the veto as a realistic solution, and upon prohibitionists as an increasingly costly electoral liability. Herbert Gladstone believed 'we are plagued with obstinate faddists who are too strong for the leaders ... I could wish to get rid of them through defeat'. He turned out to be a better prophet than Harcourt who 'always maintained that Temperance Reform was the only question that interested the electors'.[38]

The general election of 1895 was a crushing defeat for Liberals and the Alliance, the Unionists being returned with a majority of 152. This result was widely interpreted as an overwhelming public rejection of the Veto Bill. Campbell-Bannerman was convinced that 'one-half of the losses they had encountered in England were caused by the dread of this Bill' and Hamilton, although upset that the Liberals had fared so poorly, congratulated electors for showing 'very good sense in ... declining to re-elect the principal bores and faddists who belonged to the last Parliament'.[39] W.S. Caine lost his seat at East Bradford and only 175 members of the new House of Commons were pledged to the veto. The worst single blow for Liberals and the Alliance was the defeat of Harcourt at Derby by over 1,100 votes, reversing a majority of nearly 2,000 in 1892. While Harcourt blamed bad trade, the machinations of the Midland Railway Company and the 'disgraceful' behaviour of the Church and clergy for his defeat, W.E. Gladstone was convinced that it was caused mainly by Harcourt's espousal of the Veto.[40] Immediately after the election the *Westminster Gazette* asked Liberal candidates for their views on the causes of defeat. Fifty-four of the 74 successful candidates who replied believed that the veto had harmed them, fourteen thought it had done no great harm and six had found it positively helpful. Of the 175 unsuccessful candidates who replied, 134 had been harmed by the veto, sixteen felt it had done no harm and seven had found it helpful.[41]

The trade had amply demonstrated its political muscle and its ability to overshadow the efforts of prohibitionists when it felt its interests to be seriously threatened. Its electoral organisation had been improved and it had gone into the election with the intention of showing Liberals 'that their ship will never float again unless they root from its keel the rotten plank of vetoism'. Harcourt and Lawson were shown to be mistaken in assuming that the trade had done its worst in 1892. The Alliance was forced to admit that the Veto Bill had contributed to the Liberal defeat but insisted that this was because it had never been judged on its merits. As it never reached a second reading its provisions had not been exhaustively debated and were consequently not well understood. This made it easy for the trade to depict it as an imperative measure designed to shut all public houses rather than something which provided for a local option. However in using this defence the Alliance was tacitly admitting that prohibitionists had been unable to counter the barrage of trade propaganda.[42]

It was obviously important for the Alliance to minimise the electoral damage done by the veto. Prohibitionists pointed out that poor Liberal organisation in the constituencies, bad trade, opposition from the Church under the threat of Welsh disestablishment and of Catholics over the voluntary school question, the presence of Independent Liberal Party candidates which split the progressive vote and the unpopularity of Home Rule, had all contributed to the defeat. They claimed that Liberal leaders, on the lookout for a scapegoat to explain their defeat, had unfairly singled them out for blame. They also claimed that Herbert Gladstone, Henry Fulford and Courtenay Warner had begun to mobilise opposition to the veto at least eighteen months before the election by urging Liberal candidates to soft pedal on the issue and avoid pledging themselves. The Executive argued that in consequence its offers of aid had often been rejected by Liberal candidates and thus prohibitionists had not been able to demonstrate their fighting qualities. In an attempt to strengthen this argument, W.S. Caine attempted to show statistically that strong veto candidates had fared better in the election than those who had sat upon the fence.[43]

These claims must be treated with some scepticism. Herbert Gladstone had certainly entertained growing reservations well before the election but as we have seen he was by no means alone in this. There is no evidence to suggest that he organised opposition or tried to influence the views of candidates. As has already been noted, many constituency organisations rejected the veto of their own accord, despite the efforts of Ellis to persuade them not to do so. Nor are the arguments of the Executive a convincing explanation for the lack of fight displayed by prohibitionists. Liberal candidates in many constituencies complained that they had taken a firm stand on the veto but had not received enough assistance from prohibitionists to counteract the trade campaign. Campbell-Bannerman contrasted the effective electoral work of the trade with 'the noisy fussiness of the Teetotallers'.[44]

Whatever the real causes of the Liberal reverse, the fact remained that many in the party *believed* the veto was to blame and acted accordingly. W.E. Gladstone was the first to pose the obvious question. 'I do not feel sure', he confided to Harcourt after the latter had been defeated at Derby, 'that local option may not in future be better propelled by independent action than by a Liberal Government'.[45] While he was no longer in a position to influence the course of events, his son was. After 1895 Herbert Gladstone rapidly became the focal point around which opposition to the veto gathered. Elected in 1895 as a supporter of the measure he declared at a later constituency meeting that he could 'no longer adopt the Veto policy as a question of practical politics'. This was accepted with only two dissentients. Gladstone was concerned that continued Liberal support for it was futile because

if we get a majority strong enough to get a Temperance Bill through the H. of C., the H.L. will stand firm on Compensation. If they force us to the country, the Trade will make a record effort against us and will probably prove once more that, plus the Ch. of England and the whole Tory party, they are too strong for us. That would be disastrous in the interests of reform.[46]

Worried that the Alliance had forced the Liberal party into a corner he came to believe, as did the Fabians, that the prohibitionist vote had become 'too dear at the price'. For the sake of effective reform and the party, the veto had to be dropped.

Herbert Gladstone did not publicly declare his views until the end of 1897 but when he did he immediately won enthusiastic backing from the *Speaker*, the *Westminster Gazette* and the *Daily Chronicle*. However opposition to the Alliance had been building up from various quarters well before this. Its influence in English urban constituencies, traditionally its main power base, continued to decline as more Liberal candidates unfavourable to the veto were elected. A clear indication of this decline can be gathered from the resolutions passed at the annual meeting of the NLF. From 1896 onwards the veto was noticeably absent, despite strenuous attempts by the Alliance to keep it there. Whittaker had informed the Alliance Executive before the 1896 meeting that several members of the General Purposes Committee of the NLF wanted to drop it quietly. He urged that Alliance agents be confidentially informed of this so they could work quietly to ensure that delegates from their respective areas would prevent this happening. Significantly the attempt to mobilise Alliance support within the NLF backfired. The Executive's confidential instructions to its agents were made public and prompted a reaction against such backroom manoeuvering.[47] The Veto Resolution did not appear.

At Westminster, Harcourt's position within the Liberal party had been weakened by his commitment to the Alliance. Kay-Shuttleworth pointed to 'want of confidence' in him over the veto 'as among the more active causes of the [electoral] disaster'. Likewise Kimberley complained to Ripon that 'this folly about local veto is in itself proof of his utter want of judgement. Was ever man in such a fool's paradise!'.[48] Harcourt himself was not prepared to throw over his old commitments entirely but he realised the futility of taking any new initiatives. He explained his position to Spence Watson:

> I have told Wilfrid Lawson that I do not think it would be at all expedient for me in the position I occupy to make a pronouncement *ex Cathedra* at this juncture on the condition of the Temperance question. My views on the subject of popular control are, I need not tell you, unchanged, though I have no obstinate *amour propre* as to my own particular method of giving effect to it. The great difficulty we have in dealing with the matter, which I fear is not removed, is the great want of unanimity and coherence in the different sections of the Temperance reformers. The first object I think ought to be the endeavour on their part to come to some clear and definite understanding. Men like Caine and others decried the Bill I introduced and in this state of affairs it is not surprising that we failed.
>
> When the troops are a little more disciplined I shall be quite ready to carry my musket to the front, but at present it seems to me that my intervention would do more harm than good.[49]

The Alliance could expect no further active help from this quarter. These attacks on the veto must be seen against the wider back ground of change within the Liberal party. *The Times* saw the Liberal defeat in 1895 as a 'condemnation of a policy of patchwork without principles'.[50] Most Liberal leaders agreed and wished to repudiate not just the veto but the whole of the Newcastle programme. This reaction against programme politics involved not just the dropping of the many demands contained in the Newcastle Programme but also the subduing and disciplining of the sectional interests which had been pushing them. While leaders found it difficult to come up with an acceptable alternative, a progressive minority began to try and persuade the party to replace the old Gladstonian economic and civic individualism with a new, more systematic creed of social progress. Such attempts were much influenced by the views of Sidney Webb who complained that the liberalism of Harcourt and Morley was 'not the progressive instinct of the twentieth century'. He argued that

the Gladstonian section of the Liberal party remains ... axiomatically hostile to the State. ... Hence in politics they are inveterately negative, instinctively iconoclastic. They have hung up temperance reform and educational reform for a quarter of a century, because, instead of seeking to enable the citizen to refresh himself without being poisoned or inebriated, and to get the children thoroughly taught, they have wanted primarily to revenge their outraged temperance principles on the publican and their outdated Nonconformist principles on the Church. Of such Liberals it may be said that the destructive revolutionary tradition is in their bones; they will reform nothing unless it can be done at the expense of their enemies. Moral superiority, virtuous indignation, are necessaries of political life to them; a Liberal reform is never simply a social means to a social end, but a campaign of Good against Evil. Their conception of freedom means only breaking somebody's bonds asunder. When the higher freedom of corporate life is in question, they become angrily reactionary, and denounce and obstruct every new development of common action.[51]

However the importance of such pleas for new approaches should not be over emphasised. They made little headway in the party before the turn of the century because the traditional sections were not willing to be pushed aside without a fight. The Alliance found itself in a situation where it had lost the support it once enjoyed among leading Liberals, and it had been thrust aside as irrelevant by the 'New Liberals', but it still enjoyed the support of 'the great body of the party'. It was a measure of the achievement of the Alliance as a pressure group that, whereas its supporters in the early seventies consisted of a small group of Radical MPs, by the nineties it could count on the backing of the rump of the party. But by the same token, the fact that the more progressive elements in the party no longer espoused the cause as their predecessors in the seventies had done, was an indication that the appeal of the veto was waning. For the moment however sectional interests were numerically too important and too firmly entrenched for Liberal leaders to risk alienating them completely. Emy has noted that 'reform in the sense of legislation stemming from the growth of progressive sentiment in the House, was dependent upon changes in party composition'. This could only happen slowly. It had taken a long time for a party composed of veto supporters to emerge and such people could only be replaced gradually by those with different views. In the short run the best that Liberal leaders could hope for was a compromise.[52]

The search for a compromise revolved around the *Royal Commission on the Licensing Laws* set up in 1896. Despite the growth of strong links between the trade and the Tories, pressure from Anglican bishops and the Westminster Licensing Reform Committee, consisting mainly of Liberal-Unionists, persuaded Salisbury to set up a Royal Commission. Most of those appointed to the Commission openly represented the interests involved. There were eight 'neutrals', eight temperance men, including T.P. Whittaker and W.S. Caine and eight from the trade; Lord Peel, the former Speaker, was appointed chairman. Nor surprisingly the life of the Commission was acrimonious and when it reported in 1899 no unanimity of view had been reached.[53] A *Majority Report* signed by most trade and neutral members proposed a ratio of licences to population of the kind first mooted by Bruce in 1871, coupled with full financial compensation to dispossessed licence holders to be drawn from the trade. The *Minority Report*, signed by Peel and most temperance men, disagreed with the *Majority Report* principally over the question of compensation. It proposed that a veto over licences would operate freely after seven years and without compensation, but some financial compensation would be awarded to licence holders dispossessed before the time limit was up, although not at the full market value.

The *Majority Report* lacked either popular or political appeal. The trade preferred the *status quo* and Salisbury, faced with two conflicting sets of recommendations, chose to do nothing. The *Minority Report* in contrast formed the basis of a campaign by Whittaker designed to unite temperance organisations behind its proposals and persuade the Liberal party to accept it as its programme. Herbert Gladstone, wishing to retain the support of Liberal drink interests, still believed the Minority proposals to be too extreme. A bout of intensive negotiating followed. Whittaker proposed that Scotland get the veto after five years, Wales after seven, and consideration of its merits for England to be postponed for seven years; he was not unduly concerned how much compensation was paid providing it came from trade sources. Gladstone thought that an agreement on this basis was possible and began to sound out the trade. In the event, things did not work out in the way Whittaker had hoped and his strategy failed. Liberal leaders, under pressure from Gladstone, refused to commit themselves to details and, worse still, the attempt to unite the many temperance organisations behind the scheme, failed. The Alliance was hopelessly split by these proposals. The bulk of the Executive was prepared to swallow its views on compensation and back Whittaker but Lawson and the minority would not and fought against it. Lawson was joined by the Good Templars and militant prohibitionists in the north of England and the 'Celtic fringes' who felt that they had been betrayed by temperance leaders and exploited by Liberal politicians. The resulting schism was deep and lasting, and permanently undermined the strength of the Alliance. Good Templar dissidents in England set up a rival National Prohibition Party in 1899 and the Scottish Prohibition Party was founded two years later. The most dramatic evidence of conflict came in Kilmarnock Burghs where W.S. Caine had been adopted as a Liberal candidate in 1898. Caine's willingness to compromise on reform attracted the hostility of local prohibitionists and he was forced, two years later, to withdraw his candidature.

Herbert Gladstone eagerly seized his chance to weaken the Alliance hold over the Liberal party by adding fuel to these faction fights. Rather than have Lawson attack the Liberal party for breaking its promise over compensation and the veto for England, he tried to ensure that Lawson's anger was directed against his erstwhile colleagues. Gladstone told Campbell-Bannerman:

> I think that the sooner you make it clear that the Veto for England is postponed, the better. It will bring the parties of Lawson and Whittaker into conflict and will help us with our brewers and all moderate Liberal reformers. The battle axe [Lawson] will have first to descend on the heads of the nearest traitors in this case Caine

and Whittaker. For the Peel Reporters are the men who threw the Veto overboard.[54]

The wheel had come full circle. For almost thirty years Liberal leaders had bemoaned the lack of unanimity within the temperance movement but by the end of the century they were actively encouraging it.

It is arguable that pressure for temperance reform was stronger between 1900 and 1914 than it had been during the previous thirty years, as the Acts of 1902, 1904 and the abortive Bill of 1908 bear witness. After the Liberal victory in 1906 licensing reform was still seen as an 'imperative concession to nonconformity',[55] just as it had been in the 1880s and 1892. However the difference was that the Alliance could no longer dictate the terms. Its position as the dominant temperance party had come to an end. After 1895 it could no longer hope to attract the support of a Liberal leader as receptive as Harcourt, nor persuade the party to introduce another simple Veto Bill without provision for compensation or licensing reform. As a measure of its decline, the Alliance could no longer whip up enough opposition to defeat the Licensing Act of 1904 in the way it had done with a similar proposal in 1888, nor could it generate enough support for the Liberal Bill of 1908 to make the Lords doubt the wisdom of rejecting it. The election of 1895 marked the end of Alliance hegemony in the world of temperance.

Prohibitionists were wrong in assuming that the reverses suffered by the Alliance between 1895 and 1900 were no more than temporary political setbacks. They proved to be irreversible because they were accompanied and to some degree caused by more fundamental social changes which undermined the foundations on which the political effectiveness of the Alliance was based. By the end of the century the strength and enthusiasm of Nonconformity, on which the Alliance drew so heavily, was being eroded by a growing secularism, defections to the Anglican establishment, and the disappearance of old disabilities. The influence of the great provincial cities, the true home of prohibitionists, was also being eclipsed. The Alliance had been founded at a time when there was still much truth in the claim that 'what Manchester thinks today London thinks tomorrow' but by the end of the century this was no longer true. As the machinery of central government expanded and London increasingly monopolised communications, information, culture and education, there was a weakening of provincial consciousness, pride and independence.

Furthermore by 1900 the skilled artisan was no longer the distinctive political force that he had been thirty years earlier.

Industrially he had suffered from the erosion of traditional skill differentials and the invasion of some skilled occupations by the semi-skilled; politically his voice had been swamped by the widening of the franchise in 1884. The 'New Unionism' of the eighties focused attention on labour problems rather than the political, social and moral questions which had so attracted 'Labour aristocrats' in earlier decades. The Labour party carried this process a step further by providing a political medium for the articulation of specifically working-class demands.[56] Finally, the credibility of prohibitionists as social reformers was fatally undermined. Foreign experiences with permissive prohibition had convinced all but the most militant prohibitionists that the veto could never lead to the alcohol-free utopia depicted in Alliance propaganda. Where it was not adopted it could do nothing to alleviate the evils of excessive drinking and it was least likely to be adopted in the large cities where reforms were most urgently needed. The prohibitionist diagnosis of the drink problem, on which the demand for a veto was based, was also shown to be unduly simplistic. The investigations of Charles Booth, Seebohm Rowntree and others provided new insights into the nature as well as the extent of poverty and in the process the role of drink in creating poverty was minimised. Drunkenness was increasingly seen as a manifestation of a squalid environment, not a cause of it. By 1898, Fabians could justifiably claim that

local option is to social reform in the same relation as charity to social suffering. As the ignorant and well-meaning person attempts to cure poverty by giving coppers to beggars, so the local vetoist tries to cure drunkenness by shutting public-houses.[57]

Notes

1. Lawson to W.V. Harcourt, 2 September 1893, *Harcourt Papers* (Box 4).
2. Quoted in *41st Annual Report 1893*, pp. 48-52 (original emphasis).
3. George Livesey to James Whyte, 19 October 1893, 23 November 1893, in *Minutes*, 1 and 29 November 1893.
4. Lawson to Whyte, 4 November 1893, in ibid., 8 November 1893; *42nd Annual Report 1894*, pp. 18-21; Lawson to Harcourt, 5 February 1894, *Harcourt Papers* (Box 4).
5. Lawson to Whyte, n.d., in *Minutes*, 21 March 1894.
6. Lawson to Harcourt, 18 April 1894, Harcourt to Lawson, 19 April 1894, *Harcourt Papers* (Box 4).

7. Lawson to Whyte, 26 and 29 April 1894, in *Minutes*, 2 May 1894; ibid., 30 May 1894.
8. Edward Pearson to Whyte, 1 May 1894, in *Minutes*, 2 May 1894; *Alliance News*, 26 January 1894, pp. 56-7.
9. Lloyd George quoted in D.A. Hamer, *Liberal Politics in the Age of Gladstone and Rosebery* (1972), p. 193; Lawson to Harcourt, 9 February 1894, *Harcourt Papers* (Box 4).
10. *Minutes*, 20 June 1894.
11. *42nd Annual Report 1894*, pp. 6-11.
12. Hamer, *Liberal Politics*, chs. 6-8.
13. NLF, *17th Annual Report* 1895, p. 94; W.L. Amery to Harcourt, 13 December 1894, *Harcourt Papers*.
14. Lawson to Harcourt, 5 February 1894, Harcourt to Lawson, 7 February 1894, *Harcourt Papers* (Box 4).
15. Lewis Harcourt Journal, 29 January 1895, p. 944, in ibid.; H.S. Leon to Harcourt, 10 March 1895, and T.E. Ellis to Harcourt, 27 October 1894, in ibid.
16. Lawson to Harcourt, 25 October 1894, *Harcourt Papers* (Box 4).
17. Lewis Harcourt Journal, 30 October 1894, 1 November 1894, 11 November 1894, pp. 825, 930-1, 844, in ibid.
18. Ibid., pp. 860, 864.
19. Lawson to Harcourt, 25 November 1894, *Harcourt Papers*.
20. Ibid.
21. NLF, *17th Annual Report 1895*, pp. 95-8.
22. Lewis Harcourt Journal, 13 December 1894, p. 844, *Harcourt Papers*.
23. J. Malins to Harcourt, 9 November 1894, in ibid.; *42nd Annual Report 1894*, pp. 41-45, 50; *Westminster Gazette*, 25 September 1894.
24. A.G. Gardiner, *Life of Sir William Harcourt* (1923), vol. 2, p. 307. Gladstone subsequently tried to repair the damage by insisting that he still supported local option.
25. Spence Watson to Harcourt, 7 February 1895, Harcourt to Spence Watson, 11 February 1895, *Harcourt Papers*.
26. J.B. Thornley (Alliance district agent) to Whyte, 12 June 1894 and 7 July 1894, in *Minutes*, 13 June 1894, 11 July 1894.
27. T.E. Ellis to Executive, 25 December 1894, 4 May 1895, in *Minutes*, 9 January 1895, 7 May 1895; Lawson to Whyte, 10 January 1895, in ibid., 16 January 1895.
28. H.S. Leon to Harcourt, 10 March 1895, Beaufoy to Harcourt, 2 April 1895, *Harcourt Papers*.
29. W. Williams to Executive, 24 November 1894, in *Minutes*, 28 November 1894; Sir Edward Hamilton's Diary, *Sir Edward Hamilton Papers*, Add. MSS. 48666, f. 115.
30. Ibid., 29 January 1895, f. 1; Lewis Harcourt Journal, 29 and 30 March 1895, pp. 1070-1, 1075, *Harcourt Papers*.
31. Sir Edward Hamilton's Diary, 23 and 30 April 1895, *Sir Edward Hamilton Papers*, Add. MSS. 48666, ff. 106, 114.
32. Lawson to Whyte, 11 June 1895 in *Minutes*, 12 June 1895.
33. *Daily Graphic*, 8 April 1895, cutting in *Harcourt Papers*.
34. Sir Edward Hamilton's Diary, 11 February 1895, 23 April 1895, 29 May 1895, *Sir Edward Hamilton Papers*, Add. MSS. 48666, ff. 16, 106; Add. MSS, 48667, f. 5; S. Gwynn and G.M. Tuckwell, *The Life of the Rt. Hon. Sir Charles W. Dilke* (1917) p. 566; P. Stansky, *Ambitions and Strategies* (1964), pp. 135, 139-44, 148-9.
35. Quoted in D.A Hamer, *John Morley: Liberal Intellectual in Politics* (1968), p. 303.
36. Sir Edward Hamilton's Diary, 30 April 1895, *Sir Edward Hamilton Papers*, Add. MSS. 48666, ff. 114-15.
37. Ibid., 5 May 1895, f. 120.
38. Ibid., 17 July 1895, Add. MSS. 48667, f. 72; C. Mallett, op. cit., p. 156.
39. Stansky, *Ambitions and Strategies*, p. 179; Sir Edward Hamilton's Diary, 25

July 1895, *Sir Edward Hamilton Papers*, Add. MSS 48667, ff. 79-80.

40. Gladstone to Harcourt, 15 July 1895, Harcourt to Gladstone, 16 July 1895, *Harcourt Papers*.

41. *Westminster Gazette*, 13 August 1895.

42. *Licensed Victuallers Gazette*, quoted in *Alliance News*, 17 July 1895; ibid., 26 July 1895, pp. 480-1.

43. Ibid.; *43rd Annual Report 1895*, pp. 10-13; John Newton, *W.S. Caine M.P. A Biography* (1907), pp. 279-81.

44. *Alliance News*, 2 August 1895, p. 496; D.A. Hamer, *Politics of Electoral Pressure. A Study in the History of Victorian Reform Agitations* (1977), pp. 277-83, looks at specific instances where constituency organisations jettisoned the veto.

45. W.E. Gladstone to Harcourt, 15 July 1895, *Harcourt Papers*.

46. H. Gladstone to Campbell-Bannerman, 12 April 1899, 19 November 1899, *Campbell-Bannerman Papers*, Add. MS. 41, 215, ff. 66, 145.

47. Hamer, *Politics of Electoral Pressure*, ch. 13; *Minutes*, 13 November 1895, 27 November 1895, 11 December 1895.

48. Kay-Shuttleworth to Spencer, 23 July 1895, Kimberley to Ripon, 20 July 1895, both quoted in Stansky, *Ambitions and Strategies*, pp. 179, 182.

49. Harcourt to Spence Watson, 22 January 1897, *Harcourt Papers*.

50. *Times*, 22 July 1895.

51. Hamer, *Liberal Politics*, chs. 9-12; Sidney Webb, *Nineteenth Century*, September 1901, pp. 369-70.

52. *Spectator*, 6 May 1899; H. Emy, 'The Liberal Party and the Social Problem 1918-1914' (London University PhD, 1969), p. 182.

53. David M. Fahey, 'Temperance and the Liberal Party — Lord Peel's Report 1899', *Journal of British Studies*, vol. 2, no. 2 (1971), pp. 132-59 has examined the Commission and its implications in detail. The following paragraphs briefly summarise his findings as they relate to the Alliance.

54. H. Gladstone to Campbell-Bannerman, 12 December 1899, *Campbell-Bannerman Papers*, Add. MS. 31, 215, ff. 171-2.

55. Emy, 'The Liberal Party', p. 224.

56. This is discussed in more detail in A.E. Dingle, 'The Agitation for Prohibition in England' (Monash University PhD, 1974), pp. 432-59.

57. *Fabian Tract No. 86*. For the attack on prohibitionists as social reformers see A.E. Dingle, 'The Rise and Fall of Temperance Economics', *Monash Papers in Economic History*, no. 3 (1977).

Chapter 8

THE ALLIANCE MACHINE

Historians of reformist pressure groups usually concentrate upon the campaign which their particular group waged and on its impact on society, to the neglect of more mundane aspects of internal structure and control. However by ignoring 'such grubby aspects as organization and finance' they run the risk of overlooking a central feature of such groups and their understanding of them will consequently be much diminished.[1] There is a close connection between the internal structure and operation of a pressure group and the kind of campaign it mounts, as political scientists have long realised. Just as the profitability of a business concern is determined partly by the efficiency with which it is run, so also is the effectiveness of any reforming campaign determined partly by the efficiency of its managers. Furthermore the nature of any campaign, the tactics employed and the attitudes embodied in it, are determined as much by the characteristics of the group mounting it as they are by the wider social or political environment which it seeks to reform, and consequently it cannot be fully comprehended unless the composition of the group is studied.

Leaders

The Constitution drawn up in 1853 stated that 'the Alliance shall be under the direction of a President, Vice-Presidents, General Council, and Executive Committee', but did not establish who would exercise control over whom. The President, Vice-President and Executive were to be elected at the annual general meeting of Council, but the Council itself could be 'augmented to any extent and in any manner the Executive Committee may direct'.[2] In practice the Council did not play a significant part in the determination of policy. Consisting of 500 members as early as 1855, it rapidly grew too large and unwieldy to act as anything other than a rubber stamp for decisions arrived at elsewhere.

The first President, Sir Walter C. Trevelyan exerted no influence on either the day-to-day running or the policy of the Alliance. His importance was measurable rather in terms of the prestige and finance he gave to the organisation. Sir Wilfrid Lawson, President after 1878, inherited an existing power structure which he made no attempt to change. He saw his role as largely a parliamentary one and always insisted that the Alliance had the option of either supporting the measures he introduced or not as it wished. He in return reserved the same right for himself in regard to any actions initiated by the Alliance. He disclaimed that he was either responsible to it, or a representative of its views in any way.[3]

Lawson's aloofness was rooted in his attitude towards prohibitionists. He did not count himself as one of them, nor could he have easily done so because his background was so different from that of the average Alliance man. In talking to Liberal leaders he constantly referred to 'our friends' and emphasised that 'it is only because circumstances have brought me into close relations with the prohibitionists that I feel I am able to point out how they are *likely* to view matters'. There was much truth therefore in Hugh Price Hughes' observation that Lawson 'has never been the real leader of the United Kingdom Alliance, though he has made a very amiable and witty figurehead'.[4] Lawson was never as closely identified with the average prohibitionist as were Cobden and Bright with the average supporter of the Anti-Corn Law League. Yet because of Lawson's social position and his familiarity with parliament, an asset conspicuously lacking among prohibitionists, he was important in determining policy. The Alliance had to work through him, and his lack of responsiveness to the desires of advanced prohibitionists in the 1880s and 1890s put the Executive in a difficult position and contributed greatly to the internal dissensions of that period. Lawson only wished to exercise *some* of the functions of a leader. He was glad to have the force of the Alliance behind him when it agreed with what he personally wanted to do. When it disagreed with him he was unwilling to abandon his own preferences but still wanted to retain the mantle of leadership.

In practice it was the Executive Committee which determined policy and controlled the day-to-day operations of the Alliance. It consisted almost entirely of Manchester residents with sufficient leisure and means to devote a considerable amount of time to Alliance affairs. Between 1872 and 1895 a total of 64 men were members, with between 25 and 30 serving at any one time. Biographical information provides some clues as to the nature of the leadership they provided.[5] Of the 48 members who could be traced, 20 derived their main income from business, usually their own, and of these, 14 were engaged in some branch of the textile industry. Ten were members of the professions, including five Anglican and Nonconformist ministers, two lawyers and three architects and surveyors. Of those whose religions are known, 19 were Nonconformists and five were Anglicans. At least 14 were active in some sphere of local government as councillors, aldermen, J.P.s or Guardians. Seventeen were office holders in temperance societies other than the Alliance and eleven took an active interest in philanthropic activities other than temperance, usually in their own locality. Most had taken part in other reforming crusades of various kinds. Thirteen were Liberals and three of these became Liberal-Unionists; two were Conservatives. Three sons followed in their father's footsteps and became members of the Executive.

With the exception of William Hoyle through his writings and James Raper, the Westminster lobbyist, most were unknown outside their immediate locality. One of them, W.J. Crossley, the treasurer, ended a letter to W.E. Gladstone by declaring, 'my name may be quite unknown to you — I am a Manchester man — that is all — '. Most were, as the prohibitionist John Kempster candidly admitted, 'just such a list of names as we can get upon any temperance society in any town in the country'.[6] Because the Executive adhered rigidly to the principle of collective responsibility it is difficult to identify the contribution of any individual on it, and consequently it gives the impression of having been a peculiarly anonymous, faceless body. Its members were efficient organisers and administrators, something one might expect to flow naturally from a business background. Their links with the northern business world and Nonconformity enabled them to attract Nonconformist backing and financial support, but they were not well equipped to extend the influence of the Alliance beyond this somewhat restricted orbit. Their most significant weakness was a lack of familiarity with or understanding of the political life of Westminster. While several attempted to get into parliament, only Benjamin Whitworth succeeded, and he was almost entirely inactive while in the Commons.

The Executive was elected each year at the annual general meeting and the re-election of serving members was usually routine. Owing to the practice of collective responsibility, no individual could be identified with any action likely to alienate Council members sufficiently for them not to re-elect him. The only exception was T.C. Raynor, and he had identified himself by speaking and voting against a veto candidate in an election.[7] Members retired or resigned of their own volition but were not voted out of office. Nor did the Executive as a whole ever lose the confidence of the Council sufficiently to be voted out *en bloc*. Even during the troubles surrounding the Home Rule split, dissidents backed down rather than move a motion of no confidence in it. The crucial power enjoyed by the Executive was its right to choose new members who would then be endorsed by Council. This, combined with the fact that most served for lengthy periods, meant that it was virtually self-perpetuating. Only new members with the 'right' views need be chosen, so maintaining unity and continuity. A comparison of membership in 1872 and 1895 throws up no discernible differences in composition, indeed seven of those serving in 1872 were still there in 1895. Not only was the Executive not changing, it was growing older. Towards the end of the century there was a tendency for it to attract those whose views and interests diverged increasingly from the mainstream of social thought. This was not because they differed in any respect from earlier members, it was rather that the main thrust of social thought and policy was taking new directions and prohibitionist leaders were increasingly divorced from it.

The highly centralised, oligarchical control exercised by the Executive had much in practice to recommend it. In the heat of a campaign when rapidly changing circumstances required quick responses, the Executive was usually able to make them. The private determination of policy also enabled the views of other groups and individuals to be canvassed with a minimum of publicity. The continuity of views and membership provided stability and allowed a body of expertise and a wide range of contacts to be accumulated. However there were also drawbacks. Because the Executive was secure and controlled internal lines of communication, it was impossible for policy to be modified or reversed by those who disagreed with it. With no channel through which to bring about change or organise support, dissidents were reduced to registering their disapproval as individuals only.

Rank-and-file Alliance men were satisfied with the leadership provided by the Executive until the early 1880s, but subsequently there were an increasing number of complaints. Initially these were relatively mild requests that the Executive should give 'a little more power, a little more representative power ... to the workers in this movement all over the country'. When no effort was made to do this, the attacks against what was seen as its growing 'officialism' became more frequent and determined, culminating in the campaign by William Saunders which has already been mentioned. When militant prohibitionists realised they could not persuade the Executive to pursue a more positive policy in the Commons, they began to press for changes within the Alliance which would give them more say in the determination of policy. The Executive initially attempted to suppress such demands; Saunders complained that the greater the heat generated by this issue, 'the more rigid appears to be the exclusion of all references thereto in the columns of the *Alliance News*'. Eventually the volume of complaints could no longer be ignored and the Executive was forced to search for a compromise. The result was the establishment of a Consultative Council of forty members representing local prohibitionist feeling throughout the country. It was to be convened by the Executive to deliberate on important issues and formulate policy but it failed to satisfy either Saunders or the Executive. It did nothing to undermine the absolute authority of the Executive which could sabotage its deliberations by withholding information from it, or simply refuse to convene it when a contentious issue arose. On the other hand as the Executive had feared, it provided an ideal forum for internal bickering, thus distracting attention and energies from the campaign. Ambitious or quarrelsome prohibitionists were provided with an ideal platform from which to air their ideas and grievances.[8]

From the early 1880s the Executive failed to maintain that unity and drive which had so characterised its earlier efforts. The leadership, both collectively and as individuals, had spent its formative years in the largely hostile environment of the fifties, sixties and only slightly less hostile seventies. In the more favourable climate of the eighties it seemed incapable of new initiatives; in some ways it was unable even to recognise that circumstances had changed. Attempts to preserve a non-party stance became increasingly irrelevant, particularly after the Home Rule split. Indeed this exacerbated tensions among prohibitionists who were not encouraged to face up to the fact that they must rely on the Liberal party, however dilatory it might be. The Executive's lack of understanding of Westminster and national party politics became a growing handicap as the focus of the campaign shifted from the constituencies to the Commons and Lawson's increasingly erratic parliamentary leadership magnified the problem. From the early 1880s onwards it appears to have lost its way. It managed to retain control of the Alliance, but with the exception of the compensation battles when it acted decisively, it was no longer capable of giving a strong lead and a sense of direction to the campaign.

Agents

In order to convert the policy decisions of the Executive into practical activity at the local level and also ensure concerted action on a national scale, the Alliance relied heavily on a staff of fulltime salaried agents. The number of employees increased steadily from 1853 onwards as funds became available, stabilising at around 30 from the early 1870s. These included the secretary and his office staff in Manchester, the editor of the *Alliance News* and his staff, the parliamentary and metropolitan superintendent, but the most numerous and important group were the district agents. From 1873 onwards there were usually around 19 of them, each in charge of the campaign in their own region of the country.

Within his area, it was the function of the district agent to publicise the Alliance and its activities as widely as possible, usually by means of frequent meetings in the main centres of population. This involved speaking up to five times each week, usually in the evening, as well as the attendant travelling and organisation. Subscriptions had to be canvassed, substantial contributors provided with literature, persuaded to speak at meetings and generally kept favourably disposed towards the Alliance. Local electoral organisation was entrusted to them; temperance voters had to be kept up to the mark and the electoral registers kept up to date. It was his duty to bring pressure to bear on recalcitrant MPs by persuading constituents to write letters, and send deputations and petitions to them. The problems faced by regional agents seem to have varied considerably from district to district. Generally where Nonconformists were numerous, support for the Alliance was considerable, and this greatly eased the work. Subscriptions were forthcoming, voluntary help was available and meetings easy to organise and well attended. Where this was not the case, the work was much less congenial. When speaking engagements necessitated being away from home overnight, this meant staying in an hotel rather than enjoying the free hospitality of a local supporter. R.H. Campbell, the agent for Kent and Sussex, explained the difficulty experienced in organising meetings.

My arrangements are to a great extent dependent upon the following contingencies — I. My meetings must not clash with others. II. I must take the days on which the rooms are at liberty in which the meetings are held. III. I must avoid, as far as possible, the nights on which the Good Templars Lodge meet, in the town where a meeting is held, and taking the fact into consideration, that in Kent and Sussex there are now over 100 Lodges, it is often a great difficulty to arrange satisfactorily.[9]

The most obvious feature of an agent's work was its demanding nature. The physical and mental strains were considerable, and the most common reason for the resignation of agents was that their health was no longer sufficiently good to allow them to continue. Illness resulting from overwork was an occupational hazard; sometimes it was cumulative, as a result of a long period of hard work, sometimes it resulted from specific events. Richard Coad became seriously ill because he 'slept in a damp bed in Birmingham', while John Newton was reduced to 'a state of nervous irritability' as a result of a strenuous period of electioneering.[10] The work was also destructive of family life as the agent frequently needed to be away from home for considerable periods of time and this then forced his wife to act as an unpaid secretary.

Within the temperance world a position as an Alliance agent carried much prestige and was greatly sought after. Unlike the Anti-Corn Law League which found it difficult in its early years to recruit agents of sufficient calibre,[11] the Alliance was never short of applicants of the required quality. There existed a large reservoir of talent from which to choose the creation of the temperance movement since the 1830s. All those appointed had previously been active in some branch of temperance work, either as agents or voluntary workers, and consequently most were in middle age before becoming Alliance agents, but once appointed they tended to stay for long periods of time. If they did move, they used their position with the Alliance as a stepping stone to a higher position in the temperance hierarchy. W. Jones became secretary of the Irish Church of England Temperance Society, and W. Wilkinson became secretary of the Irish Temperance League. There was no fixed salary scale for agents. The starting salary of a new agent could vary between £80 and £150 a year, depending on his reputation, but was usually around £120. From then onwards increases depended on his effectiveness, and eventually reached about £200 per year with a fortnight's paid leave. This placed them comfortably at the top end of the lower-middle-class income scale, but was probably less than they could have earned had they been prepared to give up temperance work. W.S. Caine, a businessman himself, believed that, 'if they chose they could get other positions in commerce, or in the insurance world … at three or four times the remuneration that they are getting from a cause that they will not leave, because they love it'.[12]

Undoubtedly agents did regard their work as something more than simply a source of income. Most, if not all, were committed to temperance work and only left it for more remunerative employment because of circumstances outside their control. Alliance work allowed them to live and work in a congenial and familiar environment. Several were Nonconformist preachers and at least eleven were members of the Independent Order of Good Templars. The District agent was a major figure in the local temperance community. When E.C. Brambley moved to a new district after spending five years at Norwich, he was presented with a gold watch and chain by local temperance men, and his bible class gave him an inkstand. He was praised as 'the life of the temperance movement in Norwich and the controlling energy of the movement in the Eastern counties'.[13] Such demonstrations were common. Paradoxically this close identification between agents and the 'world' of temperance and Nonconformity limited their usefulness to the Alliance. It meant that they were not well equipped for spreading the gospel among groups or individuals outside their own range of religious experience, social environment or level of income. There is no suggestion that agents made, or even attempted to make converts from among the unskilled *residuum*. Most had grown up in the temperance world and taken the pledge when young. The reformed drunkard, conspicuous in the early temperance societies, was notably absent. Similarly when an attempt was made to win the support of someone of wealth or influence, the Executive preferred to undertake the task itself, or entrust it to another eminent supporter of similar religious or political persuasion to the person being approached. Agents were ideally equipped to preserve the existing basis of Alliance support, but not to extend it.

The high esteem in which the Executive held its agents was not shared by outsiders. The *Newcastle Journal* complained of 'those fiery-eloquent, glib-tongued, and slightly abusive gentry, who now swarm over the country with their cooked statistics, threadbare pictures of intemperance and popular clap-trap'. In an age when movements for social reform and philanthropy were dominated by wealthy amateurs, a 'paid agent' was often used as a term of abuse. The trade levelled several complaints against Alliance agents. First, it claimed that their approach to the problem was less than sincere. Because they had a financial stake in what they were doing, they had no wish to see the Alliance finally succeed. Secondly, because they had 'to depend on "sending the hat round" for what they earn, they are bound to keep things up to the sensational pitch, even if they have to do so by maligning their neighbours, and conspiring against their property'. While there was probably little truth in the first accusation, the second is more difficult to rebut. There was undoubtedly some justice in the complaint of the *Saturday Review* that agents tended to adopt a 'holier than thou' attitude. The paper observed that 'it must be very pleasant to feel that the maintenance of oneself and family is bound up with the success of a righteous cause, and thus to make sure of success at once in this world and the next'.[14]

While the Executive did not accept such criticism it took care to ensure that district agents had no say in the formulation of policy. Any attempts by them to do so were frowned upon. There were however a small number of salaried officials whose relationship to the Executive was less clearly defined and who did influence policy. James Hayes Raper began as a member of the Executive, then became the Alliance parliamentary agent at a salary of £500 per year until 1878, before once more rejoining the Executive. His familiarity with Westminster, its moods and procedures, was invaluable and no initiatives were taken in this direction before he had been consulted. Thomas H. Barker was the secretary of the Alliance from 1853 until his death in 1889, also on a salary of £500 per year. 'He was not only an official of the Alliance, he was one of its founders ... and from first to last took an influential part in its innermost counsels, having much to do in determining and carrying out its policy'. Henry Sutton, editor of the *Alliance News* 'ingeniously turned almost every event of the day into an argument for the prohibition of the liquor traffic', and through his editorials helped mould the attitudes of thousands of prohibitionists. The Reverend Dawson Burns, a founder member of the Alliance, became its Metropolitan Superintendent, London Correspondent of the *Alliance News* and an important voice in the temperance world through his writings.[15]

From the 1880s onwards, closer links between the Liberal Party and the Alliance brought about a change in the emphasis of agency work. Before the demise of the Permissive Bill, energies had been directed towards attracting support for it from any quarter, but once Liberals had pledged their support for local option, agents were increasingly concerned to work for the return of Liberal MPs and the defeat of Tory MPs. This increasingly involved them in party politics at the constituency level. Liberals found it convenient to utilise their services, particularly during elections. Agents had much to offer; they had usually been working their area for many years and knew its politics and personalities intimately, and they were also experienced in election work and could deliver a bloc of temperance votes to a sympathetic candidate. Because of their usefulness, agents enjoyed a growing influence in local Liberal politics and they increasingly joined local selection committees hoping to ensure that temperance sympathisers were selected as candidates. Several went further. E.C. Brambley frequently attended NLF conferences as a regional delegate and three agents were endorsed as parliamentary candidates, although none of them were elected.[16]

This open alignment with the Liberal party alienated some prominent prohibitionists who were either Tories or who wanted to avoid any involvement with party politics. In an attempt to avoid dissension the Executive instructed agents that they 'should not take office on the Committee of any political party', but did not punish those who transgressed.[17] The political activities of agents caused periodic squabbles from the 1880s onwards but the Executive did not take sterner disciplinary action against them because it seems to have realised that while it must observe the letter of its constitution and remain politically neutral in order to retain the support of moderates, agents were nevertheless adopting the right course.

Auxiliaries

The Anti-Corn Law League provided the Alliance with a precedent for the establishment of local auxiliaries throughout the country. The Executive assumed that these would perform the same functions as an agent. In addition they would be a tangible sign of local support and a means by which local temperance men could feel that they were extending their influence to the national level. They were established with astonishing rapidity; by 1855 there were 111 and by 1857 they had increased to 176. This was a reflection of the initial burst of enthusiasm following the formation of the Alliance, but most were ephemeral and became inactive almost as soon as they had been formed. Often they ousted long established local temperance societies but were unable to fulfil the community functions which the older organisations had provided; their *raison d'être* was not to fulfil local needs, but to promote a national campaign. In the smaller centres particularly this does not appear to have been enough to keep them in existence. Most of the early auxiliaries made little contribution to the campaign. The Executive soon realised that they were more trouble than they were worth and made no attempt to revive those that were flagging or extinct.

By the 1870s only a handful remained but they continued to play an important, if sometimes disruptive, role in the campaign for the rest of the century. In England their number fluctuated between eight and thirteen, the most important were in London and Birmingham, with others in Leeds, Sheffield, Hull, Leicester, Portsmouth, York, Bristol, Newcastle-on-Tyne, Bath, Barrow-in-Furness and Brighton. The Executive was never particularly happy working with auxiliaries. Frequent splits within their leadership reduced their effectiveness, embarrassed the Executive and cost it a great deal of time and effort acting as a mediator in situations where the Alliance had nothing to gain and much to lose in the form of support and subscriptions. George and Richard Cadbury refused to give their very substantial donations to the Birmingham auxiliary because they disagreed with the views of some of its leaders. Auxiliaries also displayed a tendency to become involved in purely local political issues where the interests of the Alliance were not involved. The Executive usually only became aware of this after the event, when the damage had been done. As money became scarce, the Executive picked on auxiliaries as the first target for economies. It finally came to the conclusion that 'districts are more efficiently and successfully worked under the care of agents than when entrusted to local bodies'. To this end it began to discourage the formation of new auxiliaries and in 1885 unsuccessfully attempted to take over the Sheffield auxiliary which had been the scene of much squabbling among local temperance men. Reductions in grants and the responsibilities of auxiliaries helped hasten their decline. John Kempster, honorary secretary of the London body, complained that 'there is some danger of seriously diminishing interest in our work. The duties and responsibilities of the Committee become very slight and formal when so little work remains to be directed by them, and so small a sum placed at their disposal ...'[18]

Relations between Manchester and London were frequently strained for another reason; London was potentially an alternative headquarters for the Alliance. There were sporadic attempts by other auxiliaries to decentralise Alliance operations. It was suggested for example that the annual general meeting should sometimes be held in other large towns, and also that auxiliaries should have a greater say in the determination of policy, but the Executive firmly dismissed all these suggestions. However London was a different matter for a permanent base there was vital for the parliamentary campaign; J.H. Raper pointed out that 'U.K.A. could not exist as a *National Organisation* without *London Offices* proximate to Parliament. It *could* exist without an Office in Manchester'. When economy measures were being discussed, one prominent supporter suggested the abolition of the Manchester offices. The leaders of the Anti-Corn Law League had been subjected to similar pressures.[19]

The precedent established by the Anti-Corn Law League in the use of auxiliaries did not prove a happy one when copied by the Alliance. Relations between the Executive and the auxiliaries during the last thirty years of the century can be seen as an intensifying battle over centralised control versus local autonomy, with the Executive gradually gaining the upper hand.

Income

Finance was the life-blood of the Alliance. Its income at any time limited and determined to a large extent what actions it could take. The Executive was well aware of this and the *Minute Books* are filled with references to 'the state of the finances'. This sometimes obsessive concern with finance has left the historian with a valuable mine of information. An examination of the sources of income provides clues as to the nature and sources of support for the Alliance, while patterns of expenditure indicate the priorities of the Executive and allow some conclusions to be drawn about the costs and effectiveness of the campaign.

Table 1 outlines the financial history of the Alliance between 1868 and 1899. It is clear from the table that the Alliance reached its financial zenith long before its political influence had reached a peak.[20] Income rose steadily throughout the sixties before rising dramatically to nearly £23,000 in 1872, almost double the level for the previous year. During the next four years income remained buoyant and then declined annually to reach about £15,000 by 1881. Apart from minor fluctuations it then remained at about this level for the rest of the century. Despite vigorous fund-raising efforts, annual income in 1899 had fallen to a level only marginally above what had been achieved in 1871. Consequently, at times when the Alliance should have been in a position to exert itself to the utmost, over compensation in 1888 and 1890, and on behalf of the Veto Bills in 1893 and 1895, it was unable to do so. Its finances were already seriously undermined with a permanent and growing deficit being accumulated each year. Lack of money proved a crippling handicap. This was a far cry from the vast inflows of money enjoyed by the Anti-Corn Law League in the 1840s, but it is the dominant theme running through Alliance activities from the late 1870s onwards.

Donations were the main source of Alliance funds, accounting for over four-fifths of all income in 1872. As with many other Victorian

Table 1: **Actual Yearly Income and Expenditure of the Alliance**
(Current prices)

Year	Income (£)	Expenditure (£)	Yearly surplus loss (£)	Accumulated surplus loss (£)
1868	12,431	11,712	+ 719	+ 1,724
1869	12,573	12,893	− 320	+ 1,404
1870	13,293	12,387	+ 906	+ 2,310
1871	13,985	13,101	+ 884	+ 3,194
1872	22,987	22,460	+ 527	+ 3,721
1873	22,177	20,874	+ 1,303	+ 5,024
1874	20,694	20,141	+ 553	+ 5,577
1875	18,634	21,284	− 2,650	+ 2,927
1876	19,974	20,419	− 445	+ 2,482
1877	18,224	18,179	+ 45	+ 2,527
1878	17,176	18,067	− 891	+ 1,636
1879	16,018	16,056	− 38	+ 1,598
1880	15,515	15,403	+ 112	+ 1,710
1881	15,185	15,192	− 7	+ 1,703
1882	15,149	15,295	− 146	+ 1,557
1883	15,011	15,174	− 163	+ 1,394
1884	15,102	15,087	+ 15	+ 1,409
1885	14,362	14,278	+ 84	+ 1,493
1886	13,738	14,302	− 564	+ 929
1887	14.176	14,073	+ 103	+ 1,032
1888	14,893	16,120	− 1,227	− 195
1889	15,525	15,289	+ 236	+ 41
1890	15,519	15,380	+ 139	+ 180
1891	14,656	14,952	− 296	− 116
1892	14,446	16,710	− 264	− 380
1893	16,779	16,926	− 147	− 527
1894	15,366	15,513	− 147	− 676
1895	15,860	15,938	− 78	− 753
1896	15,519	15,401	+ 118	− 635
1897	15,582	15,855	− 273	− 908
1898	15,299	15,553	− 254	− 1,163
1899	14,448	14,722	− 274	− 1,437

Source: Annual Reports.

charities, most appear to have been solicited rather than given spontaneously. The Executive showed great ingenuity and resourcefulness in extracting money. Its main weapons were the district agents who spent much of their time canvassing for funds. Once a person had made a donation he was a marked man and was expected to continue to hand over his money from year to year. Continuous visits by agents and begging letters were designed to ensure this was the case. Agents concentrated on small subscribers giving less than £10. If there was a possibility of a much larger donation from someone of great wealth, Alliance men of greater reputation and influence were called on. J.W. Owen, the electoral secretary of the Alliance, wrote:

> Yesterday Mr. Coad and I were at Taunton, making calls — we went to the house of the President of their Temperance Society, who is a rich man ... unfortunately he was out of town, or we had good hopes of £5, — but on second thoughts we thought it was better to ask Mr. B. Whitworth to write to him, and his letter would considerably increase what he would have given us ... he is a great admirer of Mr. Whitworth, and very likely to reply favourably.[21]

Some members of the Executive spent a great deal of their time trying to persuade business acquaintances to subscribe to the Alliance. William Hoyle exploited his connections within the northern cotton exchanges to this end; a visit by him to Bradford resulted in a donation of £500 from Angus Holden. Charles Thompson was so successful at this kind of work he acquired the name of 'Beggar General'. Even such lofty figures in the temperance hierarchy as W.S. Caine, were prepared to canvass for funds. Those who went after new donations were not easily turned away; 'some people to whom they applied refused them at first, but when they talked nicely to them they generally brought out the money'. Sometimes, one suspects, more in an effort to get rid of the intruders than from genuine conviction. Some collectors positively gloried in this work; Charles Thompson believed 'it was a great charity to those who had so much wealth to relieve them of a portion'. Less direct, but no less effective pressure was applied at Alliance annual meetings. After the usual appeal for funds 'subscription papers' were handed among the audience to be filled in. During intervals between speeches these were handed back to the secretary and the large donations from Lawson, Trevelyan, Whitworth and others were read out to encourage others to emulate such generosity. In the enthusiasm generated in Manchester each year perhaps not a few subscribers were persuaded to demonstrate to all their generosity by increasing the amount of their donation.[22]

A problem peculiar to all organisations relying largely on donations is the uncertainty surrounding the size of their income from year to year. This makes long term planning a hazardous process. Such difficulties are particularly acute for bodies like the Alliance which used so much of its income to pay for the services of agents; it is much easier to increase or decrease the output of literature according to the availability of resources, than it is to do the same thing with people. The Alliance sought to get around this problem by adopting the technique of the 'guarantee fund'. Used successfully by the Anti-Corn Law League, this was a means of ensuring future income by asking subscribers to donate a certain sum of money spread over the number of years for which the fund was to run. The first Alliance Guarantee Fund was started in 1865, to run for five years with an initial target of £30,000, later raised to £50,000. This was successfully achieved thus ensuring the organisation an annual income of around £10,000 each year between 1865 and 1870. A second five-year fund of £100,000 was announced at the end of 1871 after major donors had been quietly contacted to gauge their reactions. This also was a success, £58,000 having been promised within the first few days.

Donations to this second Guarantee Fund were dominated by a small number of large subscribers. An examination of income in the peak year of 1872 shows that 44 individuals each giving £100 or more accounted for almost half of all income from donations. No less than 17 of these lived in Lancashire, including 10 from Manchester, while another 16 came from other northern counties, particularly Yorkshire. Twenty-six are known to have been Nonconformists but only three were Anglicans. At least 27 derived their major source of income from business, including 18 who were involved in some branch of the textile industry. The Church and the professions were not represented and only two, Lawson and Trevelyan, derived their wealth from land. It was largely the benevolence of northern manufacturers which allowed the Alliance to expand in the early 1870s.

Further guarantee funds were mooted at various times in the 1880s and 1890s, but preliminary enquiries among leading subscribers indicated that they would not reach their targets and so none were formally launched. Consequently from 1877 onwards the Alliance was once more in a position where it did not know from one year to the next what its income would be. Large subscribers were asked to state as early as possible how much they were willing to give in the following year but this was a dubious guide as the gap between promises made and the amounts actually given gradually grew wider. Towards the end of each year, whenever it appeared that expenditure was likely to outstrip income, district agents were forced to spend more of their time canvassing for funds. Fund-raising efforts were intensified and sometimes they betrayed a hint of desperation.[23] This was an indication that the relative stability of Alliance income from the beginning of the 1880s was deceptive, for it was only sustained by sometimes massive diversions of resources away from the campaign to the collection of subscriptions. In the early seventies enthusiasm and optimism had readily been translated into extra income, but subsequent advances did not evoke the same response. Between 1871 and 1872, income had grown by £9,000, but the first passing of the Local Option Resolution and a Liberal victory in 1880 resulted in a fall in income of nearly £500. The first compensation victory in 1888 brought in an extra £700, but only after strenuous fund raising, while the second victory in 1890 brought no increase at all. The Liberal victory in 1892 resulted in a £200 fall in income, the first Veto Bill in 1893 an increase of £300, and the second Veto Bill in 1895 an increase of only £500.

Table 2: Number of Large Contributors to Alliance Funds

	Giving £1,000	£100-999	£10-99	Total nos.
1872	3	41	237	281
1877	4	15	122	141
1882	2	17	124	142
1887	2	10	110	121
1892	0	11	137	148
1897	0	9	115	124

Source: Annual Reports.

The Alliance consistently advanced two reasons for the falling off in income evident from the late seventies; namely 'the decrease of some of its more wealthy and generous friends ... [and] the depressed condition of the textile industries and other large industries throughout the country'.[24] While this is only a partial explanation, it does isolate one distinctive trend. Table 2 clearly indicates a decline in the number of large subscribers. The proportion of all donations provided by large subscribers showed an equally marked decline. Those giving £10 or more in 1872 provided 72 per cent of all income from donations, while those giving £100 or more provided 48 per cent; twenty years later these percentages had fallen to 38 and 16 respectively. This was due in part to the death of subscribers. Of the four people, Lawson, Benjamin Whitworth, Sir W.L. Trevelyan and James King of Rochdale (who donated under the psuedonym XYZ) who each gave £5,000 to the second Guarantee Fund, only Lawson was still alive by 1894. Of the 44 people who had given £100 or more in 1872, at least 27 had died by 1892. Large numbers of those who embraced temperance and prohibition as young men in mid-century were being lost to the movement as the century drew to its close.

The most worrying feature for the Alliance was its failure to replace these losses. It was forced to recognise that 'it does not always follow that the son is equal to the father in these matters'.[25] The prohibitionist movement failed to appeal to the younger generation of wealthy manufacturers, to the extent that it had done to their fathers. Only two sons of donors in 1872 emulated the generosity of their fathers. Reasons for this can only be speculated upon. Money in the seventies came from first generation industrialists, usually Nonconformists, for whom the Alliance was a means of social amelioration and a method of political self-assertion. With the second generation, there was perhaps a decline in reforming zeal, and other more direct means of wielding political influence. The move from Nonconformity towards the Anglican church was only one symptom of a shift in interests and lifestyles. Those with philanthropic impulses were increasingly bypassing the Alliance. The spread of the joint-stock company may also have had an effect. The wealthy head of the family firm became less common and managers and directors needed to consult shareholders' interests before donating large sums to reformist pressure groups, particularly those with a radical flavour.

Death was not the only reason for a decline in large donations. Many subscribers were unable to maintain the size of their donations because of a drop in their own incomes. Economic historians still disagree about the existence and nature of the so called 'Great Depression' between 1873 and 1896. Most are agreed that it was not so severe or complete as contemporaries thought, but regardless of what was happening at the national level, individual manufacturers sometimes found themselves in trouble. The most dramatic instance was the failure in 1893 of Shaw's Brow Iron Co. from which W.S. Caine drew most of his income. Charles Watson of Halifax was forced to reduce his annual donation due to a big fall in his income from his railway shares while William Hoyle, who 'had made up his mind to leave no fortune to his children if he had also to leave the liquor traffic in the country',[26] was forced to give less because of the poor state of the cotton trade. Lawson himself, a large landowner drawing his income from rents, also seems to have felt the impact of depression in agriculture. From giving £1,000 a year up to 1882 (apart from the donations of other members of his family) he could then manage only £500 a year up to 1887, nothing in the following year and only £20 in 1894 and 1895.

The reasons for fluctuations in the amounts given by other large subscribers are more difficult to determine. Benjamin Whitworth who had given £1,000 per year up to 1878, then gave nothing more apart from two donations of £20 in 1881 and 1882, before his death in 1893. This may have been due to a drop in his personal income but this is unlikely; alternatively he could have become disillusioned with the movement, or merely complacent. Both were the cause of lost subscriptions from other individuals. William Saunders refused in 1888 to give more to the Alliance because of his failure to persuade the Executive to democratise the organisation, and because of what he felt were failures of leadership. Similarly Edward Whitwell reduced his donations because the Alliance failed to take a strong stand on the question of Sunday closing.[27]

There was a feeling within Alliance ranks that some wealthy supporters were not pulling their weight. 'There is no doubt whatever', said W.S. Caine, 'that we do not, in proportion to our wealth and in proportion to the advantages that we have derived from Temperance, subscribe as we ought to'. He believed that as a minimum every teetotaller should subscribe not less than the amount which he would otherwise have spent on drink. Jonathan Hargrove fulminated against the 'scores of men who have got fat through our movement. Where are they now? What is the good of Pope Q.C. for instance?'. Caine reflected on the list of two hundred or so subscribers from Manchester itself. A few gave very large amounts, but most only a pound. He believed that 'there are lots of men among the hundred who could just as well give £100 as they can give a sovereign. People seem to think that their conscience is cleared if they subscribe, and they give the traditional guinea.' He also complained that he spoke at many large temperance meetings in other cities to audiences of over a thousand well dressed and well fed temperance men, yet these same towns gave few donations to the Alliance. In Durham for example he attended 'a very choice meeting indeed. I might have been in a fashionable West End church, to look at the people', but the town had only eight Alliance subscribers giving a total of £4.[28]

Although their relative importance would be difficult to assess, all these factors probably contributed to some degree to the decline in the number of large subscribers. As against the 44 who gave £100 or more in 1872, there were only 11 twenty years later, seven of whom came from the northern counties, including three from Manchester. Three came from London and one from Worcestershire. Six were in business, but only one in textiles. Two, the Crossley brothers, drew their incomes from the same family engineering firm. On this evidence the great northern textile magnates had deserted the Alliance. Five of the 1872 donors were still alive in 1892 but were no longer prepared to give so liberally.

The Alliance increasingly saw its typical subscriber as someone earning between £150-400, who gave £1-2 a year. The loss of large subscribers was offset to some extent by a growth in the number of these small donors. In 1872, 4,832 of them had given amounts of more than five shillings but less than £10 each, whereas by 1892, their number had almost doubled to 8,743. These people were becoming the financial backbone of the movement, increasing their proportion of all subscription income from 28 per cent in 1872, to 62 per cent twenty years later. The Executive had always been concerned to attract small subscribers because they gave the movement a more representative character, suggesting that its support was broadly based. Large subscribers even went so far as to split up their donation among members of their family in order to make it appear more 'representative'. It is likely that many small subscribers were salary or wageearners and consequently their incomes were less susceptible to economic fluctuations than were those of large donors reliant on the profits of business and commerce. During the 'Great Depression' incomes assessed for income tax continued to rise and this, combined with the fall in prices, suggests that salaried employees were enjoying rising real wages. An increasing reliance on small donors made the Alliance more secure, because it was less vulnerable to the death or defection of one wealthy individual, but it also meant that agents spent more of their time collecting subscriptions. This left them less time for campaigning. A decline in the average amount given by each small subscriber, from 22 shillings in 1872 to 18 shillings in 1892, worsened the situation. In May 1879 for example 700 donations were collected, but they amounted to only £360.

A comparison of subscription lists in 1872 and 1892 suggests several tentative conclusions. Support for the Alliance was becoming geographically more dispersed. In the 1870s most small subscribers lived in the north and west, particularly in the industrial areas. Lancashire

alone provided 22 per cent of all income from this source and Yorkshire 14 per cent. By 1892 an increasing number of small donations
came from the south and east, particularly from London and the
Home Counties. London had become the most important single
source of income with 9 per cent of the total as against 4.5 per cent
from Manchester. While the philosophy of prohibition was barely
holding its own in the industrial areas of its birth, it was winning new
converts among lower-middle-class clerks and small retailers in the
south. Prohibition appears to have attracted such people because it
was a means by which middle-class values and associations could be
acquired and a clear line drawn between them and the unrespectable
working classes. By the nineties it had also become a philosophy of
social amelioration which did not threaten the massive state intervention implicit in increased taxation, unemployment relief and the
provision of pensions. It was becoming the refuge of the individualist
in an increasingly collectivist age.[29]

Expenditure

In the early years of the Alliance campaign clear priorities were established in the allocation of funds, with expenditure on printed propaganda consistently taking over half the total budget. However as
income gradually rose, the agency network was extended and salaries
absorbed an increasing proportion of funds, from 15 per cent in 1854
to 30 per cent by 1872. In the early 1870s the greatly increased income
provided by the £100,000 'Guarantee Fund' allowed a rapid expansion
of activity but the same priorities were observed. Salaries, agency
expenses and spending on public meetings doubled, while spending on
printed propaganda, the *Alliance News*, tracts, books and pamphlets
more than tripled. Despite this burst in expenditure, the growth of income had been such that a large surplus was left after each year's
operation, reaching a peak of over £5,500 in 1874 (see Table 1).

The Guarantee Fund came to an end in 1876 with the Alliance still
far from victorious and thereafter income fell. In the same year the
Executive concluded that it was over-extended and began to look for
ways of cutting expenditure. Spending on printed propaganda was
pruned back drastically and grants to auxiliaries were reduced. These
reductions were 'arranged so as to be the least painful to the officials
and Agents' in order to 'keep the agitation as comprehensive and as
efficient as possible'.[30] This became the pattern for the rest of the
century and the costs of the agency network, which had absorbed only
30 per cent of income in 1872, took nearly 50 per cent by 1897. During

the same period salaries of all kinds rose from 30 to 50 per cent of expenditure. Thus from 1876 onwards there was a complete reversal of earlier priorities. This change stemmed from the changing nature of the Alliance campaign. As it moved away from a mass agitation aimed at parliament and towards a policy designed to capture the Liberal party by electoral activity, manpower became more important than the printed word.

The necessary reduction in expenditure was carried out efficiently up to 1885. The network of district agents remained intact and annual losses were only very small, as can be seen from Table 1. These were more than adequately cushioned by the accumulated surpluses of the early seventies, so a credit balance of more than £1,000 was always available for the next year of operations. The Executive was helped in this by the lack of any issue requiring a major campaign effort. The 1880 election did not involve any increase in expenditure, and Lawson's passive approach in parliament also helped. However 1886 was a bad year; while expenditure did not rise, income fell to its lowest level for almost twenty years, and the result was a deficit of over £500. The finances of the Alliance came under serious attack for the first time from other temperance societies. They complained that it had absorbed most of the funds available to the temperance movement but had nothing to show for it. The Executive took this seriously and because of 'the failure of the finances' began planning drastic economy measures. Three agents and two other employees were dismissed and the grant to the London auxiliary was further reduced.[31] Worse was to follow in 1888. Several large subscribers were forced to reduce their donations, amounting in all to about £1,800, and further reductions were planned, but before these could be implemented the fight against the Tory compensation proposals began. Expenditure increased by £2,000 and despite a special anti-compensation fund which brought in £1,200, the year ended with an operational deficit of £1,200. As the accumulated reserves of earlier years had been exhausted, the Alliance ended a year in the red for the first time. This was a shattering blow to the morale of the Executive and Charles Thompson threatened to resign unless the situation improved.[32]

The Executive considered that a further £2,000 per annum was needed if the Alliance was to be kept on a sound financial footing. This was not forthcoming, but any further reduction in expenditure involved dismantling some part of the agency network, thus impairing the efficiency of the organisation and its ability to mount a national agitation. This could not be countenanced because of the need to mount major campaigns against the compensation proposals of 1890 and in favour of the Veto Bills of 1893 and 1895. In all these battles the Alliance was crippled by a lack of finance and this does much to explain why in propaganda campaigns the trade was usually able to gain the upper hand. Unable to back down and thereby sacrifice its credibility, the Executive simply had to accept the growing deficits which were being incurred. By 1898 these amounted to over £1,000. Despite its 'rigid rule never to anticipate our income', the Executive was forced in 1895 to raise a bank loan of £1,200 to enable the campaign to continue.[33]

The financial plight of the Alliance would have been even worse had not the Executive increasingly run the organisation along business lines. Members utilised their business background and experiences in devising ways of ensuring that propaganda activities yielded some return. In 1872, public meetings cost £2,535 and income from the sale of tickets amounted to only £175, giving a net loss of £2,360; by 1892 the cost of public meetings had been reduced to £367 and the income from tickets to £126, giving a net loss of only £241. During the same period the net loss on the sale of pamphlets, books and tracts fell from £1,705 to £217. The most significant savings resulted from improved management of the *Alliance News*. A weekly copy of the paper was sent free to all who subscribed ten shillings or more. This imposed a degree of financial inflexibility on the organisation because some part of its income was always earmarked for this purpose and could not therefore be put to other uses; by the 1880s and 1890s this amounted to between 10 and 12 per cent of total income. By building up the paper as an advertising medium, advertising revenue was increased fivefold and a considerable loss was turned into a small profit.

The Executive prided itself on its financial management. Benjamin Whitworth claimed that 'the Government might certainly learn the art of economy from the Alliance'.[34] As the emphasis switched from printed propaganda to manpower, the Executive claimed that this was the most effective and economical method of pursuing its objectives. Operating on 'the principle of the lever', agents could initiate activity at the local level which would then snowball into a national campaign.[35] In 1886 expenditure amounted to about £44 per 100,000 people in England and Wales, and the agency network accounted for about £24 of this. With the outlay of such a modest sum the Alliance was able, two years later, to lead a successful national campaign against compensation. This was a spectacular example of what could be achieved by a careful use of modest resources but it does not fully illustrate the implications of the decision to concentrate on manpower rather than the printed word.

By adopting this policy the Alliance found it difficult to respond flexibly in the face of fluctuations in income from year to year. It was much more difficult to vary the number of skilled agents it employed than it would have been to vary the output of printed propaganda. On the other hand, because the work of district agents was divided between agitation and subscription collection, fluctuations in yearly income could be minimised by diverting more of the time of agents to canvassing for funds during bad years. The danger however was that the organisation could slip into a situation where its continued existence was reliant on an undue diversion of the time of agents away from campaigning to fund raising. Then, when a major agitation had to be mounted, income would fall drastically. This was exactly the position which the Alliance found itself in and its financial fragility was cruelly exposed by the fight against compensation in 1888. From this time onwards it takes on the appearance of a body whose major effort is geared to self-preservation. W.S. Caine frankly acknowledged that income in these years was 'simply keeping the machine going, and the least extra pressure ... drives them to the bank'.[36] Brewers were wrong in accusing agents of wishing to perpetuate the Alliance campaign, they should instead have blamed the Executive, whose orders the agents were simply carrying out. The decision to retain the agency network in the face of a falling income allowed the organisation to continue, but deprived it of any opportunity of reacting flexibly to changing circumstances. Some of the hostility it faced in these years stemmed from this. However much the Executive might have wished to redouble its campaign, it was financially incapable of doing so. Paradoxically its apparent lack of action alienated some subscribers, thus further reducing income and consequently the strength of the agitation which could be mounted.

Notes

1. David Owen, *English Philanthropy 1660-1960* (1965), p. 129, quoted, and taken to task by Brian Harrison, 'Philanthropy and the Victorians', *Victorian Studies*, vol. IX, no. 4 (June 1968), p. 365.
2. *1st Meeting of Members of the General Council* (1853), p. 2.
3. *Alliance News*, 25 Oct. 1879, p. 672.
4. Lawson to W.E. Gladstone, 27 Sept. 1891, *W.E. Gladstone Papers*, BM Add. MSS. 44513, f. 185; quoted in Fahey, p. 151.

5. The following observations are based on biographical information in A.E. Dingle, 'The Agitation for Prohibition' (Monash University PhD, 1974), appendix 1.

6. F.W. Crossley to W.E. Gladstone, 6 September 1896, *W.E. Gladstone Papers*, B.M. Add. MSS, 44523, f. 233; *Alliance News*, 22 Oct. 1881, p. 674.

7. See above, p. 100.

8. *Alliance News*, 22 Oct. 1881, p. 674, 2 April 1887, p. 224; *Minutes*, 8 Feb. 1888, 8 March 1893.

9. R.H. Campbell to T.H. Barker, 19 Feb. 1873, loose in *Minutes* for 1873.

10. *Minutes*, 22 Nov. 1893.

11. N. McCord, *The Anti-Corn Law League, 1838-1846* (1958), p. 176.

12. *Alliance News*, 30 Oct. 1893, p. 708.

13. Ibid., 4 Aug. 1877, p. 482.

14. Ibid., 4 Nov. 1871, p. 727; *Licensed Victuallers Gazette*, 24 Dec. 1870; *Saturday Review*, 19 Oct 1872, p. 498.

15. *37th Annual Report 1889*, p. 7; W.E. Adams, *Memoirs of a Social Atom* (1903), vol. 2, p. 387.

16. See Dingle, 'The Agitation for Prohibition', pp. 485-90 for further details.

17. *Minutes*, 5 June 1889.

18. Ibid., 30 April 1884, 30 April 1890, 2 July 1884, 24 June 1885, 12 Feb. 1890.

19. Ibid., 21 July 1886; McCord, *The Anti-Corn Law League*, pp. 178-9.

20. If income and expenditure are expressed in constant prices (as Brian Harrison has done in *Drink and the Victorians* (1971), p. 230) the period of peak income is pushed back to the mid-1890s. Although the price fall experienced during the 'Great Depression' was undoubtedly real and considerable, it was selective; the salaries of skilled labour and rents appear to have fallen hardly at all. It was the misfortune of the Alliance to have spent most of its income on those goods and services where there was no significant fall in price. See S.B. Saul, *The Myth of the Great Depression 1873-1896* (1969), pp. 14-15, 30-34.

21. J.W. Owen to T.H. Barker, 24 May 1879, loose in *Minutes*.

22. *Alliance News*, 25 Oct. 1879, p. 675, 16 Oct. 1886, p. 664, 17 Oct. 1885, p. 662.

23. For an example, see Dingle, 'The Agitation for Prohibition', pp. 514-15.

24. *31st Annual Report 1883*, p. 61.

25. *Alliance News*, 22 Oct. 1881, p. 677.

26. Ibid., 28 Oct. 1876, p. 690.

27. W. Saunders to Executive, n.d. in *Minutes*, 1 Aug. 1888; ibid., 2 Oct. 1889.

28. *Alliance News*, 30 Oct. 1891, p. 708; *Minutes*, 15 May 1895.

29. *Alliance News*, 2 Jan. 1891, p. 9.

30. *Minutes*, 9 April 1879.

31. *Alliance News*, 30 Oct. 1886, p. 698, 704; *Minutes*, 14 July 1886.

32. *Alliance News*, 13 Oct. 1888, p. 815.

33. Quoted in Harrison, *Drink and the Victorians*, p. 234.

34. *Alliance News*, 29 Oct. 1870, p. 346.

35. Ibid., 19 March 1887, p. 192; 26 March 1887, p. 208.

36. Ibid., 30 Oct. 1891, p. 708.

Chapter 9

CAMPAIGNING

By the mid nineteenth century reformist groups seeking to bring about change through the mobilisation of public opinion were numerous and knowledge of their methods was widespread. It was the Anti-Corn Law League which most clearly influenced the Alliance in its early years. Not only had it won a great victory, it had done so with the help of some who later joined the Alliance. Samuel Pope, J.H. Raper, Joseph Brotherton and Archdeacon Sandford had all been active in the League campaign. By developing the same kind of organisation and adopting similar methods, prohibitionists expected that good would triumph over evil in the sphere of drink as it had with free trade.

The Alliance declared in 1853 that its object was to 'call forth and direct an enlightened Public Opinion' to procure prohibition.[1] Its early progress owed much to the ease with which it could adopt techniques which had already been tried and tested by others. There were obvious advantages in being able to do this, but there were also drawbacks as it encouraged a belief that more of the same signified progress. There was a temptation to go on using established methods in a mechanistic way without exploring possible alternatives. At one time or another the Alliance used most of the techniques employed by other groups; public meetings, mass demonstrations, petitions, the distribution of tracts, pamphlets, newspapers and other literature, deputations to politicians and other influential people, were all tried.[2] It assumed that in this way the weight of public opinion would bring about a speedy victory and was puzzled when this did not happen. The very longevity of its campaign meant that the social and political environment in which it operated was changing, and differed increasingly from that which had faced the League. The growth of the newspaper press after the repeal of paper duties, the growth in literacy consequent upon the spread of formal education, an expanding electorate as well as the emergence of more clearly defined political parties, all posed new problems and opened up new opportunities. As its perceptions of how it might succeed changed, the Alliance abandoned some techniques as inefficient and modified others in order to make more effective use of the resources at its disposal.

Public Meetings

The public meeting was a central feature of most reforming campaigns in Victorian England. It was a way of attracting support and also of demonstrating to governments the extent of such support. The Alliance used it more extensively than any other campaign technique. As early as 1855 more than 500 Alliance meetings were held during the year throughout England, Wales, Scotland and Ireland. By 1877 the number had risen to over 2,000 with an aggregate attendance of nearly 500,000 and by 1888 it was nearly 4,000 with an attendance of over a million.

The sheer number of meetings is impressive, between eight and ten every day of the year from the 1870s onwards, but such figures need to be interpreted with caution. Attendance at individual meetings varied enormously from as few as 30 people to the 80,000-100,000 who turned up at the few mass demonstrations staged in London. Estimates of attendance were provided by agents and temperance men and are likely to have erred on the optimistic side. The vast majority of meetings were small, with an audience of 50-200, most of whom were already temperance men.[3] Because of the regularity with which meetings were held, such people would find no difficulty in going to several during the course of a year. The figures for aggregate attendance must be seen in this light; if 30,000 prohibitionists (the formal membership of the Alliance as early as 1856) went to an average of ten meetings each year this alone would give an aggregate attendance of 300,000.

Nineteenth-century reformers have been accused of having a faith in speech making that was 'often pathetic'. While few had great oratorical gifts, 'lecturing helped them think that they were accomplishing something'.[4] To what extent did this verdict apply to the Alliance? To be precise about the impact of such activity is impossible, but some inferences can be drawn. It has been suggested that the quality of a reforming movement's argument varies inversely with the strength of public support for its policy. Until the movement has a sure footing it needs to defend itself by argument; but once it is accepted and makes progress, it tries rather to bludgeon its opponents by assertions about the rightness of its cause and the inevitability of its ultimate victory. Certainly the educational content of Alliance speeches was always far smaller than that of teetotal lectures such as Livesey's famous 'Malt Lecture' of the 1830s, or of Anti-Corn Law League speeches of the

1840s.[5] The 'factual' approach was favoured. This meant the use of often half-digested statistical information on the volume of drinking, of expenditure on drink and of the extent of crime, lunacy and poverty that resulted. This, coupled with quoted testimonies from doctors, magistrates, and anyone else who had denounced drink, was considered to be 'proof' of the evil of drink, and the desirability of prohibition.

A feature common to all Alliance meetings, whatever their size, was that they were rather boring and repetitious to anyone not already half convinced of the viewpoint being advanced. The *Saturday Review* claimed that the Alliance possessed 'the longest-winded speakers and the most patient hearers that were ever combined for any public project'. Hugh Mason pointed out that there were so many meetings that it was no longer possible to bring out fresh arguments in favour of prohibition; 'yet I do think that you are perfectly content to hear even the same arguments reiterated and repeated'. These arguments were always framed in a way which was designed to appeal mainly to those who had already given up the use of drink. Joseph Chamberlain pointed out that while the Alliance case might convince total abstainers, they 'might not be so persuasive with persons like himself, who had never yet been able to see any inherent wrong in the moderate use of drink'.[6]

There was much truth in such a claim. The Alliance was convinced that it had a great deal of popular support; the demand for local option it insisted came 'absolutely from the people themselves'. Lawson identified his supporters as 'the flower of the working classes in all the large towns of England'. The evidence of their own eyes convinced Alliance leaders that their meetings attracted the most intelligent and industrious of the working classes. G.O. Trevelyan addressed his audience as 'you, the aristocracy of the working classes'.[7] These people were the product of wider economic social and religious movements in mid-nineteenth-century Britain. Nonconformity, the rise of the 'labour aristocracy', and the early 'moral suasionist' phase of the temperance movement had thrown up groups for whom prohibition as a philosophy was likely to appeal, and on whom the Alliance could draw for support. Imbued with the Smilesian ethic of self-help and the desire for social elevation, such people had already identified drink as a barrier to their advancement. Consequently by the 1870s the Alliance was operating in an environment containing a pool of potential supporters whose outlook was identical in most respects to that of prohibitionists. Here we find the reason for the relative lack of educational content in Alliance speeches when compared with those of the early temperance movement. For Joseph Livesey with his 'Malt Lecture', the object of his reforming desires faced him. He needed to demonstrate to his audience that drink was bad for them and that they should therefore abstain from it. He and his fellow workers had done their work sufficiently well to allow prohibitionists to assume that this basic educational task had already been fulfilled. Alliance audiences were for the most part already abstainers, and they now had to be persuaded to support the Permissive Bill as the best means of saving the country from the drink curse.

To what extent was the Alliance successful in spreading its message among the more traditional and, as it believed, drink-sodden elements of the working class? As the voice of the working man was hardly ever heard on the subject, conclusions are difficult to arrive at. While prohibitionists were undoubtedly sincere in wishing to save their fellow men from drink slavery, most did not display the missionary zeal so evident in groups such as the Salvation Army. Temperance men emphasised the distinction between themselves and those below them. They did not live in the slums, indeed teetotalism was a means of escape from them. Therefore if they did penetrate the slums in a missionary role, they came as strangers and were regarded as objects of ridicule or curiosity, fanatical representatives of an alien culture. This seems to have been true in the 1870s and has remained so up to the present time.[8] The gap always proved too wide to be bridged. W.S. Caine lamented that while Alliance meetings were always unanimous in support of the Permissive Bill, nine out of ten people 'did not have the remotest idea what it was'; he was implicitly recognising the dichotomy between the 'rough' and the 'respectable' portions of the working class and the gulf between them. Philip Snowden pointed out that temperance teaching from temperance platforms 'is given to the people who do not require conversion, and if it reaches the ear of the sinner it fails to strike conviction because of the prejudice against its source'.[9]

Drinkers undoubtedly attended Alliance meetings, especially the mass demonstrations and the larger provincial meetings, but it is difficult to determine if they were persuaded by what they heard as they were given no opportunity to voice their views. Alliance meetings were always superbly orchestrated. Resolutions to be submitted were always carefully prepared beforehand, and the result was usually a near unanimous verdict in favour of local option. All criticism was regarded as destructive and ruthlessly suppressed. Opposing speakers were shouted down and interjectors thrown out of the meeting; even reports of meetings in the *Alliance News* omitted any reference to speeches or interjections hostile to the purpose of the meeting. All doubters and opponents were classified as tools and lackeys of the drink trade and prohibitionists had no scruple about intimidating them into silence. Without any avenue through which to voice legitimate criticism, opponents either kept quiet or resorted to physical violence. At times when the political temperature was high many meetings were disrupted and riot and injury sometimes resulted. This enabled prohibitionists to pose as defenders of 'public order and the right of free speech in public assemblies ... rights too precious for Englishmen ever to yield to the clamour of a drunken band of public-house rowdies'.[10]

Most meetings throughout the country were small, orderly, and given over almost entirely to preaching to the converted. They were not primarily meant to attract support, nor were they seriously intended to impress politicians with the extent of popular backing for prohibition. A central feature of the campaign from the 1870s onwards, they were primarily a device to sustain morale. A difficulty facing all reform movements whose focus of attention is Westminster is one of generating and maintaining the enthusiasm of supporters in the face of so distant an objective. By meeting constantly to declare their faith in prohibition they could retain their enthusiasm and feel that they were making an active contribution to the campaign. They could also create an identity and the unity of outlook so necessary for sophisticated forms of agitation such as organised electoral action. 'It may be taken for granted', declared the Executive, 'that it is essential to the success of the prohibition movement that a strong body of well-instructed and thoroughly-convinced Temperance reformers should exist in each centre of population'.[11] These gatherings of the faithful relied heavily on the artefacts of nineteenth-century Nonconformity. Meetings were held in chapels, Nonconformist schoolrooms, temperance halls and Good Templar Lodges. This provides a clue to the membership of these prohibitionist elites. Those who used the chapel on Sunday could most easily find their way there during the week. Alliance activity at the local level fitted comfortably into the pattern of Nonconformist community life.

The most important of these inspirational gatherings was the annual general meeting held in Manchester. Prohibitionists met together in a congenial atmosphere remote from the hostility their ideas often provoked elsewhere. They could enthuse each other and optimists could indulge in wish fulfilment with little fear of contradiction. 'At these meetings strong meat was what they liked', declared Councillor Tugwell of Scarborough, and it was usually provided in abundance. Speeches were filled with exhortations to greater effort and prophecies of imminent success. Lawson and Pope found the enthusiasm of Manchester invigorating after the machinations and deceits of life in London. 'Let us go to our homes', urged William Hoyle, 'and innoculate all the constituencies of the country with the spirit that animates us today'.[12] The hurdles facing prohibitionists did not appear insurmountable while they were among friends in Manchester.

Literature

All nineteenth-century reformist pressure groups realised the power and potential of the written word and used it extensively. The prominent Halifax prohibitionist, Charles Watson 'believed in the printing press' and was convinced that any reform movement, 'always had to go hand in hand with the printers'. The tract was the earliest and most pervasive medium of propaganda; in the days before mass circulation newspapers it was cheap, easy to produce and distribute. Some prohibitionists were obsessively devoted to it; A.E. Eccles distributed fifty million at his own expense between 1853 and 1909, and Charles Watson distributed eight million in one year alone. They had marked well the words of Neal Dow, the pioneer of prohibitionist legislation in Maine, who had said that 'temperance literature had to be scattered knee-deep in Maine before they enacted the Maine Liquor Law'.[13]

Initially the Alliance produced general educational tracts and moral tales for widespread distribution among the masses. By the 1860s however prohibitionists were coming to the conclusion that it was not the masses who needed education, but those of higher social status who continued to demonstrate their indifference to the drink problem. Consequently tracts and pamphlets were increasingly directed towards a specific event, a specific problem, or a particular group of people. The recipients were MPs, clergymen, doctors, trade unionists and others of similar official or social status. This was very much a policy of 'horses for courses'. Those commissioned to write such works were usually in contact with those to whom they were directed, for example Canon Farrer wrote *On the Duties of the Church*, and William Hoyle a whole series on drink and depression which were directed at the business community. This approach was precise and economical. Once a target had been chosen resources were directed towards reaching it, and it alone. It avoided the waste inseparable from broadcast tract campaigns of the kind mounted by the Anti-Corn Law League. While the Alliance would have liked to indulge in these, it increasingly found that they were beyond its means. When an Alliance Convention in 1887 wanted to deliver to every elector in the country 'a packet of literature bearing on the object and policy of the Alliance', the Executive estimated that the exercise would cost slightly more than the total Alliance income for that year.[14]

However an economical way was found of reaching a wider audience with educational material. 'People's editions' of substantial works were printed, advertised widely, and sold cheaply. The most successful project of this kind was William Hoyle's book *Our Natural Resources and How They are Wasted*. First published in 1871, by 1873 it had gone through four editions, each of 10,000, in a fairly expensive 'library or drawing room' form costing three shillings and sixpence. This was followed by a cheap shilling edition of 20,000 which sold out rapidly. In June 1873 a 'people's edition' of 100,000 was issued at 4d a copy and by October 60,000 had already been sold. The Alliance claimed that it was 'one of the cheapest books ever produced in the English language'. It also had a lasting impact. A quarter of a century later J.A. Hobson ruefully complained that he had never addressed any audience on socioeconomic subjects without having Hoyle's 'fallacious argument brought up by some "temperance" member of the audience ... whose sole intellectual equipment for the study of society consisted in the little stock of facts and figures ... gathered from the writings of Mr. Hoyle'.[15]

The newspaper press always occupied an important position in the Alliance approach to popular agitation. 'The Pulpit is a great force, the Platform is a mighty power', declared the Executive, 'but the Press is a uniting agency that educates and gives intelligent direction to both'. It believed that 'the general press is the highway to the homes and minds of the general public, and is read where special appeals are never heard'.[16] Consequently it was important that the Alliance case was given a frequent airing in the general press. Liberal provincial newspapers, particularly the *Western Morning News* and the *Eastern Morning News*, both of which were owned by the prohibitionist William Saunders, gave it wide and fairly sympathetic coverage. This was a great help, but its propaganda value was limited because the circulation of such newspapers tended to be limited to groups of people who were already predisposed towards the Alliance. They went mainly to provincial Radicals and Nonconformists who usually required little persuading of the merits of the Permissive Bill or the veto.

The London daily press always remained much less sympathetic. In the minds of prohibitionists this was but one aspect of the dichotomy between 'provincial' and 'London' opinion. Alliance arguments were never sufficiently persuasive to attract consistent editorial support from any of the London-based national dailies. Nevertheless, in order to remain in the public eye and hope to influence legislators it was necessary to get a hearing in the national press. In the easy financial conditions of the seventies it was possible to do this by buying advertising space but the shortage of funds in later years made this approach prohibitively expensive. It was perhaps to the advantage of the Alliance that the behaviour of prohibitionist 'extremists' was so often deemed newsworthy by the national press because this allowed the resulting criticisms to be rebutted, usually at great length, in the letter columns of the newspapers concerned. The press was also prepared to publish and comment upon general items on drink and temperance such as William Hoyle's yearly 'National Drink Bill'. *The Times* always inserted this, but consistently refused to draw from it what the Alliance considered were the correct conclusions. In the absence of editorial support, what prohibitionists most needed were not debates in the letter columns of the press, but the systematic and widespread publication of temperance news.

The Alliance was slow to face up to this problem, but when it did, its solution showed a great deal of professionalism and ingenuity. A London press agency, initially known as the News Correspondence Agency, but later the Alliance Press Agency, was established in Fleet Street in 1889. This collected and prepared temperance news from both Britain and overseas for distribution to the daily and weekly press throughout the country. All correspondence to the press was also directed through this central point for wide dissemination. A syndicated 'Prohibition and Temperance Notes' and a 'London Letter' were distributed to over 200 newspapers each week in addition to the distribution of individual news items both by post and telegraph. Much of the material appears to have been rather mundane but was welcomed and inserted by the news-hungry provincial press. On occasion the agency also managed to achieve national prominence, playing for example a major role in the battle against compensation in 1890. It also achieved several 'scoops', including the report of Gladstone's intention to vote for the Scottish Veto Bill, which were eagerly snapped up by the national press. The agency was sufficiently success-

ful to attract the attention of the trade which compared its own inadequate efforts in this direction with the resourcefulness of the
Alliance.[17]

The Alliance's own newspaper, the *Alliance News*, played an
important part in the campaign for prohibition, but was used in a
different way than was the general press. Founded as a four-page
weekly in 1854, it grew to 16 pages by 1871 and 20 pages by 1888. It
was 'the backbone of the entire organization ... the vitalising means of
communication between the Executive and the members and friends
of the Alliance all over the world'. It was in short an instructional
manual for prohibitionists. Through its pages they were informed of
forthcoming meetings, of actions taken in parliament, of when and
how to form electoral associations, begin petitions or send deputations
to local MPs. The active prohibitionist was expected to read it
regularly. If he omitted to do so, he '*must* be much less fully equipped
for his work than he ought to be'. The chances of this happening were
minimised by its gratuitous circulation to all who gave ten shillings or
more to Alliance funds each year. The paper was thus a link in the
chain of command from Manchester to the localities, performing
complimentary functions to those of the agency network. It was also a
means whereby the Executive could exert its authority and control the
flow of information to Alliance supporters. Any material likely to be
controversial or divisive was omitted from its pages whenever
possible.[18]

As the campaign came to rely increasingly on the activities of an
elite of prohibitionists in each region, particularly from 1872 onwards,
the *Alliance News* became increasingly important. It proved an ideal
means by which prohibitionists could preserve the exclusiveness,
purity and morale so necessary to motivate them when surrounded by
a drink-sodden environment. Through its pages they were informed of
products they might want, services they might require and entertain-
ment they could enjoy, all free from the taint of alcohol.

There were periodic requests that the *Alliance News* should also be
used as a medium through which to make converts. In 1885, as a result
of the promptings of William Hoyle, an attempt was made to trans-
form it into a popular national weekly with a circulation of
50,000-100,000 copies. Despite its low price, the Executive frequently
boasted that it was 'the *largest and cheapest penny weekly paper in the
entire kingdom*',[19] there were several reasons why it could not easily
become an effective propaganda weapon among the unconverted. Its
appeal was too narrow. It carried little general news and while the

lengthy reports of speeches at innumerable local meetings pleased prohibitionists who saw their views being given wider circulation, they did not interest anyone else. The basic difficulty was a conflict of function. What prohibitionists wanted from the newspaper in order for it to fulfil its primary purpose was not compatible with any attempt to win new support. When 'lighter' material and more general news was included at the expense of reports of local meetings, even the editor complained of the 'peculiar wants of the modern reader', who needed 'his literary bread cut up into small and neat slices, each buttered on one side, and, if possible, sugared on the other'.[20] The rapid growth of the provincial press also meant that any attempt to increase circulation ran into severe competition.

Circulation figures for the Alliance News were never published, but information contained in the annual financial statements allows some estimates to be made. In 1869-70 total circulation amounted to nearly 15,000 of which nearly 5,000 was a 'gratuitous' distribution to subscribers. This grew to a total of nearly 20,000 in 1891-2 with a 'gratuitous' distribution of 11,000, before falling back to 15,000 with a 'gratuitous' distribution of over 10,000 by 1894-5. When the extent of 'gratuitous' distribution is taken into account, it can be seen that an increasing proportion of the circulation was going to existing Alliance men rather than the unconverted. This was a reflection of the growth of small subscribers to Alliance funds towards the end of the century. By 1895, only about 5,000 copies each week were likely to reach the unconverted, half the number that had done so a quarter of a century earlier. Despite efforts to the contrary, the propaganda role of the *Alliance News* declined with the passing years. Increasingly it became an 'in house' newspaper.

'Fervent Prohibitionists'

The most potent weapon in the Alliance campaign armoury was the fervent and convinced prohibitionist himself. The Alliance always sought to teach by example and the prohibitionist was a living demonstration to his fellow men of the benefits to be gained from renouncing the use of alcohol; in addition he was a means by which the prohibitionist case could be taken into places and among people where it was not known. In a society divided along class lines, the ruling elite did not, in the normal course of events, come into contact with the temperance movement which was socially, geographically and theologically alien to it.[21] Most politicians did not attend temperance meetings, and it is unlikely that they read the temperance literature sent to them in such large quantities, but it was these very people which the Alliance had to win over if it was to succeed. There were two ways in which this could be done; prohibitionists could approach them in person, and they could also attempt to win over those agencies in society which were likely to influence the opinions of politicians.

Many examples of direct approaches to politicians have already been noted. A feature of these approaches from the 1870s onwards was the assumption that politicians were more likely to be persuaded by pressure of numbers rather than by force of argument. This was most evident in deputations to those considered hostile to the Alliance. The Executive tried to get 200 prohibitionists to serve on a deputation to Bass in order to 'show him the necessity of either voting for the [Permissive] Bill or of pairing'. Cross was subjected to similar treatment while Home Secretary in 1875. He agreed to see a small deputation, but much to his surprise 120 prohibitionists turned up in an attempt to browbeat him. He pointed out to them that 'the force of a deputation did not lie in its numbers, but in the arguments it adduced', but to no avail. The Alliance continued to delight in treating politicians harshly and gloried in the presence of 'truculent teetotallers in the Lobby threatening those who came to perform their constitutional duty'.[22]

Prominent men outside the political sphere were approached with much greater finesse. It was important to win the support of 'opinion makers' because they not only influenced the opinions of politicians, but that of the nation as a whole. The Alliance concentrated particularly on religious bodies, philanthropists and the medical profession. This was a reflection of the basic tenets of the prohibitionist faith; drink was poisonous physically and socially, and the attack on it was at once a moral crusade and a major social reform. Prominent men in these fields were initially sent Alliance literature and if they showed any interest, they were then asked to see a deputation. Whenever possible, the deputation included someone who had professional, religious or social links with the person being approached. The support of Henry Brougham and Cardinal Manning were the most notable successes achieved by these means,[23] but there were many others, particularly within the Church. The Alliance was concerned at what it believed to be a 'beer and bible' alliance during the 1874 election and immediately attempted to attract the support of prominent Anglicans. Within a few years the bishops of Manchester, Gloucester, Lichfield, Exeter, Peterborough and Newcastle had all been won over. Sir H. Kay-Shuttleworth later pointed out that 'whole classes of well-intentioned good Christian men ... would join ... *if it were understood* that they were not committed to any legislative proposals beyond local option'.[24] The Executive was quite willing to oblige and treated such people with the utmost care and consideration.

Annual conferences were the scene of much Alliance activity. Prohibitionists were present at the National Agricultural Labourers Conference in 1872 and 1873 and also at the Co-operative Congress. In 1874 the Alliance financed a soirée for delegates to the Trades Union Congress in order that they might meet a delegation of prohibitionists. The main focus for such activity was the annual denominational conference of the various Nonconformist churches where pledges of support for the Alliance were almost invariably given. Because of its links with conservatism, and its political influence, the Anglican church was also an important target, but because its assemblies were inaccessible to the Alliance, other methods of influence had to be used, the most favoured being the ministerial conference. The most successful of these was convened by the National Temperance League and organised and financed by the Alliance in November 1874. Over 900 ministers attended and decided to draw up a 'Clerical Memorial' which recognised the right of local control and demanded legislative action on the drink question. Circulated by the Alliance, this was signed by over 7,800 clergymen before being presented to the Archbishop of Canterbury in 1876. It was eventually signed by 13,584 clergymen, almost two-thirds of all the Anglican clergy, including 15 bishops, 22 deans and 67 archdeacons, and was later printed by the Alliance and used as propaganda. After receiving the Memorial, the Archbishop of Canterbury demanded a thorough investigation of the drink problem and instigated the setting up of the Select Committee of the House of Lords on Intemperance. The Alliance then did its utmost to influence the course of the enquiry. It initiated the formation of the United Temperance Committee in London, upon which all the major national temperance societies were represented, in order to provide the Lords Committee with 'the best possible evidence on the various points relating to intemperance and its causes'.[25] Several Alliance men, including A.E. Eccles, William Hoyle, Dawson Burns and R.M. Grier gave evidence, as did medical men opposed to the prescribing of alcohol. Ultimately all these efforts came to nothing because the *Report* of the Committee published in 1879 strongly favoured a trial of Chamberlain's scheme of municipal control and attacked the Permissive Bill, but by their drive and initiative prohibitionists had forced the question of temperance reform into areas where it had not previously been much considered.

There was less room for such initiatives in the medical field simply because the Alliance did not possess the required expertise. Only F.R. Lees through his writings had any influence on the prescription of alcohol by doctors. The use of alcohol as a restorative had become widespread from the 1830s onwards, but by the 1860s was increasingly challenged as a result of experiments by medical men into the properties of alcohol and its effect on the human body. What the Alliance and other temperance societies did was to publicise the results of such work as widely as possible. Articles opposing alcoholic prescription by prominent medical men such as B.W. Richardson and Norman Kerr were featured prominently in the *Alliance News*, and annual meetings of the British Medical Association were attended by prohibitionists who distributed literature and ran public meetings addressed by doctors who were opposed to the use of alcohol. By the 1870s alcoholic prescription had been effectively challenged and its use in hospitals declined markedly. Manning was probably exaggerating when he claimed in 1882 that temperance men had 'either conquered or converted the doctors', but they had played their part by publicising medical advances.[26] In their approach to philanthropists and social reformers prohibitionists were much less reticent than with the medical profession because they regarded prohibition as the fundamental prerequisite for any attempt at social amelioration and wished to impress this upon all other reformers. The annual congresses of the National Association for the Promotion of Social Science provided the best opportunity to do this. Initially Alliance efforts were hindered by aristocratic and trade influence, but it made its first major step forward by winning the support of Henry Brougham, the Association's president. By the 1880s temperance men had triumphed, and temperance legislation had become virtually the Association's only remedy for the social evils of the day.[27]

Self-interested pressure groups such as trade unions and professional associations seek to act as spokesmen for particular sections of the community and are usually regarded as such by the governments they seek to influence. Reformist pressure groups seeking to promote the 'national good' on the other hand assume the role of spokesmen for the millions, but have difficulty in persuading governments that they represent anyone other than their formal membership, which might be very small.[28] We are left then with the problem of deciding whether the Alliance was leading a mass popular movement which had originated spontaneously in local communities and was subsequently given leadership, direction and stability, or whether it was an organisation which sought to generate the manifestations of popular support and impress the existence of these upon parliament. The crux of the problem lies in deciding if the initial and sustaining impetus came from local communities, or from the centre, from Manchester. Did the Alliance manufacture opinion, or simply articulate and direct it? In practice this is a difficult distinction to draw. The Alliance did not publish membership figures but from the evidence of subscription lists and the circulation of the *Alliance News* it would appear that formal membership never rose above 30,000 at any time and was normally nearer 20,000. While it always claimed to enjoy wide popular support it needed to do more than point to packed meetings of temperance reformers in order to persuade governments that this was so. It also had to demonstrate that the drinker was prepared to support local option. While it could attract 50-100,000 people to mass rallies in London, many of them presumably drinkers, the trade could attract similar numbers to argue the case against prohibition. Politicians attempting to assess the popular mood were understandably puzzled as to the real degree of support enjoyed by both sides. They were suspicious of the claims made by pressure groups because the techniques of manufacturing public opinion had reached high levels of sophistication by the last quarter of the nineteenth century. A student of the phenomenon noted that

> The Association for the Total Suppression of White Hats! The Anti-Flower-in-the-Button-Hole League! ... The Local Option Snuff Federation! ... For each and all of these associations the moralist might easily find a *raison d'être*; and for each and all he would be able, in the present temper of the public, to obtain powerful committees, patrons, presidents and vice-presidents, auditors, treasurers, honorary secretaries, and the rest of the familiar machinery used by the imposing body of hobby-rides and zealous conductors of other people's business who are active in every part of the Empire.[29]

Many considered that the Alliance was just such an organisation and were given some justification for doing so by the pronouncements of prohibitionists. When W.E. Gladstone expressed his bewilderment over the real tenor of public opinion, W.S. Caine exasperatedly asked him to 'tell us what evidence will satisfy him, and I promise it shall be forthcoming in full measure, pressed down, and running over, before he has time to prepare another Queen's speech'.[30] He was quite confident that the Alliance could engineer whatever demonstration of opinion Gladstone might require.

The very structure of the Alliance was more appropriate to the manufacture of public opinion than to the leadership of a grass-roots popular movement. It was highly centralised, with control remaining firmly in the hands of the Manchester Executive; the direction and force of the agitation was determined here rather than in the localities. The lines of communication and instruction radiated outwards from the centre, thus allowing the Executive to begin a nationwide agitation at a moment's notice and with machine-like precision. This is not to suggest that the Alliance was insincere in what it did, or that there were not large numbers of enthusiastic prohibitionists spread throughout the country. Undoubtedly there were, but they were never numerous enough to sweep all else aside. The Alliance was never able to generate a momentum strong enough to sweep everything else off the front page of the national press and make local option the burning political issue of the day, in the way that free traders and Chartists had done. Prohibition surfaced only when other questions did not dominate the political stage.

Alliance claims to be leading a mass popular movement grew less credible as the campaign progressed. The crucial turning point came in the early seventies. Attempts during the sixties to bring the pressure of public opinion to bear on parliament as a whole culminated not in the enactment of legislative prohibition, but a moderate licensing measure. The Alliance did not conclude from this that the weight of public support it had mustered was inadequate, but rather that the politicians themselves were obdurate and refused to reflect the views of their constituents. The main barrier to prohibition, it believed, was not a lack of public backing, but the hostility of Westminster. On this analysis, instead of redoubling its efforts to win mass support, the Alliance decided to develop new methods of bringing pressure to bear on the politicians themselves.

The policy of organised electoral action adopted in 1872-3 was designed for this specific purpose. It was adopted because traditional approaches had failed. The ensuing concentration on this method of agitation explains much that was distinctive about the Alliance and its tactics in the last quarter of the century. Electoral work required the creation and maintenance of a body of enthusiastic and disciplined political activists in every constituency, rather than widespread popular support. The Alliance primarily needed to attract support from those with money to keep the organisation functioning, and those with votes to apply the pressure. The average working man often had neither. Even if he possessed the vote, he was unlikely to ignore all other political considerations and cast his vote solely for prohibition. His main use was to turn up to the occasional mass meeting in order to provide an audience and give vocal support. At other times his lack of singlemindedness was likely to be a hindrance rather than a help; as long as he was not actively hostile to local option, this was all the Alliance required. Supporters of pressure groups are not a homogeneous commodity. Some possess money, others political contacts, social prestige, administrative skills, or voting power. From the early seventies, the Alliance developed a method of agitation which made best use of its strengths, the money and voting power of middle-class provincial Nonconformists and 'labour aristocrats', to bring pressure to bear on its main target, the MP, without needing to rely much on manifestations of mass popular support. By these means it could, as *The Times* complained, 'exercise a power over the House of Commons out of all proportion to its real strength'.[31]

While the Alliance continued to use campaign methods originally designed by others to attract and demonstrate the existence of widespread support, it increasingly put them to new use. The agency network, public meetings, and the *Alliance News* were all increasingly geared to the needs of the prohibitionist activists. They could not effectively fulfil this function and also attract the uncommitted, hence Alliance attempts to win new supporters were limited mainly to those who were already members of the 'temperance army'.[32] Brian Harrison has suggested that in the 1860s there existed a group of well under 100,000 active teetotallers and at least a million adult abstainers. By the end of the century the numbers of such people had increased considerably for adult membership of the two largest teetotal societies, the Independent Order of Rechabites and the Sons of Temperance, had risen from 23,109 in 1870 to 356,457 in 1910, and there were somewhere between three million and six million total abstainers in all.[33] It was from among these people, many of whom were already 'institutionalised' as members of temperance societies, that the Alliance hoped to increase its support. It had left the primary task of conversion to teetotal principles to other agencies, but once this had been achieved, sought to politicise these people by drawing them into the campaign for prohibition. This campaign relied not on mass popular support, but on teetotal support. While it sought by legislative means to save the working man from drink slavery, the task was entrusted to a teetotal elite who had no need of local option.

Notes

1. *First Meeting of the General Council of the UKA*, 1853, p. 2.

2. The use of these techniques is discussed in some detail in A.E. Dingle, 'The Agitation for Prohibition' (Monash University PhD, 1974), pp. 539-604.

3. *37th Annual Report 1889*, p. 45.

4. Herman Ausubel, *In Hard Times* (Columbia 1960), p. 75.

5. Brian Harrison, *Drink and the Victorians* (1971), pp. 227, 235.

6. *Saturday Review*, 19 Oct. 1872, p. 497; *Alliance News*, 11 Feb. 1871, p. 92; ibid., 25 Nov. 1871, p. 775.

7. *Hansard*, 3rd series, vol. 278, c. 1283; *Alliance News*, 18 Nov. 1871, p. 748; ibid., 27 January 1872, p. 72.

8. For attitudes in the 1860s see (Thomas Wright), *Some Habits and Customs of the Working Classes by a Journeyman Engineer* (1867), pp. 131-51; for 1900s, Robert Roberts, *The Classic Slum*, pp. 94-5; for the 1930s, Mass Observation, *The Pub and the People* (1943), ch. 11, esp. pp. 327-8.

9. *Alliance News*, 8 March 1873, p. 155; Philip Snowden, *Socialism and the Drink Question* (1908), p. 80.

10. *Alliance News*, 6 May 1871, p. 289.

11. *36th Annual Report 1888*, p. 33.

12. *Alliance News*, 19 Oct. 1872, pp. 735-6, 21 Oct. 1871, pp. 666-7.

13. Ibid., 17 Oct. 1874, p. 661, 22 Oct. 1881, p. 678.

14. *35th Annual Report 1887*, p. 19.

15. *21st Annual Report 1873*, p. 34; J.A. Hobson, 'The Economics of Temperance: A Rejoinder', *Commonwealth*, vol. 1, no. 9 (Sept. 1896), p. 318.

16. *Alliance News*, 15 Jan. 1887, p. 40; *7th Annual Report 1859*, p. 3.

17. *Breweries and Distilleries*, Nov. 1890, quoted in *39th Annual Report 1891*, p. 54.

18. *20th Annual Report 1872*, p. 64; *32nd Annual Report 1884*, p. 39.

19. Quoted in B.H. Harrison, ' "A World of which we had no conception". Liberalism and the English temperance press: 1830-1872', *Victorian Studies*, vol. 13, no. 2 (1969), p. 138 (original emphasis).

20. *Alliance News*, 7 Feb. 1885, p. 81.

21. Harrison, ' "A World of which we had no conception" ', pp. 125, 143.

22. *Alliance News*, 26 April 1873, p. 230, 19 June 1875, pp. 388-9; *Hansard*, 3rd ser., vol. 278, c. 1292.

23. For Brougham, see Harrison, *Drink and the Victorians*, p. 237, for Manning, see A.E. Dingle and Brian Harrison, 'Cardinal Manning as Temperance Reformer', *Historical Journal*, vol. XII, no. 3 (1969), pp. 488-9.

24. Kay-Shuttleworth to Barker, 18 Oct. 1887, in *Minutes*, 19 Oct. 1887.

25. Ibid., 19 July 1876.

26. Harrison, *Drink and the Victorians*, pp. 306-7; Sir Victor Horsley and Mary Sturge, *Alcohol and the Human Body* (5th edn, 1915), pp. 4-5; *Alliance News*, 6 May 1882, p. 274.

27. B.Rodgers, 'The Social Science Association 1857-1886', *Manchester School of Economic and Social Studies*, vol. 20 (1952), pp. 305-6.

28. Allen Potter, 'Attitude Groups', *Political Quarterly*, vol. 29 (1958), pp. 72-82.

29. Blanchard Jerrold, 'On the Manufacture of Public Opinion', *Nineteenth Century*, vol. 13 (1883), p. 1080.

30. *Hansard*, 3rd ser., vol. 278, c. 1297.

31. *Times*, 9 May 1873.

32. The phrase was used in *Alliance News*, 20 Oct. 1883, p. 662.

33. Harrison, *Drink and the Victorians*, p. 317; J. Rowntree and A. Sherwell, *The Temperance Problem and Social Reform* (8th edn, 1900), p. 5; G.B. Wilson, *Alcohol and the Nation* (1940), p. 257.

Chapter 10

CONCLUSIONS

Despite the Alliance campaign legislative prohibition of the drink trade never became a reality in England. With the benefit of hindsight this is hardly surprising. Prohibition has not been conspicuously successful in any of the modern nation states in which it has been tried, and nineteenth-century England offered what was in many ways the least promising environment in which to try so drastic a social experiment. It challenged at many points a society in which drink and the drinking place performed a wide variety of indispensable functions without offering any practicable substitute. It also threatened the very existence of a powerful vested interest which was unwilling to stand by and be a spectator to its own demise. Such obstacles were too great for the Alliance to overcome.

The attractions of an alcohol-free utopia were not sufficiently persuasive for most people to accept that drink was intrinsically evil. It was excessive drinking which gave them cause for concern and which they regarded as a fit subject for reform and consequently there was never any concensus that drink should be completely prohibited. For this reason permissive prohibition stood no chance of being widely adopted even if it had succeeded in reaching the statute book. By the end of the century this fact was plain even to the Alliance. In retrospect its programme can be seen as a curious half-way house between the individualism of early Victorian England and the collectivism of the twentieth century. By seeking to enlarge the social responsibilities of the state, it helped undermine the foundations of the former and prepare the way for the latter, but of itself it was neither one thing nor the other and in an extended time perspective its appeal proved transitory. The Permissive Bill, local option and the veto were symbols of provincial pride and independence and Nonconformist morality. As the strength of such drives were eroded, so also was the demand for prohibition.

Given the magnitude of the task it had set itself the remarkable thing about the Alliance campaign was not that it failed, many Victorian reforming crusades failed to attain their stated objectives, but that it so nearly succeeded in placing permissive prohibition on the statute book. Having failed up to 1871 to generate enough mass support by traditional methods to ensure the passing of prohibitory legislation, the Alliance then changed direction and began a campaign designed to capture a major political party which could then be used as a vehicle through which to achieve reform. The task was a difficult and laborious one, as this study has shown. Alliance leaders were often tactically inept and rank-and-file prohibitionists frequently squabbled among themselves over the lengths to which they should go in exerting pressure, but enough pressure was exerted to eventually persuade the Liberal party that the support of the Alliance was important and worth paying for. This result was achieved not by the force of argument and logic which prohibitionists could muster to their cause, but rather by their ability to exert *political* pressure. On the one hand they were able to win over Liberal constituency organisations to their point of view, and on the other, they were willing to withdraw their electoral support from politicians who did not agree with them. This was the work not of a mass popular movement, but of a relatively small group of well organised and dedicated political activists.

The success of prohibitionists as political agitators was based on two factors. First and most important were the qualities they themselves brought to the task. They were enthusiastic, dedicated and persistent, and the Alliance was at once an embodiment of their aspirations and also a vehicle through which these qualities could be organised and directed. Secure in the knowledge that they were pursuing the right course they were able steadfastly to ignore the torrent of ridicule and criticism poured on them by politicians, the press and polite society and proceed with their campaign. Secondly, their task was made easier by the vulnerability of the Liberal party to outside pressure, particularly after the Home Rule split. Liberal leaders were wrong in assuming that an exclusive concentration on Ireland could head off sectional demands indefinitely. Eventually the very survival of the party required that they be given some tangible satisfaction. As D.A. Hamer has noted, 'the Liberals could not live with sectionalism, but nor could they live without it'.[1] The Alliance can take no credit for creating conditions so favourable to it, but it did identify them and exploit them with dogged persistence.

The social cost of the Alliance campaign was the absence of any reform which effectively grappled with the reality of excessive drinking in late Victorian England. The Alliance always claimed that it supported moderate measures which fell short of prohibition and indeed that it 'prepared the way for legislative proposals which would never have been put forward had its enlightening and stimulating influence been withheld'.[2] There is some truth in the first part of the claim to the extent that partial reforms, particularly the Sunday Closing Bills for Ireland and Wales, undoubtedly enjoyed the active and wholehearted support of prohibitionists, but any measure which posed as an alternative rather than an adjunct to prohibition was not treated so favourably. The Tory Bills of 1874, 1888 and 1890 were openly and vigorously attacked, and the last two defeated. On the Liberal side, neither the Bruce Bill of 1871 nor Chamberlain's Gothenburg resolution enjoyed the active support of the Alliance. Its position could best be described as one of critical but passive approval. The Executive made no attempt to mobilise active support, preferring on both occasions to reserve its energies for the Permissive Bill. This action must be seen in the context of a society where debate on reform was dominated by two competing groups, the temperance movement and the drink trade; any measure which aroused the hostility of the latter, but did not win vigorous support from the former, was doomed to fail.

What of the second part of the Alliance claim, that its campaign created an environment favourable to the emergence of moderate reforms? This was certainly true up until 1871 as Brian Harrison has pointed out,[3] and it was instrumental in ensuring the introduction of the Bruce Bill in that year. However its failure to support this moderate measure marked a turning point. Thereafter the Alliance kept temperance reform in the political limelight not only by its constant demands for action but also by its unwillingness to entertain any compromise short of prohibition. While it provided the impetus to legislate, it also frustrated any attempt to do so by unduly restricting the range of alternatives available. In 1892 the *Speaker* complained that prohibitionists 'had had their own way during the last twenty years which have passed since the abandonment of Bruce's Bill, and they have accomplished nothing'. That the Alliance was responsible for the stalemate became obvious even to some of its supporters. George Cadbury left the organisation because he recognised that 'the unwillingness of the United Kingdom Alliance to work for moderate measures in the direction of temperance falling short of Direct Veto was the reason why so little has been done'.[4]

Chamberlain complained that in advocating the Gothenburg resolution he had 'organisations to the right of me, to the left of me, and I was left in the middle to be supported indeed by a great body of impartial and intelligent opinion', but because he lacked organisational backing he had been 'totally unable to compete' with either the trade or the Alliance.[5] In saying this he was emphasising the defects of a political system which assumed that reforms in the public interest could emerge from the clash of competing pressure groups, but he also pointed to a more pervasive way in which the Alliance inhibited the emergence of alternatives. Because it was the dominant temperance body in politics it could monopolise political debate with the advocacy of its own solutions and its control over the means of communication within the temperance world allowed it to stifle alternatives. H.E. Bruce complained that the continual promotion of the Permissive Bill prevented proposals being aired or chosen on their merits.[6] Independent voices possessed no means of making themselves heard.

It is no coincidence that the end of the nineteenth century witnessed a broadening of the debate on temperance reform. Restrictive licensing provisions were once more being widely discussed, most notably in the *Royal Commission on the Licensing Laws*. The aim was no longer to prohibit, but to improve drinking habits and ensure the 'maximum prevention of misconduct'.[7] The benefits of public control and ownership were also increasingly canvassed, first in the form of municipal control, a revival of Chamberlain's ideas, and later in the form of national control. The campaign to provide counter-attractions was also given a boost with the establishment of the People's Refreshment House Association (1896) and other private trust companies attempting to run public houses in the public interest. This widening of the debate came in response to a clearer understanding of the nature of the problems to be solved stemming from the work of many investigators working outside the temperance movement from the late 1880s onwards, but it was made possible by the dethroning of the veto in 1895. The Alliance was no longer strong enough to dominate the debate and it could not remain immune to the fact that it had lost the initiative. Immediately after the 1895 election the letter columns of the *Alliance News* were filled with demands that it moderate its demands and show a willingness to support restrictive licensing reform. Differences of opinion among Alliance leaders over compensation and the Reports of the *Royal Commission on the Licensing Laws* have already been mentioned. Soon afterwards, T.P. Whittaker, a prominent Alliance leader, defected in order to campaign for the Gothenburg system. Formerly a leading opponent of municipal control, he rapidly became one of its most fervent advocates. All these developments were evidence that the Alliance had lost control over the debate on temperance reform.

Prohibitionists were effective political agitators but poor temperance reformers. Their determined advocacy of an idealistic but hopelessly impracticable solution prevented the passing of any workable measure of reform. Paradoxically it was those very qualities of determination, indifference to criticism and inflexibility that made them such effective agitators which also made them ineffectual as practical reformers. Thus we are left with the task of offering some explanation for the dominance of these characteristics. They stemmed partly from the nature of the Alliance as an organisation, and partly from the social background of prohibitionists.

Few if any Victorian philanthropic bodies operated in an environment conducive to the calm and patient social enquiry now thought necessary for the effective diagnosis and elimination of social ills.[8] The day-to-day requirements of running a large and complex organisation left little time or energy to spare for the reconsideration of fundamental assumptions. The haste and urgency of the work encouraged rigid attitudes and resistance to new ideas and influences. Only those ideas which supported existing notions were likely to be accepted, and once incorporated, rapidly became dogma. For the rest, it was easier and less time consuming to brand critics as wrong than to sit down and examine the validity of what they had to say. It is in the nature of protest groups such as the Alliance that they attract those who are more concerned to register a protest against iniquity rather than investigate it. The campaign was pervaded by a tone of righteous indignation; prohibitionists *knew* what was wrong and threw all their energies into putting it right. They would have agreed with Henry George when he remarked that 'we who know what we want have a big advantage over folks that don't'.[9]

It was important for the continued existence of organisations like the Alliance that they should always be seen to be making progress towards their ultimate objective. Failures and wrong turnings had to be ignored, hushed up or explained away for fear of losing support and finance. Alliance literature always claimed that the movement was making great progress. As early as 1874 the *Manchester Examiner* wondered,

after how many months or years shall we be allowed to say that the reports of the Alliance are all moonshine, that the stories of its progress have been so many successful experiments on our credulity ... we shall not say so yet; but there is a limit to human patience, and we shall soon cease to believe in magnificent victories that lead to nothing.[10]

However prohibitionists were less sceptical and the emotional well-being engendered by the conviction that their battle was being won was not conducive to a questioning of either the end in view or the means being employed. Alliance propagandists were well aware that claims of continual progress fostered an uncritical allegiance among supporters. From the late 1880s onwards there was no need for such subterfuge. While the Socialists began their critique of prohibition and moderates advanced their own version of reform as incorporated in the Bills of 1888 and 1890, the Alliance was at last making demonstrable progress towards its own goal. In the enthusiasm generated by the defeat of the compensation proposals and the support consequently offered by Liberal leaders, the Alliance saw no point entertaining any compromise, nor was it unduly worried by criticisms of its social diagnosis. It was seeking a political solution and by working through political channels appeared at last to be on the verge of success.

In the final analysis it was the leadership of the Alliance which determined the course taken. It was open to it to attempt to push the movement in new directions, but this opportunity was never taken. The Executive was too firmly anchored to the northern world of provincial Nonconformity and shared the social origins and background of its supporters too fully to be capable of taking new initiatives or even regarding them as desirable. Its doctrine of collective leadership made it impossible for a dominant individual to emerge and make his mark in the wider world. Consequently it failed to throw up anyone like John Bright or Joseph Chamberlain, whose radicalism and Nonconformist zeal was tempered by an awareness of political realities, and who might have been able to persuade the Alliance to support practical reform. Because the Alliance needed a spokesman at Westminster and could not find one from among its own ranks, it had to rely on Lawson. The weaknesses of his parliamentary leadership have already been mentioned, but it is difficult to imagine that anyone with a more flexible approach could have been persuaded to take on the task. The Executive's view of the world outside Manchester was conditioned by the ideas of Lawson, Pope and Raper. All three recognised the need for tactical compromise, wishing always to give Liberal governments a breathing space, but none were willing to violate the principles laid down in 1853 and abandon the demand for prohibition.

The background and social situation from which most prohibitionists were drawn provides the final and most fundamental reason for the inflexibility of the Alliance. Augustine Birrell likened the division between Nonconformists and Anglicans to 'Offa's dyke ... broad, deep and practically impassable, cutting clean through social life.'[11] Prohibitionists wished to bridge this gap in order to impose their morality on society as a whole. Their formative experience had been in a temperance movement which had identified the evils of drink and tried by various means to eradicate them. The Alliance was formed because many considered that the early attempts had failed. Prohibition was the next logical step, for if the evil could not be controlled it must be abolished. This reasoning provided the motivating force for the work of the Alliance and the critics said nothing to convince prohibitionists otherwise. Their demands had derived not from social investigation but from the intrinsic logic of the evolution of the temperance movement itself and so were not susceptible to outside criticism. The rest of society had not undergone the same formative experience. Those outside the Nonconformist world had not identified drink as wholly evil, nor had most of them been involved in early attempts at reform. Wishing only to prevent the abuse of drink they naturally turned to moderate measures of reform. From their point of view the demand for prohibition appeared excessive and the persistence of the Alliance was interpreted as fanaticism. Conversely the Nonconformist voice of the Alliance insisted that 'those whom the world applauds as moderate men are ... incapable of rendering great services to mankind'.[12] A society which embraced such cultural diversity found that effective temperance reform was beyond its reach.

Notes

1. D.A. Hamer, *Liberal Politics*, p. 329.
2. *38th Annual Report of the London Auxiliary of the Alliance* (1899), p. 5.
3. Brian Harrison, *Drink and the Victorians* (1971), pp. 370, 384.
4. Quoted in *40th Annual Report 1892*, p. 26; quoted in A.G. Gardiner, *Life of George Cadbury* (1923), p. 305.
5. *Alliance News*, 13 July 1894, p. 441.
6. Ibid., 9 November 1878, p. 720.
7. N. Buxton and W. Hoare, 'Temperance Reform' in C.F.G. Masterman (ed.) *The Heart of the Empire* (2nd impression, 1901), pp. 185, 188.
8. Brian Harrison, 'Philanthropy and the Victorians', *Victorian Studies*, vol. 10, no. 4 (1966), pp. 366-7.

9. Quoted in Herman Ausubel, *In Hard Times* (Columbia 1960), p. 72.
10. Quoted in *Alliance News*, 24 October 1874, p. 689.
11. Augustine Birrell, *Things Past Redress* (1937), p. 38.
12. *Alliance News*, 24 February 1877, p. 120.

INDEX